The Making of a Detective

The Making of a Detective

*A garda's story of investigating some of
Ireland's most notorious crimes*

PAT MARRY

PENGUIN BOOKS

PENGUIN BOOKS

UK | USA | Canada | Ireland | Australia
India | New Zealand | South Africa

Penguin Books is part of the Penguin Random House group of companies
whose addresses can be found at global.penguinrandomhouse.com.

First published by Penguin Ireland 2019
Published in Penguin Books 2020
001

Set in 12.01/14.27 pt Garamond MT Std
Typeset by Jouve (UK), Milton Keynes
Printed and bound in Great Britain by Clays Ltd, Elcograf S.p.A.

A CIP catalogue record for this book is available from the British Library

ISBN: 978-0-241-98531-1

www.greenpenguin.co.uk

Penguin Random House is committed to a
sustainable future for our business, our readers
and our planet. This book is made from Forest
Stewardship Council® certified paper.

I dedicate this book to the loving memory of
my big brother, Austin Marry.

Austin and I loved to tell stories when we got together.
He was always fascinated by my experiences as a
detective and he was sure other people would be too.
It was with his encouragement and support that
I decided to write this book.

Unfortunately, we lost Austin suddenly in 2018.
His leaving us so soon has left a painful gap in all
our lives. Though he did not live to see my book
completed, I know he would be very proud
to see the story between covers.

Contents

Prologue: The Making of a Detective

When I came out of Templemore Garda College in January 1986, I wasn't a detective. I was nothing of the sort. I was twenty-four years old, with a number on my shoulder – 93E – and no way to influence the decision regarding where I'd be stationed. If you didn't have any pull among the seniors, you got the postings no one else wanted – usually protection duty. And that's what happened to me. I was sent to Donnybrook Garda Station in south Dublin, and given guard duty at the British Embassy on Merrion Road. After seven years working in the private sector, becoming a garda was a culture shock, to say the least. It was what I'd always wanted, but once I got it, I wasn't so sure. I'd had a vision of me as a uniform in public view, there to help and protect and make a difference, not as a cardboard cut-out, standing outside an embassy, achieving exactly nothing.

I remember a summer's night, the moon high and the breeze easy. I was outside the embassy and it was four o'clock in the morning and there wasn't a thing moving – not a car, not a person, not a bird, not a scavenging fox. It was just me, with absolutely nothing to protect the embassy from. So I walked out into the middle of the empty road and I lay down, in full uniform, and I looked up at the clear sky and said to myself: *There has to be more to life than this.*

I thought I'd feel like a proper garda once I'd made my first arrest. I'd learned the words off by heart and couldn't wait to use them. I finally got my chance on the beat on Clonskeagh

Road. There was an intoxicated man outside Smurfit's offices, and I arrested him for being drunk in a public place. I brought him to the station, where it dawned on me that he had been hoping to be arrested – he got a clean bed for the night, a hot meal and some entertainment with the lads on duty. One of them was getting married soon and he asked the man if he'd any advice for him. 'I do,' says my first proper arrest. 'Find a woman you don't like, buy her a house and be done with it.' He was enjoying himself, and he had me to thank for that. It was me who was taught the lesson that night, not the drunk man.

Fifteen years later, I tracked down and arrested a charming, cold-blooded killer – Colin Whelan. I count that as my first meaningful arrest. By then I had assisted on many investigations into violent deaths, starting with the murder of the Blanchardstown woman Marilyn Rynn in 1995. During that investigation I watched closely from the sidelines, absorbing everything the lead detectives did and said. That was the first case in which I felt I was finally on the way to becoming a detective.

Back then, there was no technical, strategic or psychological training within An Garda Síochána; no foundation course called 'How to Be a Good Detective' – it was up to the individual to want it badly enough and be intelligent enough to learn on the job. I wanted it, and I pushed myself forward onto the right teams, always listening, always learning.

The Whelan arrest was the moment I felt, for the first time, that I was a detective. I had earned it and proved it. I had pursued this killer for months in a delicate dance – him leading us first this way, then that, confident he was smarter than us, sure it would all be over soon, convinced the headstone over his wife's grave pronouncing him a loving husband would stand as a testament to his innocence. He underestimated us, and he overestimated himself. That's a common problem among murderers. It gave me great pleasure to arrest Colin Whelan for the murder of his wife, Mary Gough, knowing I had every shred of evidence necessary to secure a conviction. He's still behind bars today.

And then there was the moment when I looked into the eyes of another apparently grieving husband, Joe O'Reilly, and every fibre of my being snapped with the electricity of knowing – gut-instinct knowing – that he had deliberately and violently killed his wife, Rachel. I didn't yet have proof, and he was playing the role of chief mourner with gusto, but my instinct was telling me he did it. I remember he was preparing for a photocall – there were cameras and lights, people bustling about Rachel's parents' house – and in the midst of it sat Joe, the sorrowful man. I was staring at the side of his head, thinking it all through, and he suddenly turned and looked straight at me. We held eye contact for five long seconds, and we understood each other completely without a word: I knew he had done it, and he knew that I knew. The game was on. By this time I had formed a detective's radar, and I believed I could trust it.

I had a long and fascinating and successful and sometimes soul-destroying career as a detective. I live with regrets, and I've seen and heard things that won't ever leave me. I've helped families by solving the mystery of how their loved one died, and I've had to look into the eyes of shattered parents and spouses while telling them that I can't put the murderer away, that I don't have enough evidence. It's all part of the job.

It was never easy, but it was never dull. I never again lay on the ground and wondered why life was passing me by, that's for sure. I learned how to be a detective, a good detective, and that was what I'd wanted all along.

1. The Dead Body Effect

The house gave no sign that it had been the scene of a violent murder the night before. There should have been a sign, though, because there should have been a uniformed garda standing watch outside. I'd have expected him to be at the gate, or maybe pacing between the gate and the front door, or even leaning against the wall sneaking a fag – that was possible too. I was parked at the kerb but there was no one in sight, and certainly no uniform. From where I was sitting in the car, I could see a key sticking out of the front door lock. Anyone could walk right in. The body was still in situ.

I checked the house number again. Yes, I had the right house. So where was the cop who was supposed to ensure that no one disturbed the crime scene?

I watched for a while, just to make sure there was no sign of the garda being in danger – maybe the murderer had returned and dragged him inside? I knew it was unlikely, but still, I'd learned to expect the unexpected by then.

It was all quiet, so I got out of the car cautiously and made my way up the path to the front door. I let myself in with the key handily left there, and walked quietly down the hallway and into the sitting room. There I found the garda assigned to protect the crime scene. He was stretched out on the couch, sound asleep in his big, grey, Garda-issue overcoat. I could have danced a jig up the hallway in hobnail boots and he wouldn't have stirred. Next to him, on the floor, lay the dead body, a carving knife sticking upright from the bloody wound in its chest. I tapped the garda and his eyes opened, and he took a moment to remember where he was. Then he got up, turned the couch over on its side and said, 'That's how it was, Pat.'

It wasn't the first time I'd seen a crime scene treated with such nonchalance, and it wouldn't be the last. When you start out, dead bodies are a difficult experience. It's hard enough not to run away, let alone look away. In those first years on the force, it feels like death will never be easy to deal with, but then something happens, and what's striking is how fast it happens. Somehow, one day you're just used to it – and to an extent you wouldn't have thought possible beforehand. The dead become a natural part of your world.

In a murder investigation, the victim is your friend because they hold all the answers that will tell you who killed them. It's a strangely intimate relationship. You pay more attention to them than anyone else in your life; you drill down to the minutest details; you learn every single thing there is to know about their past, their life choices, their love life and marriage. In a way, you feel close to them, and yet they can only ever be a dead body at your feet, an unspeaking witness to a sudden and horrible crime.

When the call comes through and you realize you're going to see your first dead body, it's unnerving. The immediate thought is that you have to be professional and appear unaffected, no matter what. At the same time, your stomach is knotted tight in fearful anticipation. The day of my first call-out was in the summer of 1987, when I was a uniform garda. A report of any incident always comes to a uniform first – usually whoever is manning the front desk that day – and they then pass it on to the relevant person. In this instance, my sergeant was the one it got passed on to, and he brought me along with him. As we drove towards the spot where the body had been reported, I tried to steel myself for whatever it was I was going to see. I didn't know then that it's impossible to steel yourself against the smell of decay.

A woman's body had been found in a graveyard in Dublin West. I could smell the scene before I reached it. The stench was powerful, telling us clearly that the body must have been lying out here for some time.

She was exactly where the observant member of the public had said she'd be, curled up in a brambly ditch. I felt sorry for her, lying uncovered there on her own, next to the buried dead. Had she come here to die? Or had something happened to her in this place? The scene wasn't telling us much, so the results of the autopsy would have to be our guide.

That was my first dead body, and now I had to observe my first post-mortem. The rule is that the garda who attends the scene and finds the body must also be present at the post-mortem, to identify the body to the pathologist. So along I went to the morgue on a warm July morning, just twenty-four hours after her body had been removed from the scene. I found the whole experience deeply shocking. I was twenty-six years old, a garda for less than two years, and I had notions about how these things would be done.

I was wrong.

The first shock was when they opened the body bag in which she'd been transported from the graveyard to the mortuary – reversing a journey many had travelled before her. When the pathologist unzipped it, hundreds of white maggots poured out onto the stainless-steel table and skittered to the floor. Insects don't stand on ceremony, and they'd had seven days before the body was removed from the ditch, so they had taken up residence and made the most of their good fortune. The pathologist then peeled back the plastic body bag to reveal the corpse and my stomach churned – rats had eaten her face, and the hollow, bloody mess where her face should have been was framed by her long hair. It was like something from a horror movie and I recoiled physically, desperately trying to steady myself.

The second shock was watching the mortuary attendant, who was tasked with removing her rings from her rigid clenched fists. He wrenched the fingers apart, breaking them in the process, the sound of the bony cracks ripping through the air and ricocheting off the metal surfaces. It seemed like an assault, but this crude approach was the only way the attendant could do his job.

But the most inescapable part of the whole experience was – just like in the graveyard – the stench. It was utterly overwhelming. There is a distinct smell to death, and it never leaves you. In fact, it got the better of me that day, in spite of my determination to be professional and unfazed. I had to get out of there and outside into fresh air, where I vomited and retched violently. I wasn't able to return to see the rest of the post-mortem. I just couldn't go back into close contact with that smell. As it was, I felt like it was clinging to me, seeped into my clothes and my skin. When I got home that evening, I showered and scrubbed for a long time, but I could still get that putrid smell, like it had taken root inside me. It was a deeply horrible after-effect of a difficult day. The next morning I talked over my reaction with a scenes of crime expert. He told me that the death stench gets caught in the nostril hairs, which leads to that feeling of smelling it continually, no matter if you scour yourself with a wire brush. He also described his first dead body and how badly he'd handled it, and that made me feel much better about my own 'failure'. It didn't make me a bad cop, after all. It made me a decent human being.

As for that first dead body, the post-mortem did tell us her story. She was a troubled woman who had suffered from mental health issues, and it obviously got too much for her and she took an overdose. Then she walked to the graveyard, lay down in the ditch and died. I felt it was a terribly sad ending to a young life, to feel so isolated and so hemmed in that there was nothing else but death. It was an early and important lesson about the effect of mental illness on a person, and one I carried with me into every case I worked on. As a garda, you get to hear the dead person's story, but you also get to see the end of their story played out in the lives of those they leave behind. The anguish of the loved ones is very hard to witness, and that's something that never becomes so familiar that you can be blasé about it.

After that first experience of a post-mortem, I was apprehensive about death and dead bodies. But there's no room for such sensitivity when you've got ambitions to be a detective. And in the end I got cured of it the way most recruits get cured of it – by spending a night with a corpse.

It happened when I was a young uniform in Blanchardstown and got handed the nightshift: 10 p.m. to 6 a.m. in the morgue, watching over a murder victim. When a murder is committed, the body becomes one of the evidential exhibits, and as such it must not be interfered with in any way between discovery and the post-mortem. The way that's ensured is by having it accompanied at all times by a garda. I'd drawn the short straw this time, and I entered the mortuary at James Connolly Hospital at ten o'clock, facing eight hours alone in a room full of stainless-steel drawers holding the dead.

The body I was there to mind was laid out on a white marble slab, mostly covered with a white sheet. He was a young man, and he'd been shot in the back of the head. He was lying on his back, face towards the ceiling, and his head and neck were raised on a plastic support block. At the end of the slab, behind his head, was a gully for fluids and matter to drain into.

I settled into a hard chair and stared at him. From time to time, blood dripped from the hole in the back of his head, plopping quietly onto the marble slab beneath. The sound of it got louder as the night wore on. My eyes moved from that hole to my watch and back again. Time slowed to a standstill and my every nerve was on edge. Suddenly, a noise rang out from one of the steel caskets. My heart nearly stopped in my chest. I glanced around, but I knew I recognized that sound. It was most definitely the sound of someone passing wind. I'd heard that dead bodies expel gas, and even groan sometimes, and now here was the proof, I supposed. I relaxed again, laughing a little to myself.

It wasn't a one-off, either. Over the hours of my shift, that sound broke the silence a number of times – loud farts that should by rights, I thought to myself, have woken the dead. I was grateful that there was no groaning. That would have been even more disturbing. It was a horrible sensation, to be the only living man in a room of dead bodies – especially the suddenly dead. It made me think about the fragility of life; the lad I was watching over had been playing sport when he was shot dead, full of life and vigour one second, dead on the ground the next. His life was paper-thin, and I didn't like thinking about that.

I was scared for much of my time keeping watch, but as the dawn light started its slow crawl across the metal surfaces, I realized that nothing had happened, and nothing was going to happen. They were all dead, and that was that. When I left the morgue at 6 a.m., I emerged with a sense that I could now cope with anything. The apprehension was dead too.

The truth is that humans are habit-forming, even about corpses. The effect of familiarity with death is that you become casual about it. I think some officers wear this as a badge of honour – that nothing can touch them, that they can brazen out the bloodiest crime scene with a joke and a hollow laugh. To an extent, I became like that too, but I'm not proud of it. I tried, always, to remember that I was dealing with a real person, not just a victim. It's an approach that leaves you open to more distress, but it can also sharpen your reading of a crime scene, can give you the courage to see the case through to its proper end. I think decency has a place in every good detective, and it's important not to lose sight of that, especially when violent death becomes a routine experience.

The thread that runs through all crime scenes and that anchors us to the victim is their story. It's hard to remain distant and unaffected when you get to know the person they were before they died. When a murder occurs and you spend weeks or months – or even years – piecing together a detailed picture of the victim in order to solve the crime, you form a sort of relationship with them, and that connection is a powerful tool in understanding how to solve their murder. I first learned this working on the murder investigation into the death of Marilyn Rynn.

The area where her body was found is known locally as 'the Tunnels'. It's at the top of Blanchardstown village, where a laneway leads under the road, staying underground for about fifteen feet before coming out near Brookhaven Drive, where Marilyn Rynn lived. It is sometimes called the Corduff Tunnel because it's located on the Old Corduff Road, and it's a handy shortcut that the locals use all the time.

In the early hours of 22 December 1995, it was very cold

and very dark in the Tunnels and the rain was hammering down. I can actually remember being on my shift that evening in Blanchardstown, and thinking to myself that it would be a quiet one. Between the bleak rain and the warm Christmas cheer of people's homes, who would be bothered going out to do mischief?

Regardless of the cold darkness of the tunnel, it was still the quickest route home and out of the bitter December air, which is why Marilyn headed that way after getting off the Nitelink bus. The bus stop was only a matter of minutes from her house, and it was a path she walked all the time. On this night, though, her journey ended in a call to Blanchardstown Garda Station to report a missing woman. Her brother made the call on 26 December, and by then he was very certain something was wrong because the fact that no one had heard from Marilyn was completely out of character.

It was three days before Christmas; people were preoccupied with the holiday, people were away, it was a messy time to go missing. There were false sightings that kept it a missing persons case for the next week. We had two neighbours swearing they had seen Marilyn on the morning of the 23rd, going to work as usual. This cast doubt on the 'missing person' conclusion and stalled the investigation. However, Marilyn's brother was adamant that his sister was in some kind of trouble. The idea of her missing a family Christmas was impossible. He knew something had happened to prevent her from going home and enjoying the holiday as usual.

About two days after she was reported missing, a detective went to Marilyn's house and checked it out. He saw her post accumulating on the doormat – more than usual, no doubt, because of the Christmas cards. His gut was telling him that Marilyn's brother was right, that something had happened to this woman. Nonetheless, at this point we had to proceed with it as a missing person case as we didn't have any evidence to the contrary.

We drew up a plan of the Nitelink bus, and via a media appeal and a door-to-door questionnaire – which included a question to the effect of 'Did you travel on either of the 3 a.m. Nitelink buses on 22 December?' – we asked all the passengers travelling that night to come forward and identify the seat they had occupied. Three-quarters of them did so, and we put a big 'X' on the seats they had been in. The aim was to discover where Marilyn had been seated on the bus, and hopefully jog their memories so they could tell us where she got off and what direction she went in.

On the first round, no one could place Marilyn on the bus. The investigation sagged a little at that point, but local politicians – particularly Nora Owen, TD – were determined that the mystery of Marilyn's disappearance be solved, because it was causing alarm among the local population. They pushed some more money towards the investigation, which allowed us to go around the witnesses again. This time, a woman came forward with information. She had her reasons for not wanting to make it known that she was out and about at that hour on that night, but her conscience had been nagging her to tell the truth. She put an 'X' on Marilyn's seat and, crucially, told us she had seen Marilyn get off at the top of the village. Now we had Marilyn, alive, in the village, around 3.30 a.m. The logical next step in the sequence of events was that she walked home – and never got there.

At this stage, the key evidence that was keeping this as a missing persons case was statements provided by two witnesses, both of whom lived locally, who claimed they had seen Marilyn the day before Christmas Eve. The incident room tasked me with talking to them again, to find out just how certain they were of what they had seen. They were very decent people, eager to help the investigation, and they both reiterated their accounts of seeing Marilyn. So I decided to check out their movements on the day in question, just to corroborate what they were saying. I went to the local supermarket where they both worked and examined the clock-in cards. What I found there shocked me, but of course I was new to the game back then. At the time when they claimed they'd witnessed Marilyn walking to the bus stop on 23 December, they were in fact at work, clocked in, verifiable. They hadn't seen her at all.

So now we knew that Marilyn was on the Nitelink, that she got off in the village and that no one had seen her since. It was logical to assume that she had taken her usual route home, through the Tunnels. On 6 January, a police search team went into the Tolka River Valley, planning to cover the area in and around the Tunnels. I remember the search team and their sniffer dogs in place that morning, ready to conduct the in-depth search. The signal was given and the group of men in search overalls followed the dogs into the thick brambles and bushes. We all settled down to wait, but it turned out to be the quickest search for a body I've ever witnessed. It took just fifteen minutes for one of the dogs to find the body, abandoned in the undergrowth.

Marilyn's naked body had been dragged and thrown into a tangle of bushes, her skin tinged blue by the extreme cold weather that had gripped the country over the Christmas period. Her handbag was discarded not far off, along with her clothes, and there were marks on her neck that suggested a violent death. The scene made it immediately clear that this was now a murder investigation, and the Garda Technical Bureau (GTB) was called in.

By this stage in my career, I was finally in a position to take part in a murder investigation. I was a detective in training by now – still a long way to go to earn the full title, but definitely on the way. My progress through the ranks had been slow compared to others, because I had no pull whatsoever. If you had family members who had been in the force or some other useful connection, it was possible to move up relatively quickly. But I was the first in my family to become a garda and had no connections of any kind. The only thing I had was my work ethic, and the desire to become a detective and prove myself to those higher up the chain.

I'd spent three years as a uniform, and in that time I did my level best to solve any case I was involved in. One of my best moments came when I was on the beat in Blanchardstown, and Mulhuddart National School was burned to the ground one night in an act of arson. The local community was extremely upset about this, and I went over with other colleagues to check out the scene. I had recently completed a ten-week scenes of crime training course, which included how to read an arson scene, so I went around the remains of the building carefully, seeing what I could find. In one room there was a lone desk, still standing, though badly burnt. Its drawers were open and it looked like it had been rifled through. On a hunch, I bagged some of the charred papers that lay inside and sent them off for fingerprinting. Sure enough, back they came with a match to someone on file for previous wrongdoings. That someone was a local lad we already knew had been seen in the field behind the school on the night of the fire.

I went to talk to the principal and she confirmed that the desk was hers and that she always kept it locked – and that prior to the fire she had locked it securely, as usual, and kept the key on her person. To my mind, that meant the suspect could not have put his fingerprints on those papers other than on the night of the fire, after he'd bust open the desk. The rest of the evidence gathered supported this, and the young man was arrested and charged. He was adamant that it wasn't him, right up to the courthouse. He entered a not-guilty plea at the arraignment, and as a result the defence, prosecution and witnesses all gathered for the trial. I was the second witness and was ready to go with my findings. But just before the first witness – the crime scene mapper – was about to be called, the defence counsel stood up and said there was a change of plea. As he uttered the word 'guilty', the young man looked straight at me with a look that plainly said, 'Fuck you!' It was a great outcome, and the people of Mulhuddart were delighted that the arsonist had been found and put away.

This sort of work from a uniform wasn't all that usual, so it gained me the attention of some of my superiors. I was singled out by Detective Sergeant Derek Byrne, who put me forward as a plain-clothes junior member, known in the force as a 'buckshee' detective. That meant I wasn't a real detective yet – that I was there to prove I could become one. So I was an eager buckshee in 1995 when Marilyn Rynn was murdered. (I always wondered how buckshees got their name. As far as I can make out, it's because they weren't paid a full detective's allowance – 'buckshee' is a slang word meaning 'free of charge'.)

Once a murder has been announced on the news, everyone knows there will be a murder conference at 10 a.m. the following morning, and anyone who wants to be involved makes it their business to be there at the appointed time. Once it was clear that the Rynn investigation was a murder case, I made my way to the murder conference along with the other detectives and buckshees, knowing this was a good opportunity to learn and to hopefully prove my worth. In 1995 the K District comprised Cabra, Finglas and Blanchardstown, with divisional headquarters in Santry, and all murder investigations in these areas were run through the incident room in Cabra. It was operated by one of the best incident room managers in the force, Detective John Lyons, and I learned a huge amount from watching him.

A real incident room isn't anything like the ones you see on television in crime dramas. There are no whiteboards, no pictures of the victim and suspects stuck up with thumb tacks, and no frantically scribbled lines to connect the evidence. It's actually a very calm place, at the eye of the storm of the crime and the investigation. The only furniture is a very long table that seats about twenty people. Chairs are reserved for the detective inspector leading the investigation and for the incident room team, but for everyone else it's first come, first seated. If you come late, you stand by the wall.

The incident room murder conference is a place to describe and discuss, and you do not speak unless you're spoken to – especially if you're a buckshee. The DI leads the proceedings, recording everything in the Jobs Book. This is the bible of the investigation, listing every job to be undertaken, with a name beside each one. Job 1 is the first report to a garda of the crime, whether by a member of the public or a colleague, and then the jobs are listed in chronological order – as many as it takes to conclude the investigation. As each job is completed, it's marked on the 'bingo card'. This is a grid showing all the job numbers, and when you state that your task is complete, an 'X' is put through that particular job number.

There are key roles to be filled for every murder investigation, including crime scene mapper, crime scene photographer, scenes of crime officer, exhibits officer, family liaison officer, press officer, and technical analysts for CCTV and phones. The incident room is where all the information and evidence gathered is shared, dissected and evaluated. In any incident room, the victim becomes very real to the investigators, because we pore over every detail about them that we can find. It was during this process that I first realized and understood the strange relationship between victim and investigator – how you come to regard them as very real, very 'alive', even though you know them only in death.

As the information started to come into the incident room from the various lines of inquiry in the Marilyn Rynn investigation, a very clear picture of the victim emerged. She was an independent woman, forty-one years old, very happy in her own company and living alone, but also a great friend, sister, aunt and daughter. She loved gardening and keeping fit. She worked at the National Roads Authority and was a respected and much-loved colleague. It seemed that everyone who had met Marilyn enjoyed her good humour, her work ethic, her reliability and her great zest for life. She was a woman who had never harmed anyone – kind, trustworthy, intelligent and gentle. Her lonely, brutal death was totally at odds with her busy, caring life.

The Rynn case is famous in policing and justice circles as the first time DNA evidence was used in Ireland to secure a conviction – generating headlines such as *Killer trapped by his DNA* – but that's far from the whole story. The solving of the riddle of Marilyn's murder was also down to methodical detective work and perseverance. The senior officers knew the value of being on the ground and talking to people in the area, so door-to-door inquiries were made a priority. For door-to-doors, a questionnaire is compiled and every officer sticks to it, so that we capture the same information from every interviewee. In the Rynn case, about 2,000 statements were taken – a vast amount of information to sift through, which was the job of the incident room team. As it happened, one of the doors we knocked on was the killer's. This is how I came to appreciate that taking a witness statement is an essential skill, one learned through experience, and that it can catch a killer as reliably as any technology.

When Garda John Carr knocked on the door of a house in Edgewood Lawn, a slightly built young man with long hair in a ponytail and a beard opened it and welcomed him inside. Asked about the night of the murder, the young man said he was at home that night, he hadn't got much to add to the investigation and he didn't know the dead woman. They talked some more, but then the man's wife came into the room and the detective explained why he was there. The woman was well aware of the murder, like everyone else around there, and she said she felt very sorry for the dead woman's family. Then she looked at her husband and said, 'Didn't it happen the night you were out?'

Now the detective was all ears, because this differed from what he'd just been told. So he looked at the man for an explanation, and the young man pleasantly described how he was out that night, at his office Christmas party, and ended up having to walk home. In fact, now that he thought of it, he did see a woman matching Marilyn's description. She was walking through the Tunnels in the company of a tall blond man – but that's all he could say about it. Then the next morning he got up, put on his clothes from the night before and went to work, all as usual. So now the detective started making more notes, because this last detail was interesting. It was raining cats and dogs that night he had walked miles home – why would anyone put on the same damp clothes the following morning?

The young man's name was David Lawler, and although he didn't know it, he had just become a person of interest to the investigation.

A person of interest occupies a sort of limbo between becoming a suspect and remaining a witness. The strategy used is TIE – trace, interview, eliminate. If you can't eliminate someone, but nor do you have any evidence to suspect them, they are a person of interest. As such, they can't be arrested, but they will be asked to submit a DNA sample in the event that samples are collected. They are on shaky ground, in other words, and it could give way beneath them if we find them out in a lie.

In order to move from a person of interest to a suspect, there must be 'good cause to suspect'. This is important because a suspect can be arrested and must give a DNA sample, which can be taken forcibly, if necessary. In the Rynn case, there were two known criminals who could have been in the frame. One was a very dangerous, violent man who was living rough in the Tolka River Valley, not far from where the body was found. The other was spotted in CCTV footage at a diner Marilyn had gone to that night before taking the bus home. He was in the queue behind her, and again he had a criminal record.

As it happened, DNA testing ruled out both of these men. And that was another lesson I took away from the investigation – not to jump to conclusions, even when something looks probable. This applies to forensic evidence as well, which might not be as straightforward as it at first seems. For example, a person could have legitimate access to a crime scene, meaning their DNA features at the scene, but they are in no way involved in the murder. This is a relatively common occurrence, depending on who finds the body and what their first instinct is – a relative might drop to their knees and hug the victim, or touch them to try to find a pulse. An open mind is an incredibly important asset to a murder detective.

One of the things that interested me about the Rynn case was how much misinformation the door-to-door interviews turned up. That was another important lesson – beware of the witness with a desire to help. It's an odd aspect of the 'dead body effect', this wanting to be useful to the point of giving false information, but it happens regularly in investigations. You'll get a witness who is one hundred per cent certain they saw something significant, when they saw nothing of the sort at all. But it isn't lying, it's more like a false memory that comes out of their need to be helpful and to be seen to be helpful. Or perhaps it's a desire to be important to the investigation, to be a key witness. It's hard to say, but it's a phenomenon I've seen many times, and as an investigating detective it's essential to keep the possibility of it happening in mind.

The Rynn interviews were the first time I encountered it. There were the neighbours who swore they had seen Marilyn leave for work when she was, in fact, dead at that time. Then there was the woman who insisted she'd received a phone call from Marilyn after the 22nd. Even when we had the evidence, we couldn't convince her that she was misremembering – she kept insisting she was right. In 2,000 statements, you're always going to get a certain amount of misinformation.

I can remember when the detective who had interviewed Lawler during the house-to-house returned to the station. I was sitting in the detectives' office when he handed me the witness statement he had just taken and said, 'Read that and tell me what you think.' I read it. It was a statement by a David Lawler, who said he'd been out that night and come home late, and had walked behind a woman who fitted Marilyn's description. He said she was with a tall, blond-haired man. He said they went under the Tolka bridge and that was the last he saw of them. He said he went home, slept, dressed in last night's clothes and went to work.

The detail about putting on the previous night's clothes the next day was odd enough to raise a suspicion. I looked up at John Carr and said, 'Well, it's our first sighting of her on foot and he's putting himself in the area.' John told me how it was only when Lawler's wife came into the sitting room and remarked that her husband was out that night that Lawler came up with this whole scenario. 'Well, that's interesting, to say the least,' I said. 'Why would he lie? I mean, you only lie to cover the truth.'

In the incident room, we could see key pieces of information emerging from the mass of fact and fiction. We knew that Marilyn had left her office Christmas party at the Old Shieling Hotel in Raheny at around 2 a.m. She had taken a taxi to O'Connell Street in the city centre and met friends for a cup of tea at Eddie Rocket's diner. Then, she headed to Westmoreland Street for the 3 a.m. Nitelink out to Blanchardstown. She was an independent woman who loved socializing with friends, so this trip wouldn't have been out of the ordinary for her. We knew she'd got off the Nitelink at about 3.30 a.m. and headed off on foot towards her home. We knew that somewhere between the bus stop and her house she had been dragged off the path, raped and strangled. Her killer had left her naked body in the undergrowth, her clothes and handbag discarded nearby. The attack likely happened between 4 a.m. and 5 a.m., when the Tunnels were empty and silent. They were probably the only two people out and about at that hour. One woman walking home, and one person watching and tracking her, intending to do her harm. What we needed to know was: who?

On 15 January, the crime was reconstructed for *Crime Line*, RTÉ's crime-reporting programme that sought the public's help in solving crimes. They did a good job of giving a very clear visual story of the murder and there was a huge public reaction to it in the form of outrage and calls to the incident room, but nothing much actually came of it in terms of leads and evidence, from our point of view.

The Forensic Science Laboratory in Dublin (now FSI – Forensic Science Ireland) had introduced DNA technology for Garda investigations in 1994. This was a new science at the time, but we were well aware of its potential to provide rock-solid evidence. The state pathologist, Dr John Harbison, had taken samples from the body at the scene, and from these he had identified traces of semen. Based on this, Detective Inspector Derek Byrne (as he now was), who was leading the investigation, decided to get buccal swabs (a swab from inside the cheek or mouth) from a wide range of men, to compare against the DNA of the semen found in Marilyn's body.

I was put into a team of four, in charge of coordinating the taking and submitting of these samples, which was an important job to be involved in and made me feel I was well on the way to being accepted as a full detective. I wanted to do a really good job, so I focused all my attention on doing it right.

We started collecting buccal swabs from all the men who fell within our framework of possibility. We had the DNA taken from Marilyn Rynn's body, so the next step was to prepare a DNA profile from each sample and see if there were any matches. This represented a mammoth task. Nowadays, the whole process is very quick and efficient, but it was a new science back then and the exercise was very time-consuming – generating just one single profile took eight hours. So the procedure was that we sent thirty samples at a time, generating thirty DNA profiles, all of which were compared against the original sample. The lab would stop once it hit a match.

In the end, we secured over 350 samples for DNA testing, including 100 from men with known histories of sexual assault. As a person of interest, David Lawler was asked to supply a sample. He agreed without hesitation, saying, 'No problem. I hope you get the bastard.' We didn't know it then, but Lawler was an early adopter and avid user of the Internet, and he had trawled online for information on DNA testing. He had read that semen lasts for fourteen days in the open air, at which point its DNA can no longer be identified. Marilyn's body was found fifteen days after the crime. And so Lawler was only too happy to cooperate and provide a buccal sample, because he felt safe in the knowledge that the DNA evidence would be too degraded to use. His sample was sent off with all the others.

The results for the first batch of thirty samples came back all negative. Another long wait ensued as we waited for batch two to be tested. In July, we got good news: the lab reported a match. Contrary to Lawler's belief that the DNA would be degraded, the freezing temperatures had ensured the samples were preserved. He hadn't factored in the bitter December air.

The lab informed DI Derek Byrne of their findings, and he told no one. That was a good call, because he had to ensure the media didn't get wind of it before we were ready to move. Media interest in the case was intense, and any leak would have undermined the investigation. (The issue of leaks to the media dogs all investigations, and I'd certainly had my fill of it by the time I retired.) So the DI was perfectly right to hold his cards close to his chest. Based on the information he'd received, he ordered that a search warrant be secured for Lawler's home. The search was carried out, but didn't uncover much that was evidential. Nonetheless, all the elements were now in place.

During any such investigation, the detective inspector leading the case is in regular contact with the DPP (Director of Public Prosecutions) from the moment a suspect is identified. It's a very close relationship between the investigation team and the DPP. The DPP's office assigns a senior officer – usually the director or the deputy director – and that senior officer is apprised of all developments as they occur. All of the conversations between the DI and the DPP are conducted confidentially, as they should be. Ultimately, it is the DPP who decides whether a suspect is to be charged with murder or not. In order to make that call, they must have knowledge of all evidence available and also be confident that it was lawfully acquired. Nowadays, the family of the deceased has access to the DPP's decision-making, via the senior investigating officer (SIO) in charge of the investigation, and they can query those decisions within a certain time limit.

The role of the DPP is crucial in every investigation, so it's essential that the SIO keeps them properly and fully informed. In the later years of my career, I was the DI who communicated with the DPP on the cases where I was SIO. In the Rynn case, that job fell to DI Derek Byrne. He continually updated the DPP's office on the situation with David Lawler, and once the interview process was complete, as is the protocol, he asked the DPP to make the decision. The DPP subsequently issued a direction that Lawler should be charged with the rape and murder of Marilyn Rynn.

On 6 August 1996, David Lawler was arrested and brought to Cabra Garda Station to be formally charged. When he was brought into the interview room and told by two senior officers that there was an incriminating DNA match, the unflappable Lawler sat back and said, 'I'll tell you the story.'

He told us everything.

On 21 December 1995, Lawler went to the Telecom Éireann Christmas lunch. He worked there as a technician, installing phone and modem lines. He drank and partied for the next twelve hours, then headed off on foot. He had originally told us that there were no taxis, so he decided to walk home to Blanchardstown. Later, he confessed that he had walked to Benburb Street, a popular spot for sex workers. It was a very busy night, though, with so many Christmas revellers around, and the prostitutes were as busy as the taximen, so Lawler couldn't find anyone to hook up with. He continued on his way, walking the five miles to Blanchardstown. When he was almost home, a Nitelink bus pulled up and a lone woman got out and began walking ahead of him, towards the Tunnels. He trailed her. In the shadows of that underground path, he attacked her. He dragged her off into the bushes, forced her to remove her clothes and raped her. Marilyn Rynn got a good look at him as she tried to fight him off, and she indicated that she recognized him from around there. This was easy to do because of his distinctive long ponytail and beard, which was why his nickname locally was 'Jesus'.

This was a man with no prior convictions, not known to gardaí, with a stable home and a wife and young child, so what he did next is mind-boggling. There, on that cold, wet ground, he put his bare hands around Marilyn Rynn's neck and he squeezed relentlessly. But she was lying on her stomach, and he couldn't get a proper grip. He flipped her over, dug his thumbs into the tender spot at her throat and strangled her until her body stopped jerking. She was dead. Then he stood up, walked home and got into bed beside his wife.

The next day, he went to work and continued his life as if nothing at all had happened. When we came knocking on his door, he calmly told his lies. All the while the woman he had killed with his bare hands was lying frozen where he'd left her, hidden in the bushes. It appears he didn't give her another thought.

For the investigation team, this was a dream confession – corroborating all we had already and explaining everything we didn't. That doesn't happen very often in murder investigations. In my experience, most perpetrators opt to stay silent, leaving the burden of proof squarely on the investigators' shoulders; hoping against hope that this tactic pays off and the evidence doesn't stack up solidly enough to secure a conviction. In this case, Lawler offered it all up on a plate. I'm not sure why, but perhaps he needed to share his conquest, his 'perfect crime', in order to gain pleasure from it. Whatever his reasoning, from that moment he was a model of cooperation. He accompanied some of my colleagues out to the crime scene and showed them where he had thrown her credit cards, to make it look like a robbery gone wrong. They found the credit cards, exactly where he said they'd be.

One of the interesting things I took away from Lawler's guided tour of the crime scene was the fact that some of the items he'd scattered from Marilyn's handbag lay beyond what we call the 'preserved area'. When faced with reconstructing a crime, one of the key early decisions is assigning the area to be forensically investigated. That familiar white-and-blue Garda tape marks out the boundaries of the scene, and we concentrate all of our attention on this space. But in this particular case, the designated scene was too small, in that it missed important evidential items. I can remember filing this away in my mind as something always to be careful about if I ever got to head up an investigation, and vowing to remind myself that getting other expert opinions on the crime scene area might sometimes be advisable.

After his admission of guilt, Lawler was charged and brought to the District Court at the Four Courts. He later secured bail from the High Court, on the condition that he live with his parents in County Wicklow. Then the job of preparing a criminal trial began, which is a lengthy procedure because there is due process on both sides, witnesses to be served, and a massive volume of information to be evaluated and presented. It took fifteen months to get to the Central Criminal Court, but on 26 January 1998, David Lawler finally stood trial for the rape and murder of Marilyn Rynn. He pleaded guilty. He had no other choice, because by then the Garda's case was watertight – we had the DNA match, and we had the full story from the perpetrator himself.

The judge handed down a life sentence, which back then was eleven years (now it is eighteen to twenty-two). Lawler was removed from the court by prison officers and taken directly to Mountjoy Prison.

There is always a sense of quiet jubilation in the incident room when a case is brought to a successful conclusion, but it's tempered by sadness and a sense of disbelief at what human beings are capable of doing to one another. We were very glad to be able to give some comfort to Marilyn's family by convicting the man who killed her, but at the same time, we knew it was a cold comfort. The day David Lawler was sentenced to life in prison was a good day for us, but for Marilyn's family it was just another day without her. It's a despairing kind of business.

The Rynn case marked a professional milestone for me, being the first time I had contributed properly to a murder investigation and aided my colleagues in reaching a good out-come. The incident room and the murder conference had presented a daunting environment, but I had learned the ropes quickly. I mapped it all out in my mind – how to set up the room, how to pick the best people for each role, how to read the crime scene and plan the investigation based on that. And it was brought home to me very clearly just how crucial the skill of taking statements is in a murder case. I watched the senior officers doing it, and I figured out the golden rules: patience – let the person talk at their own pace; listen – to what's being said and what's not being said, both are equally important; never suggest anything to the interviewee – don't interfere with their telling of the story in any way; stay neutral – no matter what the crime or what you're hearing, don't show emotion; no chatting – you could give away a crucial detail or colour their story unintentionally; only question ambiguity – say 'clarify this for me'; and finally, never forget that everything you're doing, hearing and saying has to hold up in the witness box, or else you could jeopardize the whole case.

The other key takeaway for me was the importance of going back to witnesses – not to simply take their first statement as all they have to say. It's important to talk to the witnesses two or three times in order to get all the information they possess, because it often happens that they do know something of use, but they don't know they know it. It takes time, letting them talk away, in order to get a really full statement of their observations. I learned that from the bus passengers – it was absolutely worth redoing that exercise because we got the information we needed in the end. It was there, it just didn't come out in the first round of interviews.

I realized then that a detective has to have great patience and not rush things in order to solve any case. An investigation evolves in an organic way, with its own rhythm, and you have to respect that and let it take its course.

The Rynn case had a positive outcome, but later I would learn that you also have to live with failure and all it brings. We had done our jobs well, and that had brought about the conviction, which was very satisfying. We felt we had done right by Marilyn, even if no one had been able to help her in her moment of need.

It was a perfect case to come in on as a rookie detective eager to learn, and I certainly did learn. I also realized that I wanted to do it again. I wanted to investigate serious crimes as a detective, and I wanted to solve them. More than that, I felt I could. There's a motto among the gardaí that you learn in Templemore as a wet-behind-the-ears recruit: *Do fuck all, but whatever you do, do it well.* It's born out of the weary cynicism that a hierarchy creates, and you hear it repeated again and again, like a mantra, or a prayer.

I'd found what I wanted to do, and I wanted to do it well. I was ready.

2. A Disarming Killer

I had left my phone charging overnight in the kitchen. When I came down in the morning and checked it, there were forty missed calls – nearly all from my superintendent. I felt that familiar combination of racing heart and sinking stomach: it had to be a murder. I rang him immediately, apologizing the moment he answered for not having kept the phone nearby. 'Well, Detective Sergeant, it must be rewarding living in a house so big you can't hear the phone ring,' he said. I knew that tone of voice, and I knew that it was best to stay quiet. I was in the wrong, and there was no point arguing otherwise.

It was now March 2001, six years since the Rynn investigation, and in that time I had been promoted to uniform sergeant at Clones Garda Station, where I served between 1997 and 1999. At that point a vacancy arose for a detective sergeant in Balbriggan, and as I was living in Navan at the time I was glad to make the change and applied for it. I got the promotion, so in 1999 I became Detective Sergeant Pat Marry, working out of Balbriggan Garda Station and still eager to prove myself a good detective. Now here I was, listening to my superintendent describe the incident he was ringing me about, not for a moment thinking this was my chance to conduct an investigation that would put me firmly into the ranks of the detectives I admired.

As it turned out, it wasn't a murder. He told me that a man in Balbriggan had called the emergency services last night, said his wife had fallen down the stairs. She'd been rushed to

Beaumont Hospital but was pronounced dead there. The staff in the hospital had voiced some concerns about the husband and his story, so as a precaution a statement had been taken from him, the keys of the house seized and the scene preserved. But both families were at the hospital and presented a very united front, there was no history of domestic violence and the young couple had been married for just six months, after dating for ten years. In all likelihood, my superintendent told me, it was a tragic accident, but I was to get myself down to the post-mortem anyway, just to be sure. He had ordered the scene at the house to be preserved, but that was just a precaution and probably unnecessary.

The dead woman was twenty-seven-year-old Mary Whelan, née Gough, and her husband was Colin Whelan. She had been taken to the morgue on Malahide Road, Marino – on the Northside of Dublin city – where Dr Marie Cassidy, the assistant state pathologist, was going to perform an autopsy. The staff at Beaumont who had attended to Mary were concerned by some marks they'd noticed on her body, and also by the fact that her tongue was swollen. Given the version of events told to them by Colin Whelan, they couldn't understand why Mary's body was so cold – as if she had been dead longer than her husband claimed. This was particularly strange when she had been found wrapped in a duvet, which her husband said he'd put around her to keep her warm, as instructed by the 999 call handler. When a nurse noticed some fresh scratches on Colin Whelan's chest, the hospital decided to call in the gardaí. That's how I ended up on the road out to the Dublin City Mortuary.

By this stage, the idea of a post-mortem didn't fill me with dread. It was never going to be something I looked forward to, but I had witnessed a fair number of them by now and was fascinated by how the silent body could tell us so much about its final moments. When I watched an expert like Dr Cassidy methodically interrogating every centimetre of skin, I could appreciate the skill involved in this intense examination and also the dedication of the forensic pathology team to finding out the truth. On this occasion, it turned out that I didn't have to witness the full examination taking place because four colleagues from the Garda Technical Bureau were there before me and they watched Dr Cassidy work. I waited outside, ready to receive the results.

After five hours, Dr Cassidy emerged and joined me in the waiting room. She looked at me and said, 'I have good news and bad news.' Still thinking of the outcome of a tragic accident that my superintendent was predicting, I said, 'What's the good news?' She replied, 'I've completed the post-mortem in full, and if it was any other pathologist you'd have been waiting another four hours for the conclusion.' *That's me told*, I thought. 'So what would the bad news be?' I asked. Dr Cassidy said bluntly, 'You have a murder on your hands.'

I was taken aback, because this was not what I was expecting, given the rundown I'd received earlier. I asked her how sure she could be that it was murder, and in her straight-talking way she asserted that there was no doubt whatsoever that the woman had been strangled by means of a ligature. She brought me into the examination room and together we observed the various signs that led to her conclusion. She showed me a red mark on the right side of Mary's neck that was an indication of an incomplete ligature mark, then pointed out that her tongue was swollen and that the face was congested and cyanosed and there were petechiae (pinpoint haemorrhages) over the eyelids and inside the mouth. QED, apparently.

I asked if any of the findings could have occurred as a result of a fall down a set of stairs. 'Good question, but no,' came the reply. Dr Cassidy explained that death from such a fall is normally associated with a significant head injury, or possibly a fracture of the cervical spine or the bones in the neck, but no such injuries were present on the body of Mary Gough. The bruising that was evident looked, in fact, to be more consistent with being dragged down the stairs rather than falling down them. The findings were clear, she told me; there was no other possible cause.

I rang the super, Tom Gallagher, and gave him the bad news. At that stage, there was no senior investigating officer – a role that was introduced in 2008 – so as was usual then, the super took responsibility for the investigation. He ordered an incident room to be set up immediately in Balbriggan station and requested the help of the National Bureau of Criminal Investigation (NBCI) to run it. He appointed me the lead officer on the case.

It would turn out to be one of the most intricate murder cases I would ever encounter, with enough twists and turns for a shocking crime novel. It would test everything I had learned up to this point, and I had to sharpen my wits to catch a killer who was ready for us.

The first step was to examine the evidence we had. There was the scene itself, but that was minus the body, of course. When the emergency services had responded to Colin Whelan's 999 call at 12.30 a.m. on 1 March, they had removed Mary from the hallway and rushed her straight to Beaumont, so I only had their statements to piece together the exact crime scene, along with the victim's husband's account of what had happened. Colin's account was very straightforward and remained the same no matter how many times he repeated it: he had spent the evening at the gym and then with Mary; they had driven to Drogheda to collect a detox report from Mary's homeopath and got home at 9.45 p.m.; they sat in the sitting room until about 11.15 p.m., when Mary went upstairs to have a shower; at midnight, Colin heard a loud *thump, thump, thump* and went into the hallway to find his wife lying at the foot of the stairs – he said she was moaning and reached out her right hand to him; she was bleeding heavily from her nose, he thought, so he dialled 999 and reported the fall, put a duvet around his wife and a towel under her and followed the operator's instructions for CPR until the emergency crew arrived and took over.

The first emergency crew on the scene comprised six members of the Balbriggan fire service. They took over CPR, but Mary Gough was non-responsive. An ambulance arrived and transferred her to Beaumont Hospital. The crew continually tried to revive her, but she remained non-responsive. At Beaumont, a team worked intensively on Mary. They noted that she was very cold to the touch, with no pulse and no spontaneous breathing. There was a lot of blood on her face and neck, but she wasn't actively bleeding. She was also cyanosed, which means blue in colour, and that too seemed to tell a different story. Their efforts were to no avail. She was pronounced dead at 1.25 a.m. on 1 March 2001.

Once Mary was dead, some members of the medical team went out to Colin Whelan to break the news to him and console him. An observant person can be worth their weight in gold to a Garda investigation, and it turned out that one of the nurses was just such a person. Colin's shirt had a couple of buttons open, and she noticed some scratch marks on his chest. She offered to check them for him, and he explained that they must have happened when he was rushing around. She knew this couldn't be the case and reported her concerns.

In a case like this, suspicion falls very quickly on the husband, but as the investigator it's imperative to follow the evidence, rather than an easy assumption. I couldn't afford to think of Colin Whelan as the obvious suspect. Yes, he presented reasonable grounds for suspicion, but on the other hand, he was regarded as being devoted to Mary – a good husband, and also a good son and son-in-law. He had no history of violence, no history of any wrongdoing whatsoever, so it wasn't a straightforward matter. Was it possible that someone else had been in the house that night and strangled Mary? It might have sounded like a far-fetched possibility in the circumstances, but a good investigation covers every angle, even those that might seem implausible.

I went back to his initial statement, taken on the night Mary died. He had specifically said that he and Mary were home alone that night. If that was the case, it would certainly strengthen our suspicions regarding his role in her death. So I went to the Whelan home and examined the house alarm. From my life before An Garda, I had a radio operator's licence and knew a bit about radio waves. I reckoned that the main control panel would be pulse-generated, with the pulses continuously in operation, even when the alarm was turned off. I asked an engineer to come in and examine the system, to see if my thinking was correct. The engineer confirmed my thinking. He then extracted an event history/memory log from the system, covering a twelve-month period up to and including the day after the murder. The log showed that no sensor had been activated during the night in question. Even with the alarm switched off, any tampering would have registered on the control panel, and it hadn't. There was no alarm activation of any kind on the night of Mary's death, so there had definitely been no intruder. This meant I had a murdered woman alone in the house with her husband. The clues were still leading towards Colin Whelan.

The other thing that threw up an anomaly was the 999 call. The team listened to it again, and something stood out immediately. Mary had been found with a duvet wrapped around her, and checking back on Colin's statement, he said the 999 operator had told him to do this. We listened to the call carefully. There was no mention whatsoever of a duvet, or of covering Mary, or of keeping her warm. Nothing. Colin's statement to this effect wasn't true. I felt in my gut that this very interesting lie was going to prove important.

One of the worst things a detective has to do is to inform a family of the death of a loved one, especially when it's a murder. The grief and shock produced by the revelation are very difficult to witness, and there's really nothing you can do by way of help or comfort. On top of that, you know that it's your face they will see whenever they tell the story of what happened and how they found out. It's a nasty responsibility. And when it came to the murder of Mary Gough, I had to do something that turned out to be even more difficult: tell two bereaved families that we suspected their son/son-in-law had killed her.

The families were united in their grief at the loss of Mary, but also in their fondness for Colin. They had no idea about the results of the post-mortem, so it was going to come as a huge shock to them that we had our doubts about his story. I considered it carefully, turning over various options in my mind, because I thought telling them required a proper strategy. At the same time, I had the horrible feeling that no matter what I did, it was going to be akin to pulling the pin and rolling the grenade.

I decided on a two-stage approach: tell the Goughs first,

then the Whelans, all on the same day. In the first place, the Goughs were the primary family – being the victim's family – so it was right that they be told any news first, before anyone else. But there was another reason as well. Once we told the Goughs that we weren't convinced by Colin's version of events, and that they didn't tally with the post-mortem findings, they would naturally want to question him. This meant he would either have to stick to his story or change it, and that he'd have to tell it to a wider audience, who would then become potential witnesses. In this way, Mary's family would actually be our allies in getting to the truth.

Sure enough, the Goughs were utterly astonished to hear that we had suspicions about Colin's account of Mary's death. He was part of their family, and they had no suspicions about him themselves. I kept the information in this first conversation to a minimum: we weren't happy with Colin Whelan's statement vis-à-vis the post-mortem results. I said what I had to say and then I shut up, which is usually the best course of action. The family were shocked, couldn't string a response together at first, then the questions flooded out and over me, filled with anger and disbelief at what we were suggesting about their son- and brother-in-law.

As it happened, I didn't get to tell the Whelan family in person, as planned. Once we left the Goughs, they went straight around to see Colin Whelan to ask him what on earth was happening and what the gardaí were talking about. As a result, the news filtered out quickly to the Whelan family. They, too, were sure that my colleagues and I were gravely mistaken, and that it would all be cleared up quickly and Colin would stand exonerated.

The day after I told the Goughs of our concerns, Mary's brother arrived at Balbriggan Garda Station looking for me.

He wanted to know exactly what we were saying when we said we 'weren't happy' with Colin's version of events. I listened as he told me that the two families were in disarray, shocked at this sudden turn. The Goughs had gone to see the Whelans and they'd all sat around trying to unravel what could be going through the investigators' heads, and couldn't come up with anything sensible. The Whelans felt they should all ignore the gardaí, making the point that Colin hadn't been arrested, which meant it was all a storm in a teacup and needn't be taken seriously at all.

I listened to Mary's brother as he struggled in vain to reason it all out, and he got angrier and angrier at this slur on a man they all respected and loved. When he paused for breath, I swung the hammer blow: 'We are conducting a murder investigation because Mary was strangled to death.' He reeled out of the station, his world turned upside down, and I felt very sorry for him. But this shock-by-shock approach was important to the investigation, so I had to stick with it. As expected, he went straight off to tell the families what he'd just learned.

Later that day, I spoke with Mary's mother, Marie. She, too, was deeply shocked at the suggestion of Colin being involved in her daughter's death. Marie was an intelligent woman, able to size up a person, and it was obvious that she believed Colin incapable of hurting Mary. Marie's grief was huge – she had not only lost her daughter, she had also lost her best friend. They had been a tight unit, the pair of them, and when Marie talked to me about Mary, it brought her to life in a way that it almost hurt to witness. Marie's husband had died some years before, and her children were her life. With Mary's death, she had been robbed of so much.

I looked into her eyes and promised her that I would leave no stone unturned in identifying exactly what had happened to her only daughter, and who was responsible. Marie held my gaze, leaned forward and said, 'You will leave no crumb unturned, Pat.' Her variation on the usual saying made absolute sense to me, and I nodded in agreement.

With all murders, the investigating team want to give the family the answers they so badly need, and it was no different with the Gough family. I knew we'd cover every single detail in order to give them a definitive answer as to how and why Mary was killed in cold blood.

There was one other very interesting thing Marie said to me. As she spoke about Mary, and then about Mary and Colin, it was as if she were picking up different memories, looking at them and putting them down again, like shells on a beach, searching for any scrap of meaning or any clue that could make sense of this death. When her mind went back to her daughter's wedding day, she described a moment when Colin left the church to go outside and organize the post-ceremony photos. Mary started weeping, right there in the church, and Marie's immediate thought was that it was because her father wasn't there to see her big day. So she comforted her daughter until the tears stopped. But later, she wondered if that interpretation had been correct. After the wedding, Mary changed. She began to dress in a dowdy fashion that wasn't her style, and she stopped getting her nails done and wearing make-up. When Marie asked why, Mary said that Colin didn't like it. There were moments when Marie thought about these things, and the wedding day especially. Had Mary actually been crying because she'd just married someone who didn't make her happy, who wasn't right for her? It was a question that niggled at her, and she was placing her trust in the investigation team finding out the truth about her daughter's marriage.

Once the news was known to the families, Colin became

the centre of attention in a new way, with relatives asking him what had happened and forcing him to retell the story again and again. He stuck to his narrative. But, as we'd hoped, this line of questioning from both families would later give us witness statements from those closest to the couple. He was feeling the weight of scrutiny now, and we could see the emotions he was struggling to contain. In a sit-down with him to once again go over the events of that night, he banged his fist down on the arm of the chair he was sitting in and shouted, 'I am telling you what happened. Why don't you believe me?' It seemed he thought that if he said it, we would accept it, close the door on our way out and not bother him again. That was never going to happen. I could see this was a man under pressure, and for our purposes that was a good thing.

At this stage, my gut was telling me that Colin had murdered his wife, but I couldn't answer the crucial question: why? I was lucky in that the team assigned to work the case were all excellent detectives. The incident room was full of ideas and everyone was ready to work. It was very much a team effort as we sifted through a mountain of documents and circumstantial evidence. First, we tracked Colin's movements on the day of the murder, which was very easy. He had gone about his business as if he'd wanted to lay a trail of breadcrumbs for us.

He went to work as usual, ringing his wife twice during his working hours. Mary's work colleagues had talked about her incredibly attentive husband, and how he regularly rang her during the day, remarking how lucky she was to have a man like Colin. During his lunch break, he went to Brown Thomas department store on Grafton Street, and selected an expensive gift for Mary. It was a bronze ornament of a fisherman in a boat. Colin paid £99 for it, standing at a counter perfectly in view of a security camera. He told the woman at the till about his wonderful wife, and how it was a gift for her. She remembered him well because of that chat. When he arrived home at 6 p.m., Mary was busy preparing his dinner. He went out to the local gym for half an hour, then came back home to eat the meal with Mary. Then they headed to Drogheda, back home again by 9.45. Nothing unusual anywhere, and plenty of expressions of love to back up his reputation as a devoted husband.

Our next move was to secure search warrants for his workplace and the house. He ran his own company, which supplied computer programming services. He had one client – Irish Permanent – and worked from their premises on St Stephen's Green, in Dublin city centre. He was the sole employee of his company. Warrant in hand, we went to his office and definitely left no crumb unturned. His workstation was a very long, curved desk holding two PCs. We searched every inch of the desk and removed virtually everything, including the PCs, his paperwork and diary. I even poked around in the square metal dustbin beside his desk and found a crumpled-up yellow Post-it note. Someone had written on it: *Roses are red, violets are blue.* I took it, and the bin. I gave the PCs to the Computer Crimes Investigation Unit (CCIU), with instructions to advise me of anything interesting they found.

The Whelans' house in Balbriggan was gone through with a fine-tooth comb as well. When we first entered it to begin the search, I remarked to my colleagues that the place made me uneasy. It was absolutely immaculate, and the books on the shelves were stacked tallest to smallest, all aligned by height in a manner that looked like it had been measured out with a ruler. It put me in mind of the film *Sleeping with the Enemy*, where a woman is living with a man who micro-controls her existence. It was a level of perfection that was somehow troubling, giving the impression of someone who always needed to be in control. I thought about those constant phone calls that Mary's colleagues had mentioned, and I wondered just how loving they really were. I had a feeling, looking at those bookshelves, that there might be a different story behind the facade presented by Colin Whelan.

We searched the house thoroughly and took away anything that wasn't nailed down, including paperwork related to the couple's finances. And we weren't the only ones examining the crime scene in detail. The scene had been preserved after the first report of the incident, and it remained cordoned off for about three days. The Garda Technical Bureau had conducted its crime scene examination, which had turned up some damning evidence. There were blood spatters around the house – on the stairs, on the landing and in the master bedroom. This wasn't consistent with a fall straight down the stairs. The duvet was still lying in a heap at the bottom of the stairs, with a yellow towel beneath it that was bloodstained. On the floor between the master bedroom and the en suite was a dressing gown; the belt was twisted and seemed to be stained with blood. The GTB also took scrapings from Mary's fingernails. They found two DNA profiles – Mary's and Colin's.

In the incident room we began evaluating the items taken from the Whelans' home and Colin's office, and I realized that the 'why' might be staring us in the face, right there on the table among the documents. I found a life insurance policy that had been taken out in March 2000, about six months before their wedding. That was simply forward planning and not suspicious, but I followed the thread and started digging into the history of the policy. When it was first taken out it was for £200,000, a very significant sum. When I investigated further, I discovered that the policy had been upped to £400,000 in May 2000, payable on the death of either spouse within ten years. Both Colin and Mary had signed this policy, but was it definitely Mary's signature? I brought in experts from the Documents and Handwriting Section at Garda Headquarters to examine it, but the response was inconclusive: it was probably genuine, but it could be a copy. Well, that wasn't going to hold up in court as a professional opinion.

Something about that policy kept bothering me, and I couldn't let it go. The conditions didn't add up: if one spouse died, the surviving beneficiary would receive £400,000, but the policy ran for a ten-year period only. Why would a healthy young couple set up their life insurance in this manner? I'm not an expert in this area, so I decided to ask the opinions of two people who were. I sent it to a financial accountant within An Garda and also to a forensic accountant based in London. They both came back with the same opinion: the dual policy for £400,000 on each life for a fixed period of ten years with no encashment value would seem an excessive amount of life-only insurance. The policy may have been a standard one, but the amount was very large considering their mortgage was only £79,000. There were no children to be provided for and Mary's earnings were not high enough for her to warrant such a large sum. Just as I'd thought, it didn't make sense, and therefore it was suspicious. I marvelled at Colin Whelan's long-term planning: was this the oldest motive in the book – kill your spouse and collect a lump sum?

I felt we had uncovered the secrets of the case, but then the technical team got back with their findings from Colin's PC. The whole investigation team was stunned by what they'd found. There we were, watching hours of CCTV footage, talking to a hundred people, raking through documents, and all the while we had the perfect witness just waiting to be asked the questions: the computer. Silent, objective, infallible memory – a witness that could not be contradicted.

It was the first time I'd heard the phrase 'cyber affair'. This was 2001, so social media hadn't yet exploded into people's lives and changed everything. But Colin was an IT man, so he was ahead of the times; he got in on the ground floor and kept climbing. He was operating in chat rooms and dating sites, where he went by the name 'Celtic tackle'. His profile stated he was: *Colin, Irish nationality, 28 years of age, systems analyst, interestingly single and looking.*

It was all laid out for us, the stepping stones from first sticking his toe into the online dating pond to meeting a woman whom he reeled in hook, line and sinker. Helen Sheppard began chatting to 'Celtic tackle' in December 2000, and it soon turned into lengthy phone calls. Helen's mother had died not long before and she was somewhat vulnerable, turning to chat rooms for socializing and hoping for love. That's when Colin showed up, and seemed to be the man of her dreams.

Their relationship moved very quickly from strangers bumping into each other in virtual reality to two people proclaiming their love for each other and arranging to set up a real life together. Between 26 and 28 February 2001, they made arrangements to meet, but Colin cancelled, saying he had to go to Germany. He suggested he would visit her in Wales on 2 March instead. On 28 February, Colin sent Helen an email setting out his feelings for her for the first time. Later, he phoned Mary, then put the phone down and called Helen and talked to her for thirty minutes. Helen was convinced that this man was in love with her, and that they had a future together.

As a murder detective who was used to digging and digging to find even the smallest clue, the largesse of the computer evidence was mind-blowing. This was the first time in Ireland that a computer formed the central plank of the investigation and evidence, so none of us had experienced such a thing before. I couldn't believe it could be so easy to track a person's life, to track their very thinking. It was thrilling in one way, and disturbing in another.

After viewing Colin's online life, I organized a trip to Wales to talk to Helen in person. I asked the local Welsh police to set up a meeting and attend as well, which was protocol in these circumstances. They did so, and on 9 March 2001, I and two detectives from my team met with them, and then all of us headed off to talk to Helen Sheppard. Her home was in a row of terraced houses on the steepest street I had ever seen. I thought to myself that the heart attack rate must be very low, given that everyone would be fit as a fiddle from climbing up there every day. We knocked on Helen's door, and she welcomed us inside. She was a very warm person, but she looked worried and confused about us calling on her.

I walked through the house and into the kitchen, and there on the fridge door was a photo of Colin Whelan, stuck on with a magnet. I pointed at it and asked if it was him. Helen said it was, but she hadn't heard from him since 28 February. She looked at us in apprehension. 'I hope there's nothing wrong?' she said.

In a gentle voice, I told Helen that Colin was a married man. She told me she was aware of that, and that his wife had died in a traffic accident. I knew there was no easy way to break the bad news I had to give her, so I just said it plainly. 'Listen, Helen, Colin's wife died on the first of March just gone . . . and we believe he murdered her.' With that, Helen Sheppard collapsed to her hunkers and wept inconsolably.

When she had regained her composure, she was cooperative

and eager to help the investigation. We downloaded the hard drive content from her PC, which took eight hours, and we took a detailed statement regarding her relationship with Colin Whelan. She showed us one hundred greeting card emails he had sent her, which she kept filed in date order. I flicked through and came across one bearing the phrase 'Roses are red, violets are blue'. I smiled to myself.

We now had a second motive, linked to the first – once he had killed Mary, Colin could collect his big insurance payout and move on to a new life with Helen. The team was disturbed by the level of preparation and the patient execution of his plan. It was methodical and utterly devoid of emotion. I had worked on a number of murders by this time, but this was the first time I felt I was dealing with a psychopath. That wasn't a medical diagnosis given to Colin Whelan, but from my understanding of what a psychopath was, I felt that was what we were facing. Colin fitted the bill perfectly as far as I was concerned – intelligent, organized, capable of feigning emotions he didn't feel, possessing a grandiose sense of himself, manipulative and lacking remorse or guilt. It meant he was highly dangerous because he would do whatever it took to get his own way and put the world into the order that made most sense to him.

And that wasn't the end of the revelations. There was another incredible insight contained on the hard drive of Colin's computer, an insight that was deeply shocking in a case that we thought couldn't shock us any more. The technical team tracked Colin's browser history and found the websites he had been searching prior to the murder. It was clear from this that he had set out purposefully and deliberately to kill Mary and commit the perfect murder. On 2 January, he had researched 'Asphyxiation', 'choking', 'smothering' and 'blocking the air supply'. On 29 January, he searched for 'death by asphyxiation'. On 19 February, he looked up 'causes instant death'. On 20 February, he researched 'blocking the wind-pipe', 'how long to die from asphyxiation', 'lack of oxygen', 'lack of oxygen may cause death', 'lack of oxygen to the brain', 'lack of oxygen to the head' and 'manual strangulation'. It was a chilling list, and my heart went out to poor Mary, unwit-tingly living with a man who was buying her gifts and playing the loving husband, and all the while planning to kill her with his own hands. It was sickening.

From an evidential point of view, the most incriminating web search conducted by Colin Whelan was 'North Carolina Supreme Court – state – Wallace'. This concerned a serial killer called Henry Louis Wallace, who was convicted of nine counts of murder in North Carolina, USA, in January 1997. The murders were committed over a two-year period and involved the strangulation, choking and asphyxiation of women. In eight of these crimes, various ligatures – including T-shirts, a bra, pillowcases and towels – were used either as the murder weapon or as accessories to conceal the actual cause of death. In a number of cases the defendant used towels to wipe the scene clean of fingerprints and other incriminating evi-dence. In one of the killings, Wallace rolled the victim onto her back, pulling the towel tight around her neck until her face was blue. He did this in order to prevent any ligature marks occurring, which would immediately suggest strangulation. He then removed the towel and called 911. He moved the woman from the bed to the floor and began administering CPR to instructions from the 911 operator. When police offi-cers arrived, it was obvious the victim was dead.

This closely echoed the crime scene at the murder of Mary Gough. We had the towel under the body, the charade of CPR and the emergency services realizing the body was too cold to correspond to the version of events told to them. Colin Whelan was a good student, as methodical in his studies as in everything else. He gleaned all the information he needed from these websites and replicated the actions on his wife, believing he would get away with murder. The search teams had found Colin's dressing gown and noticed that the belt looped around it was stretched taut in the middle; forensic examination later showed that there were traces of Mary's DNA and mucus on it. A common feature of the Wallace crimes he had researched was the use of a towel or other piece of material to act as a buffer between the implement of strangulation and the victim's neck – thus preventing telltale ligature marks. Based on all the evidence gathered, it seemed likely that he'd planned to render Mary unconscious by choking her with the towel-wrapped belt, then throw her down the stairs to ensure a convincing scene. That plan went awry when he applied too much force and killed his wife upstairs. He then had to drag her body down the stairs, causing burn marks on her legs and bottom. From that moment, things started to unravel, but he must have thought he was still in control.

This explained something that had always seemed so out of place: the lack of neatness at the crime scene. He had left behind the towel, the duvet and other signs of what had actually occurred, which seemed utterly out of character for this man of perfection. What I realized was that he must have been working on the assumption that, after playing the grieving husband in the hospital, he'd head on home and get everything shipshape and Bristol fashion again, and no one would be any the wiser. But the professional and thorough approach of Superintendent Tom Gallagher thwarted this plan. He had ordered the scene preserved, based solely on some scratch marks on Colin Whelan's chest. It was a mark of his impressive ability as a detective that he had done this, and it was thanks to him we got this far in figuring out what exactly had happened to Mary.

Colin Whelan had played the long game, behaving as the perfect husband, convincing everyone that he and Mary were blissfully happy. I recalled the relative who'd told me how she had visited the couple for what turned out to be Mary's last Christmas, and how there was a pile of presents under the tree. But it struck her that they were not wrapped. Mary said it was all the gifts from Colin for Christmas, but obviously he intended everyone to see them clearly, rather than intending for Mary to get a lovely surprise on Christmas morning. That detail had stayed with me and now I understood why – it summed up the whole charade he had snared Mary within, and how he had fooled everyone else as well. He was clever – almost clever enough to get away with it. As the team viewed the evidence we'd uncovered, there was one comfort: we had him.

The arrest of Colin Whelan was my first meaningful arrest. That's how I've always seen it. Prior to that, I had arrested a number of people for various offences, but never for murder. In the Whelan case, I was the lead officer, and it was the moment all our hard work had been leading up to.

At 8 a.m. on Tuesday, 10 April 2001, I knocked on the door of Colin Whelan's parents' house in Gormanston, County Meath. I stepped into the hallway and went on down to the bedroom in which Colin was staying. I opened the door and he was lying in bed, awake, like he was waiting for me. I asked him to get up and dressed and come to the kitchen. There, I said to him, 'I want to explain who I am.' This might sound odd, given that we were already well acquainted, but I was always very careful when performing arrests to clearly announce my identity and my exact reason for being present. To my mind, if the arrest is carried out perfectly correctly, then it can't be questioned or undermined by the defence in a trial.

Colin looked at me with disdain, as if he thought I was being smart by saying this, and he replied, 'I know well who you are.' That was the end of the small talk. I put my hand on his shoulder, in front of his family, and said, 'I am now arresting you on suspicion of the murder of your wife, Mary Gough, at 49 Clonard Street, Balbriggan, on the twenty-eighth of February 2001 to the first of March 2001. You are not obliged to say anything unless you wish to do so, but whatever you do say will be taken down in writing and may be given as evidence.' He did not resist in any way, indeed he was very cooperative, but he said nothing at all.

I brought him to Balbriggan Garda Station, where he was questioned until 8.20 p.m. He was pleasant, but he repeatedly answered 'No comment' to the questions put to him. As he had been arrested on suspicion of a crime, we could question him for twelve hours (nowadays it's twenty-four hours), at which point we had to release him from the terms of his detention. During this period, I had to keep the Director of Public Prosecutions informed at all times, as only the DPP can direct a charge to be made. The DPP's office were already aware of the evidence we had amassed against Colin, and now they followed the progress of the questioning. We got the go-ahead to charge Colin Whelan with murder, so at 8.20 p.m. I formally released him, then immediately arrested him for the crime of murder. I charged him to appear at Swords District Court the following morning, 11 April.

While Colin was in custody that night, awaiting his court date the next morning, his brother-in-law walked into the station to find out what was going on. For the family and friends of the accused, these days are horribly difficult, particularly as they don't really know what's happening because we can't discuss the case with them. This is someone they love and trust, and we have them locked up in a cell, and they simply can't understand what's happening. Back in 2001 there were no family liaison officers (FLOs) to help relatives through this period. Thankfully, FLOs are firmly in place now, as a conduit between the family and the investigation team, which is a very important and helpful role. But on that night, there was no FLO and Colin's brother-in-law had me in his sights, naturally enough. He confronted me, pointing his finger right up against my nose, angrily telling me exactly what he thought of me and An Garda for arresting a decent, law-abiding man. He was very angry, but I knew I had to stay calm and still and just soak it up. If I didn't, I could well be heading to Swords District Court in the back of the van beside Colin Whelan.

When a murder case is going to court, the Garda Press Office releases a statement informing of that development, which is why court appearances are a media scrum, with the gardaí fighting to get the accused through the crowds gathered outside. This day was no different. Swords District Court was mobbed by reporters and cameras, and we had to clear a path through them to get Colin inside. The hearing lasted about five minutes. Colin Whelan was remanded in custody, but his barrister secured bail through the High Court later that day. This meant he could go free but had to fulfil bail conditions, such as signing in at Balbriggan Garda Station daily. The trial date was set for October 2003, which was two and a half years away. During that time, Colin would be free to go about his business, but he would have to be at the

Central Criminal Court in October 2003 to answer the charges we had laid against him.

For almost two years, Colin Whelan observed his bail conditions to the letter as the trial date crept closer. Then came a twist none of us was expecting. In March 2003 I got a call from my superintendent with the news: the previous day, Whelan had failed to sign in at the station, his family had reported him missing and his car had just been spotted on the Upper Cliff Road in Howth. My first thought was, *Jesus, he's done a runner.* I got into my car and headed out to Howth, to see the scene for myself.

The walk up from the village to the hill is a popular one, following a narrow winding path that hugs the cliffs and ends in a beautiful view over Dublin Bay. It was on top of the hill that I saw the car. It was actually Mary's car, and I noted that it was parked with millimetre-perfect precision; I'd expect no less of Colin. The passenger window was wound partway down, and when I looked through it there was a gin bottle that was almost empty and the car keys sitting on the passenger seat. I looked at the little scene he had left, then I walked over to the cliff edge and looked out to the wide blue sea, and I knew without a shadow of a doubt that Colin Whelan hadn't taken his own life, as he clearly wanted us to believe.

Unfortunately, we still had to order a full land and sea search, because we couldn't assume my hunch was correct, but I knew in my gut that it was. The car was parked so precisely that it in no way looked like the work of a distraught, suicidal man. The window had been left open so that we didn't have to smash it to retrieve the keys – another aspect of Colin's desire for neatness. The gin bottle was just a prop, and when I checked his phone it showed that his last call was to the Samaritans. Convincing? Not when the call lasted one second. This crime scene had been staged by an intelligent, controlling, manipulative man who had everything to hide. So even as the helicopters droned overhead, searching for his body, I was totally focused on figuring out where he'd really gone.

It would take me a long time to answer that question, but like everything else Colin Whelan did, I got to the bottom of it eventually. After he left his 'suicide' scene for the dim-witted detectives to find and be tricked by, he walked down to the train station in Howth. He'd chosen that station because it had no CCTV, so his movements wouldn't be caught on camera. He boarded the train to Belfast, then made his way to Belfast International Airport, where he booked a flight to Barcelona. There, he got a ferry out to the island of Majorca, his final destination.

His cleverness was integral to this plan because he'd also figured out how to get a false passport. I won't disclose exactly how he did this, but suffice to say that he picked a person of similar age and build to himself, someone he surmised would not possess a passport, and he assumed that person's identity. He must have been laughing to himself as the Mediterranean breezes ruffled his hair on the boat over to the island. He might not have executed the perfect murder, as he'd planned, but as far as he knew he'd now executed the perfect escape. He was completely free, and his wife Mary Gough was like a bad dream that he had finally woken up from.

Back in Ireland, the trail had gone cold, and we were facing a major criminal trial without the criminal. We had no idea where Colin Whelan had absconded to, and we couldn't even prove that he *had* absconded – it was still just a gut instinct. It was absolutely galling to have got this far, and then be out-witted by him disappearing. But the truth was we didn't even know where to start looking. We knew nothing of the station or the train to Belfast or the flight to Spain. It was needle-in-a-haystack stuff. So the other jobs on our desks clamoured for our attention, and Colin Whelan took a back seat. There was absolutely nothing to go on. A dead end.

It was fourteen months before a clue came our way, and another two months before I got confirmation of an authentic sighting. As can often happen, it was just a simple, random coincidence that unlocked the whole thing.

I got a call from a superintendent who had received some information from a personal friend. It might be nothing, it might be something, he said. His friend, who was from Balbriggan, had been holidaying in Majorca and went into an upmarket joint – the Squadron Bar in Portals Nous – for a drink. The barman looked familiar, and the friend was sipping his drink and racking his brains. *Who is he?* Then it hit him like a slap in the face: Colin Whelan, the guy wanted at home for murdering his wife. That's who it was!

He left the place quick sharp, wondering if Colin had recognized him. But the next night, curiosity was eating him up, so he went back to the Squadron Bar for another look, to see if he'd been imagining things. No sign of Colin anywhere. The friend asked the staff about the guy who was serving last night. 'That's Cian, from Galway,' he was told. He began to doubt himself, so he finished his holiday, went home, said nothing to anyone. But about a month later he met up with his old friend, the superintendent, and he told him about the guy he saw in Majorca who looked spookily like Colin Whelan. It wasn't much, but the super decided to ring me to tell me about it anyway.

That call came out of the blue, when I'd begun to think we'd never be able to give Mary Gough's family peace, but I had a feeling it could be something important. So I got on to the Guardia Civil in Spain, via Interpol, and sent them a photo of Colin Whelan. Then I waited. I waited for eight long weeks before I got a call back: yes, they'd checked it out, and the man at the Squadron Bar was the man in the photograph. As it turned out, the long delay in getting this confirmation played in my favour. Colin had resigned from the job the day after the super's friend had spotted him, but three weeks later he bumped into his boss and asked if anyone had been looking for him. She said no, and if he wanted his job back, it was his. That's when Colin made an unlucky assumption: he reasoned that the man from Balbriggan hadn't actually recognized him, that he was panicking for no good reason, and that the coast was clear. He agreed to come back to work at the bar. He had no idea that I was on his trail again, and that the tables had finally turned.

I got a second stroke of luck when another phone call came through. This was from a civilian, a woman – and just as before, it was a bit of random coincidence. This woman had also walked into the Squadron Bar while holidaying in Portals Nous, and she'd got talking to the lovely Cian from Galway. Then one day she was reading the newspaper, and there in black and white was a photo of a wanted man – and it's only Cian from Galway. She couldn't believe her eyes but she knew it was him, no doubt in her mind. She then did something that should have earned her a medal, and for which I was very grateful. She chatted more to Cian at the bar, and it turned out he was into rugby and would love the new Ireland jersey. Well, she just happened to have a friend who could arrange that, so why didn't he give her his details and she'd post it over to him from Ireland? He was absolutely thrilled, and scribbled his name and address on a card. She pocketed it, and when she rang me she told me I was welcome to come and collect the card.

So I did, and when we got the handwriting analysed it told us what the Guardia Civil were telling us: Cian and Colin were one and the same. *What are the odds?* I thought to myself. I had no earthly idea, but it felt like we'd just beaten them.

It turned out there was a new extradition agreement in place between member states of the EU, which meant I could rely on the Spanish police to help me achieve a quick arrest before Colin could scarper again. The extradition warrant was issued on foot of a bench warrant from the Central Criminal Court. It proved to the Spanish authorities that we had a prima facie case, which was necessary to secure their permission to remove Colin Whelan from their jurisdiction to ours. As this was the first extradition from Spain to Ireland under the new system, I would be accompanied by a detective garda from the Extradition Section of An Garda. It was essential to execute it perfectly, as it would provide a template for such extraditions in the future.

When the Spanish police came knocking, they disrupted a very nice life. Colin was popular in the bar with staff and customers, enjoyed the work, and was in a relationship with a woman who no doubt had been bowled over by his perfectly devoted ways. It was all going right for him, until it wasn't.

The plan was for me to go to Spain and be present for the arrest, so I could conduct a search and take possession of any belongings or items of interest, which was permitted under the terms of the extradition warrant. I awaited the word from the Guardia Civil that it was on and I should hotfoot it over there, but instead I got a call from the Gough family, saying there was a reporter on their doorstep telling them Colin Whelan had been arrested in Spain. I had to make some calls to find out myself and it turned out to be true – the Spanish police had gone ahead and made the arrest, which had somehow been leaked to the Spanish media, which was how the Irish reporters had got wind of it. I was highly irritated by this unexpected turn of events, but I had to move on.

The Guardia Civil informed me that, when first arrested, Whelan had insisted he wasn't Colin Whelan. His fingerprints confirmed his identity, however, at which point he admitted who he was. He was given the option of contesting the extradition warrant, but he declined and chose instead to return to Ireland to face the charges. So about a week after he was first detained, I received word that he had been transferred to Madrid airport, to await collection by An Garda Síochána – in other words, me.

On 27 July 2004, my plane landed at Madrid airport, which is the holding centre for all extraditions from Spain. It was eighteen months since I'd laid eyes on Colin Whelan, and I was very much looking forward to the reunion. At the airport, I was led down to the holding cell area, which was a surreal experience. It is located under the airport building and consists of a long corridor with cells on both sides, some with glass panes, some with bars, a prisoner in each one. I know it sounds clichéd, but I couldn't help thinking of Clarice Starling, heading down the corridor to meet Hannibal Lecter and hear about his fava beans and Chianti. It was unnerving.

In the cells I passed, detainees leered at me, or wept, or banged the glass in a fury – all watching my progress with huge interest, one way or the other. About three-quarters of the way down that long corridor, there was a cell on my right with bars. Colin Whelan was behind those bars.

I looked in and he was standing there, bearded now, facing

me, ready. We exchanged a look and, as has happened to me with other murderers, we understood each other perfectly without a word being uttered. Colin's time was up – he knew it and so did I. He had accepted his fate.

I then had to do something I'd never done before: escort the prisoner back to Ireland on a commercial flight. I hand-cuffed him, and we put his coat over his hands so that other passengers wouldn't see the cuffs and be alarmed. We were booked onto an Aer Lingus flight back to Dublin. Any Irish-registered plane is sovereign land – like an airborne embassy – which makes the captain the 'president', so when transporting a prisoner you have to present yourself to the captain and announce your presence. Once you receive the captain's permission to board the flight, you sit in the two seats at the very back, just in front of the toilets. That's where I brought Colin Whelan, and we settled into our seats, side by side, for the two-and-a-half-hour journey. The detective garda from the Extradition Section sat in the seat in front of us.

Throughout the flight, Colin was pleasant and chatty and we conversed easily. I offered him a drink, and he asked for a Coke. I took off his handcuffs so he could drink it himself, but I wasn't remotely worried about him trying anything. He had psychopathic traits, but he wasn't a killer in the impulsive sense. I knew he would be well mannered and polite with me, and he was.

We talked about this and that, and then the talk came around to what was waiting for him in Ireland – his delayed trial for murder. I asked him, 'How will this play out?' He replied, 'The barristers work for me, I don't work for the barristers.' I took this to mean he was planning to plead guilty, and I mused over why he would choose to do that. I realized that he was thinking that a guilty plea would mean a quick trial, no details, no raking over the evidence, no lurid newspaper reports – and all of that would mean less pain for his family. I looked out of the corner of my eye at him, the psychopath with a heart. He turned his head and said, 'You're very good at your job.'

When the plane landed at Dublin airport, we stayed quietly in our seats while all of the other passengers disembarked. Once we landed on Irish soil, the extradition warrant was ended and I now had to arrest him on a domestic warrant. I could have done this while in the air, given that the plane was basically an extension of Ireland, but I didn't want to give a defence barrister any room for suggesting the arrest was improper in any way. So I waited until the wheels were on terra firma – what was indisputably Irish land.

When the plane was emptied of all but staff, we stood up from our seats and I cautioned Colin Whelan and arrested him for the murder of his wife, Mary. I then led him off the plane, where a patrol car was waiting – accompanied by Airport Police – to transfer him to nearby Swords Garda Station.

On 11 April 2005, four years after Mary Gough was strangled to death in her own home, Colin Whelan stood trial for her murder at the Central Criminal Court before Mr Justice Paul Carney. I still didn't know what Colin would do, how he would plead. The Whelan and Gough families were lined up in the gallery, stressed, upset and fearing the worst – each of them with a different fear, of course. Colin was brought in, wearing an immaculate suit, and the court registrar asked, 'How do you plead?' He turned and looked directly at me as he said one word: 'Guilty.' An officer began reading out the details of the crime, and I looked over at the gallery. The Whelan family were open-mouthed in disbelief. I have never again seen a family look so confused and shocked – until that moment, they still believed fully in his innocence. In sentencing him, I remember the judge describing Mary's murder as 'the most calculating and callous killing that I have ever encountered in my time in court'.

For the investigating team, it had been a long and hard-won case, but it gave us great satisfaction to know that the Gough family had their answers. I could look Marie, Mary's mother, in the eye, and tell her that I had indeed turned over every single crumb in searching for her daughter's killer. It was a terribly sad case, though, because Colin had fooled the Whelans and the Goughs. His in-laws had loved him – he had been part of their lives for more than ten years – and they were devastated by his crime. And at the centre of it all, poor Mary Gough was denied her future because she believed a liar, because she trusted a cheat. She was entirely innocent, and she didn't deserve what happened to her.

I've never forgotten her. I got to know her so well during the investigation as we dug into every aspect of her life – she was a warm and caring person who had never caused harm to anyone. The only peace I could give her was the knowledge that the man who killed her was behind bars.

There was one final twist in this case of twists and turns, however. Some weeks after Colin was sentenced and imprisoned, I was at home in Navan when I got a phone call from Colin's brother-in-law, the man who had spoken to me in anger and disbelief at Balbriggan Garda Station when Colin was charged. He said he needed to meet me: 'I want to see you face to face.' So I invited him to come to my home and he agreed. He drove straight to Navan, and when he arrived I made us a pot of tea and we sat down to talk. He wanted to give me an apology, in person, for his behaviour that night, and he wanted to tell me that he appreciated that we had found out the truth, even though it was devastating to his family. He acknowledged the hard work of the team in solving the case, and he wished me all the best in the future. Not for the first time, and certainly not the last time, I marvelled at human nature. A detective gets to see the very worst of it – but then we also get to see the very best of it. There's some solace in that, at least.

3. 'It's a burglary in progress, Detective'

It was Monday afternoon, 4 October 2004, and I was at my desk when one of the detectives on my team came in and told me about a burglary in progress out in the Naul, about five miles from where I was sitting in Balbriggan station. I knew the roads around that area like the back of my hand, and I reckoned I'd have a fair chance of cutting them off as they made good their escape if I moved quickly enough, so I jumped up from my desk and ran. I didn't stop for a jumper or a jacket, just stood up in my tie and shirtsleeves, grabbed my car keys and a walkie-talkie, and went straight out to my plain-clothes detective's standard-issue Ford Mondeo and headed in the direction of the Naul. As I drove, the radio was relaying the messages between the first garda at the scene and the station. I listened in surprise as the garda reported that a lady had been injured by the intruder and that an ambulance was in transit. *Highly unusual*, I thought to myself. It wouldn't be the last time I had that thought about this case.

As I drove along the field-edged country roads, I was already wondering about the burglary call. From experience, I knew that 99 per cent of burglars are smart, fast and have an escape plan. They go in and get out as fast as possible. A professional burglar takes two or three minutes at most, and the last thing he wants is a confrontation with the residents. He wants to get in silently, go to the main bedroom, go to the woman's side of the bed, take the jewellery – and, if he's very lucky, any cash lying about – then get the hell out of there before any blue flashing lights arrive. Was this a burglary gone wrong?

The radio was still spitting out messages. And then the voice changed, sounded a bit more urgent, and the garda on the scene told us the lady was dead. It had all gone very wrong, I thought, putting my foot down and pushing the Mondeo towards the little townland called Beldaragh.

When I reached the scene, there were cars and people outside a bungalow set back from the road. The house was called Lambay View. Two uniforms were deep in conversation on the driveway. When they spotted me, one came over and said the husband of the lady who had died wanted to go back into the house to get his coat. 'Absolutely no way,' I told him. I asked him to take out his notebook and detail every car and person in the vicinity, taking down names, addresses, phone numbers, details of their clothing and shoes, and their reason for being present. He got to it immediately. The other uniform I placed at the front gate with orders not to allow anyone into the driveway without my say-so. I told him to document any comments made by anyone who approached him.

I headed around to the back of the house, where I met my superintendent, Tom Gallagher. From inside the house I could hear the gut-wrenching sounds of people wailing and sobbing. It was the family and friends of the victim, the super told me, including her poor mother who had found her. I felt for them, but our first priority was to preserve the scene so we could figure out exactly what we were dealing with. So I went into the kitchen and told the handful of people gathered there that they would have to leave and let us do our job. An older gentleman approached me, and the expression on his face is one I'll never forget. He looked like he'd just peered through the gates of Hell.

He turned on me, shouting, 'That's my daughter dead in there. Don't tell me to leave!' I could see it was grief and shock talking, and I understood. Nonetheless, I had to insist that they all go, which they did. I walked them out through the back door, where my super was still standing just outside. The house fell silent behind me.

Superintendent Tom Gallagher was a straight-talking Leitrim man who commanded great respect, and he was no fool. I had worked with him on the Whelan case and admired him greatly. He said to me, 'Go in there, Pat, and come back out and tell me what you see.'

I went back to my car and took out the protective-clothing kit stored in the boot. Then I went around to the back door again and put on all the gear, including a full dust suit. When I was ready I walked into the house once more, knowing it was now just me and, somewhere, a dead woman.

In the kitchen, the table was overturned and the drawers were pulled out. There was a sitting area to one side and there were DVDs thrown across the floor and cabinet doors were standing open. I could see why burglary was the first call, and why it was the wrong call. No burglar bothers with the kitchen drawers. To my mind, it looked like a non-burglar's idea of a burglary, staged and unconvincing.

I made my way down the hallway. At the end, on the left, was a bedroom, and inside that bedroom was a scene of pure savagery. I saw the body of a woman with her head near the saddle board in the doorway and her body twisted at an awkward angle. Her head, neck and face were bloodied and badly injured – I could see part of her skull because the wounds were so deep. Behind her, there was a small box with blood on it. It seemed somehow out of place in the scene.

I looked at the blood spatter in the room, and it described

a very violent death. Blood spatter analysis was relatively new at the time, but I was a fully trained scenes of crime officer; I had completed a ten-week course at Templemore in 1989 and graduated first in my class. It had taught me how to finger-print and technically examine a crime scene, including fibre-evidence collecting and all kinds of trace evidence. It was invaluable training, and I got to apply the theory to real-ity every single day on the job.

Standing in the hallway, I examined what I could see of the crime scene through the door of the bedroom. The blood went as high as the ceiling, about nine feet above the body, and all across the walls and down to the skirting boards as well. I recognized that this was blood-upon-blood spattering, whereby the blood from the injury transfers to the weapon and is then flung onto the surrounding surfaces. Once blood hits a surface, it leaves a pattern and begins to dry. I could discern blood spatter on top of dry blood. This told me that it had been a frenzied attack, that the assailant had assaulted the victim and then, after a period of time, had gone back and assaulted her again.

When I first encountered a crime scene, I spent a lot of time just observing and soaking it up. It was like a sort of meditative state, where I became still and tried to pick up on what I could feel or anything I could intuit about the scene. That may sound unscientific, but I found it an effective way to notice every detail. So I stood with the body of the deceased and I studied every aspect of her death. I tried to sense what had gone on in that room, and who might have wanted to commit such an incredibly brutal killing. One thing was certain – it didn't look like the work of someone trying to get in and out of the house as quickly as possible.

When inspecting a crime scene, the cardinal rule is, of course, not to contaminate the scene. You have to move very slowly and very carefully, observing closely before you make any movements. You can't rush into it – it's important to be mindful and to dwell on every detail you can see or interpret from the physical evidence. The scene will tell you an awful lot if you pay attention to it.

The one thing common to every murder scene I've attended is the sense of sadness. There is a sorrow in the silence that is unique, and there's a sort of cold taste of death in the place. You can feel the deceased's own grief at being taken from life too soon, taken from the people they love; it's like a final despairing cry is hanging in the air around them, with all their unsaid feelings packed into it. Standing at a crime scene is deeply affecting on a number of levels, but the investigator has to push aside that natural emotional reaction and focus on the evidence. In this case, the blood spatter evidence was telling me loud and clear that this woman had been savagely beaten, and that the beating was intended to end in her death.

Eventually, I walked back down the hallway, through the kitchen and out the back door, to the fresh air and the normal colours of the world. My super looked at me with interest. 'Well,' he said, 'what did you see?'

I looked around at the garden and I was aware of a repetitive noise – something industrial – nearby. Every crime scene gives you that feeling that the world has changed – that while everything looks the same, nothing is the same any more. 'I saw two things,' I said to him. 'Number one, it wasn't a burglary. Number two, the killer really hated that lady.'

Superintendent Gallagher nodded his head slowly. 'You're correct,' he said.

'And I'd say the victim knew her killer,' I went on. 'And, like all murders, there has to be a reason.'

He nodded again. 'Exactly.' He told me the dead woman's name was Rachel O'Reilly, née Callaly. Then he looked at me and said, 'Go talk to the husband.'

I went around to the front of the house again, and I immediately noticed a man slightly apart from everything that was going on. He was a very tall, well-built man and he reminded me strongly of Colin Whelan. He was standing on his own, away from the Callaly family, who were talking to the paramedics who had arrived on the scene.

I went over to him and extended my hand and introduced myself. He shook my hand and told me he was Joe O'Reilly. I told him that I'd be investigating the incident and that we would get to the truth of what had happened to his wife. It struck me that he didn't seem very upset, but rather seemed detached from all that was going on around him. That could have been shock, of course, but it still struck me as odd. The way he was standing away from everyone else rang an alarm bell for me too; it seemed strange not to be with the family at this time.

His first comment to me was that he had been in the house earlier and had moved a box at the scene. It was the small cardboard box beside Rachel's body, and he told me that he had picked it up and moved it. Well, I thought to myself, that covered legitimate access if we found his DNA at the scene. Now another alarm bell was ringing loudly in my head.

I asked him for his mobile number, so we could keep in touch with him, and he gave it to me. I sympathized with him and warned him that there would be huge media interest when word got out and I advised him not to talk to the media, to let the investigation team do its work. We arranged that I would visit him that evening at his mother's house, to talk to him properly.

My super headed back to Balbriggan to set up an incident room, and I followed him because I was absolutely perished with the cold, from standing out in the October weather in my shirtsleeves. Just as in the Whelan case, there was no SIO role at this time, so the superintendent was responsible for running the investigation. He knew we had a really brutal killer on our hands and that it was imperative to put this person away as quickly as possible.

An excellent team was assembled, and two incident room coordinators from the National Bureau of Criminal Investigation, Detective Garda John Clancy and Detective Garda John Geraghty, were put in place, ably assisted by Detective Inspector Dominic Hayes. As the detective sergeant at Balbriggan, which took in the area of Beldaragh, I was in charge of all detectives and plain-clothes detectives in the district, which comprised Skerries, Rush, Lusk, Garristown and Balbriggan. I was therefore given responsibility for overseeing the O'Reilly case, which included keeping the Callaly family updated and informed of developments. The specific role of liaising with the Callalys was assigned to Detective Garda Peter McCoy. It was a team I greatly enjoyed working with, and I learned a lot about structuring investigations from the expertise of Clancy and Geraghty. This was a top-class unit to be part of: level-headed, smart, no hidden agendas and all with one focus – to solve the crime. If any team could track down the killer, this one could.

The incident room was busy straight away, assigning jobs and getting the investigation moving quickly. The scene was being preserved with the body in situ, until the state pathologist (as she now was), Dr Marie Cassidy, could arrive to perform her initial examination. Superintendent Gallagher put in train house-to-house inquiries all around the area, including checkpoints where passing vehicles were stopped and the drivers questioned.

The Garda Technical Bureau made its way to Lambay View and began a thorough examination of the crime scene. Search teams fanned out from the house, looking for any clues in the vicinity, with the particular aim of trying to locate a possible murder weapon. Assigned members of the incident room team also began work on tracing any CCTV footage that might be helpful – anywhere between the Naul and Joe O'Reilly's workplace, which was Viacom in Dublin. The investigation machine swung into action, moving swiftly to capture as much information as possible.

That evening, I headed out with two colleagues to talk to Joe O'Reilly about the events of the day. He was at his mother's house in Dunleer, County Louth, and when we arrived she let us in and showed us into the sitting room. We waited for about eighteen minutes, then Joe came in, fresh from the shower. He appeared calm, relaxed and collected. I led the questioning, and my first query was obvious: could he think of any reason why someone would want to murder Rachel? He said he couldn't. I asked if it was possible that Rachel was having an affair and maybe a disgruntled wife had killed her. His reply warranted a note in my notebook: 'No, neither of us were having affairs.' It seemed odd to include himself in that when I'd asked specifically about Rachel.

I asked again about possible grievances, and then suddenly dropped in another question about the possibility of an affair, this time suggesting he might be the one who was straying. He denied it again. I felt there was more to it, but I let it go.

I asked if he'd had his mobile phone on him all day, and he said that he had. I asked for the number, and to my surprise he gave me a different number from the one he'd given me at the house earlier. When I queried this, he explained that he'd thought I'd wanted Rachel's number, and that's what he'd given me. I felt sure I'd asked very clearly for his number, so this also seemed a bit odd.

I knew he'd been in the house with Rachel's body before our arrival, so next I asked for the shoes he'd been wearing at the time. He left the room to fetch them. He was gone a good while. When he returned he handed over a pair of black boots. As I took them, I looked him dead in the eye and said, 'Are you sure you weren't having an affair?' He looked straight back at me and I held his stare.

'Look,' he said, 'I did have an affair.' I asked who the woman was and he told me: 'Nikki Pelley, a girl I used to work with.' I asked Joe the date and time of his last contact with her, and he told me it was at about midday on the day of the murder. We would hear a lot more of the name Nikki Pelley as the case progressed.

In the notes I made of this interview, I recorded that he appeared very calm and controlled and in no way upset. He never showed emotion or distress, which to me seemed remarkable for a man whose wife had been savagely beaten to death just hours before. He didn't come across as a grieving husband, that much I knew, but of course that's not a crime.

The other thing that struck me was that he didn't talk about Rachel. Usually, the family can't stop talking about their loved one – they're in shock and trying to make sense of a world without that person in it, and they normally do so by talking it all out again and again. Joe O'Reilly didn't do that. This is the time in an investigation when I usually get a good picture of the deceased, but I had no inkling at all about what Rachel O'Reilly was like from her husband. That was unusual.

One of the important tasks I wanted to achieve with Joe that first evening was to get a full record of his movements that day. Timing is of the essence when interviewing a witness. They may, for example, have pertinent information but fail to reveal it because they are not aware it is important. Or if time has passed and the media has started reporting on the incident, then the witness might hold back a piece of information they fear makes them look bad in some way. It's important to interview quickly, to get as close to the first reaction as possible, and to listen carefully and probe the statement for any weak points or potential evidence. It's a skill, and it takes time to master.

I wrote down Joe's movements on Monday 4 October exactly as he described it: he got up at 5.20 a.m. and left the spare room, where he'd spent the night. Immediately I asked if things were okay in his marriage. He said they had been a bit rocky but were all good again, and he was sleeping separately from his wife simply to avoid waking her when he got up early to go to the gym. He left the house, driving his navy-blue Fiat Marea estate, stopped for petrol and arrived at his gym on the Nangor Road at 6.20 a.m. There he met with his colleague, Derek Quearney. They sat in the car chatting for twenty minutes, then went inside and used the sauna and the showers. He headed to work after that, arriving at Viacom on the Bluebell Industrial Estate on the outskirts of Dublin at 7.15 a.m. Then he left the office at 8.15 a.m. and went to Phibsboro bus depot to talk with a particular employee. Quearney joined him on this excursion, but they drove there separately. Naturally, I wanted to know why.

Joe explained that, by driving two cars, they could both claim mileage. This was an important point, as it put Joe in his own car, the Fiat Marea, alone. Once at the depot, Joe said he couldn't find the employee he needed to speak to – that his van was empty and he could see the man's phone inside the van, so there was no point ringing him. 'Did you not check the canteen?' I asked. 'There's too many canteens,' he replied without hesitation. So if he didn't see the man he'd travelled to see, who had he spoken to in the depot? He told me he spoke to no one other than Derek Quearney.

He left the depot at 11.20 a.m., reaching Viacom again at midday. At 1.30 p.m. he received a call from the crèche to say that Rachel had not collected their younger son at the appointed time. Joe said he rang Rachel's best friend, Jackie Connor, to check if Rachel was with her, then he rang Rachel's brother and her mother, Rose, and asked Rose to go to the house to check on Rachel. He then made his way home himself, and arrived at a scene of horror.

If all of this could be corroborated, Joe O'Reilly had not murdered his wife. That was the problem, though. Even a cursory check threw up questions. No one in Phibsboro bus depot had seen or spoken to Joe O'Reilly that morning. The CCTV that covered the yard area was out of service that day, and only the internal cameras were operational. Derek Quearney entered an area with CCTV coverage at 9.26 a.m., but no camera caught sight of Joe O'Reilly at any time. There was no evidence to show he'd ever been there. If he had gone searching for the employee – say, in the canteen – he would have been caught on CCTV, but of course he'd just explained that there were too many canteens to go checking them all. As I discovered later, there were just two canteens at the depot.

I asked again for Joe's mobile number, and he once again gave me Rachel's number. I was perplexed as to why he kept giving me an incorrect number.

Without anyone to back up his story, we seemed to have almost four hours when Joe's movements could not be traced, from 8.15 a.m. to midday. His sole source of alibi was, therefore, Derek Quearney. We were interested to see if he could provide any help in placing Joe O'Reilly in Phibsboro bus depot during these crucial hours.

Two of my colleagues on the team spoke to Quearney that same day – the day of the murder. His statement gave a similar account of his movements, seeming to corroborate Joe's version, but it also included some interesting nuggets. He mentioned Joe having rows with Rachel over the phone, and he also confirmed that Joe was having an affair with Nikki Pelley, saying it was known about by others. That didn't tally with Joe's assertion that the marriage had been 'a bit rocky' but that all was well and good now. I also asked Derek to tell me Joe's mobile number, which he did, confirming the correct number.

We knew it was important to talk to Nikki Pelley, and two detectives were tasked to visit her on 4 October. They asked her to confirm Joe's mobile number and her own, and she did so, backing up the number given to us by Derek Quearney. In her statement, she admitted she was having an affair with Joe, and that he stayed over with her at her home on Tuesday and Saturday nights. Joe had told her that he and Rachel had been having marital difficulties for over a year and slept in separate beds. Beyond that, she didn't want to hear anything about his marriage or Rachel. When asked about her movements on the day of the murder, she didn't mention any contact with Joe on that day.

While those interviews were taking place, other members of the team went out to Viacom, to talk to Joe O'Reilly's colleagues. Over the course of the investigation we spoke to about thirty employees, past and present. On 4 October, those who went out to conduct the initial interviews at Viacom talked to an administration assistant who shared an office with Derek Quearney and knew him and Joe well. I remember that her statement was particularly interesting. She recalled Joe walking into the office at 12.15 p.m. and his demeanour caught her attention. She said his eyes were red and puffy, like he'd been crying. She was taken aback by how he looked, and said to him, 'Jesus, you look like shit.' He mumbled something she couldn't quite catch, shrugged and took his coffee off to his own office. The fact that he looked very different – so different that someone who saw him every day was shocked by his appearance – struck me and stayed with me.

The following day, 5 October, Rachel's body was removed from the house at about 1.30 p.m. A set of car keys was found lying underneath her. These were the keys to Rachel's own car, which was parked outside. This suggested that she had not been long in the house when the attack occurred, that she was still holding her keys, having come in from the car. The coroner directed that the body be brought to Dublin City Mortuary, and Rachel finally left the place where she had been murdered.

Outside the house, the search teams soon found something. About a quarter of a mile away, a garda spotted two bags lying in a culvert. One of them contained a camcorder; the other held a jewellery box with jewellery inside. The feeling among the searchers was that these items had been placed there to support the notion that the murder was a burglary gone wrong. But there was cash in the house that hadn't been touched, so it just didn't add up. Whoever was trying to fool us wasn't doing a very good job of it.

That same day, another team arrived at Joe's workplace

with a warrant to conduct a search. They did a thorough examination of Joe's office in particular, and came away with a tranche of documents and his laptop. This was found to contain many emails to some of his family members and Nikki Pelley in which he spoke of his anger at Rachel, how much he hated her and how he longed to break free of her and take the children away to a new life. This was very much at odds with the description of his marriage and his feelings about his wife that he'd given us.

I didn't attend the post-mortem, but it was conducted on 6 October by Dr Marie Cassidy and confirmed the suspicions she'd raised when viewing the body in situ at the crime scene. The findings were stark: Rachel O'Reilly had died from head and brain injuries resulting from being struck several times with a blunt weapon. Her skull had been fractured and her brain bruised by the force of the blows. There was evidence that she had fought for her life, suggested by injuries on her arms that could have been defensive wounds. It again reminded us that we were dealing with a very determined and very dangerous killer.

Back in the incident room, the investigation was starting to sprawl out and we were following seven hundred lines of inquiry. CCTV footage was obtained from Murphy's quarries, just down the road from Lambay View. They had a camera recording the main entrance, which also took in part of the roadway beyond it. The CCTV team were interested to see a car that looked very like Joe O'Reilly's navy Fiat Marea driving by at about 9.10 a.m., in the direction of his house. At about 10 a.m., what appeared to be the same car drove past again, this time in the opposite direction. In the course of the investigation, we checked the Pulse computer system for all Ford Mareas in the country, discovering that there were 2,500 such vehicles. The team set about tracing all of them, to ascertain the likelihood of the owner of the Marea near Murphy's quarries on 4 October being Joe O'Reilly. It was a huge task, but this is a good illustration of how far the team was prepared to go to secure evidence that would be admissible and useful in a court of law.

The incident room was kept extremely busy with the amount of information pouring in from the various strands of inquiry. In fact, it became the biggest murder investigation in the history of the State up to that point. There were regularly thirty of us around the table, all involved in a massive team effort to catch a brutal killer. But there was one piece of information we were handed that was very strange. One member of the team preserving the house for technical examination had reported that Joe O'Reilly had arrived at the house while the scene was being examined. He revealed to the garda in question that he had a dream in which Rachel appeared to him and told him something was missing from the house. She specifically told him, in this dream, that a dumbbell and a towel were missing. He was telling the garda this so he could check if this was the case. Joe said he could confirm that the towel was missing – a brown towel from the hot press – but he wasn't sure about the dumbbell.

The garda who passed on this conversation found it very odd. I found it very odd myself – especially the idea that any man alive could say a specific towel was missing from the hot press. I could barely tell you where the hot press in my house was, let alone tell you what was and wasn't inside it. This towel detail was so silly, it was suspicious.

It would turn out that Rachel appeared in a number of Joe's dreams, always with a specific suggestion about the crime scene, handily enough. Unfortunately, dreams aren't suitable for use in a court of law, so none of the 'dream evidence' could ever be used.

On Wednesday 6 October, Detective Garda Peter McCoy and I went to visit the Callaly family at their home. We sat together on the couch in the conservatory and it was plain how deeply shocked these people were. Jim, Rachel's father, cried throughout and was inconsolable. He and his wife couldn't understand or explain how anyone could have wanted to murder their daughter. It was just senseless.

Unlike my conversation with Joe, Rachel came vividly to life when I talked to the Callalys. She had been a fit and active woman, and regularly enjoyed playing hockey and softball. She worked part-time at a solicitor's office in Dublin, but also sold Avon and Tupperware products around her community. She was well liked by everyone who met her and had made good friends around the Naul. She was a devoted mother to her two sons and clearly adored them. She had wanted so much for her family, but everything she tried came up against the resistance of her husband. She was unhappy in her marriage but had been putting a brave face on it and hoping Joe would reconcile with her so they could be a 'proper' family again.

I remember Jim saying, 'You know, only a week earlier, myself and Rose sat in this very spot, talking about retirement and taking it easy now that we had our family reared, and this is something that we just didn't bargain for.'

Rose struck me as a strong woman, but I could see this had rocked her to her core. I took her hands in mine and I told her, 'All I can do is be honest with you. I promise I will do my best and I will not lie to you and I will keep you updated. I'm human and I do make mistakes but bear with me. I won't let you down.' I meant every word, and there were tears in both our eyes. Those sentences marked the beginning of a friendship that lasts to this day.

It was important to take Rose's statement, as she was the first person to find Rachel after the murder. In spite of the huge shock and grief she had experienced, Rose was very clear about what she had seen. After receiving a phone call from Joe to say that Rachel had not picked up their son from the crèche, Rose drove over to Lambay View to check on her daughter. She got there about 2 p.m. The first thing that struck her was that the two dogs were outside and they didn't rush to greet her. The patio door was open, but they hadn't gone inside and didn't follow her as she made her way towards it. That seemed odd behaviour for two dogs that normally leapt about for any visitor.

When she stepped through the patio door and into the kitchen, she noticed that the curtains were drawn, which was also unusual. Then she heard the sound of water running and saw that the tap was gushing out water. She saw that some cabinet doors were open and items were scattered on the ground.

Rose made her way through the bungalow to her grandsons' bedroom, where all appeared normal. Then she turned and saw her daughter, lying on the floor. Rachel's hair was so matted with blood that Rose couldn't tell which way her head was facing. No one can imagine what she felt in that moment, witnessing a scene so beyond the bounds of normal life. She didn't touch her daughter or disturb the scene in any way. In shock, she dialled the numbers of family members to get help. A friend of Rachel's, Sarah, arrived at that point, and together Rose and Sarah went to check on Rachel. The scene was gruesome, disturbing in the extreme, and neither woman entered the room. Sarah immediately rang 999 for an ambulance.

This was when Joe arrived home. He smiled at Rose, but when she shakily said that she thought Rachel was dead, his face changed. He ran straight down to the bedroom – which was an interesting point in itself, I thought – and he shouted, 'Jesus, Rachel, what did you do?' He dropped to his knees and scooped blood and matter from the floor either side of Rachel's head, tossing it out into the hallway. Then he put his hand on Rachel's neck to locate a pulse. As Joe cried over his wife's body, the ambulance arrived, then the police, and the shock and the grief went on and on.

It was incredibly difficult to hear this woman's account of finding her daughter murdered. It was the kind of scene that was hard enough for a seasoned investigator to observe, but the idea of looking at one's own child in this setting was almost too much to think about. I admired Rose Callaly's fortitude and I felt deeply for her distress and loss. The statement didn't end there, though; there was more to add. Earlier that day, Joe had rung the Callaly house and told a sceptical Rose that he'd had a dream in which Rachel had appeared to him. In the dream, she asked him what was next to their bedroom and answered her own question by saying, 'The spare room.' Then she asked him what was in the spare room. She then asked him if a dumbbell was missing from the room. Joe felt it was an important clue. He told Rose that the weights and dumbbells were stored in the spare room and that if a dumbbell proved to be missing, he was sure it would turn out to be the murder weapon.

In the aftermath of the murder, as the Callaly family struggled to cope with what had happened and the investigation team followed every single possible line of inquiry, Joe embarked on a series of media appearances seeking information that would help catch his wife's killer. He gave print interviews, was photographed in the house, and also gave TV interviews where he repeatedly asked for help in finding the murderer. I had clearly told him to avoid this route, but he was determined to put himself out there as the face of the investigation. I found this strange and unhelpful, and not what I would consider the priorities of a man who was devastated by his loss.

I was interested to talk to Jackie Connor, as she had been Rachel's best friend and I assumed Rachel would have confided in her. She had given a statement initially, but I wanted to go over it with her and find out if she knew anything else that might be helpful. Over the course of three days near the end of October, I spoke to Jackie for three or four hours each day, gradually getting to know her and building a sense of trust between us. At first I found her a bit distant, but quickly I realized that she was a deeply loyal person and it did not sit well with her to answer private questions on Rachel's behalf. In her mind, anything Rachel had ever told her was said in confidence, and she didn't want to betray that trust. I greatly admired this stance, but I took pains to explain that what she knew would give us unique insights into Rachel's life and might help us to solve the case. Eventually, she relented and gave me a detailed statement.

Jackie told us that Rachel suspected Joe was having an affair, but she had wanted to save her marriage. Things had been going from bad to worse, however, and on 3 October she had given Joe an ultimatum: clean up your act, or everything is going to change. Jackie was a nurse and she had headed to Lambay View after Joe called her saying Rachel was a no-show at the crèche. She was there with Rose and Sarah before I arrived. Jackie described how the blood was congealed, not fresh, and the body was cold, with limbs rigid. It was a truly awful experience for her to see her friend beaten in such a violent manner, and she couldn't think why anyone would want to do such harm to Rachel.

Jackie also told us she had been shocked by Joe's demeanour in the days after the murder. She felt he was sticking close to her, and he had asked her out to the cinema, which she found inappropriate and odd. I was watching her as she said all this and I got the distinct impression there was something else she wanted to say but was holding back. She fell quiet and I let the silence go on, not breaking in on her thoughts. Suddenly she said, 'You know, Joe told me he did it.'

I had to work hard to stay composed when I heard this. I leaned forward, all ears, and she told me that Joe had told her that he'd had a dream in which he was the murderer and could see himself committing the murder. *Another dream*, I thought to myself. *What is up with this fella and the dreams?* I appreciated Jackie's trust in telling us about this, but I knew that since the confession was part of a dream, it held no probative value.

On 11 October, Rachel O'Reilly's funeral was held. I didn't attend, but some members of the team did. They reported that while Joe appeared to be grieving, and performed the eulogy and said all the right things, they felt there was a certain detachment about him, an aloofness that bothered them. I thought back to the day I had arrived at the crime scene. That was the exact feeling I'd had about Joe when I saw him standing apart from everyone else, and it had bothered me too.

Before the funeral mass, Rachel's family and friends decided to write cards and put them in the coffin, to say goodbye. Joe was observed writing a two-page letter and tucking it inside Rachel's top. A few minutes later, the undertaker lowered the lid and screwed it shut. The coffin was brought to Balgriffin Cemetery, where Rachel was laid to rest.

This oddness in Joe reached new and very surreal heights on 13 October, after we'd handed possession of the house back to him following completion of the technical examination. He contacted the Callalys and told them he'd found a great sense of peace inside the house and wanted them to experience it too. He invited them over to visit. They agreed, and Rose, Jim, Rachel's brother Paul and his wife Denise headed to Lambay View. Rose Callaly later gave us a statement about this visit, and the entire investigation team was shocked by it. Certainly, no one there – not even the longest-serving senior officers – had ever encountered anything like it in a murder investigation.

Joe O'Reilly walked the Callalys around the house and repeatedly asked if they wanted to listen to the final messages on the answerphone. They said they preferred not to hear them. Joe told Rose about yet another dream, in which Rachel asked him if something was missing from the house, before answering her own question and saying it was a dumbbell. Joe again remarked to Rose that if this were the case and the police found it, the weight would prove to be the murder weapon. He asked repeatedly about the answerphone, and they kept politely declining. Then he went over and pressed Play on the machine anyway, and Rachel's voice filled the room, asking them to leave a message. He stared at them as the tape played, and in her statement Rose Callaly said she'd had a horrible feeling that he was cementing an alibi. In that moment, she felt she heard Rachel's voice in her mind saying, 'It was him, Mam – he done it, Mam.' At that point, Rose felt sick with this realization, but there was much worse to follow.

Joe then brought them to Rachel's bedroom, to show them how he thought the murder must have happened. He began swinging his arm in a hitting motion, showing them that 'the killer' would have hit Rachel first when she was standing, then when she fell to the floor he would have knelt down and hit her again and again. The family watched in shock as he re-enacted all this, explaining how the blood spatters occurred. He mimed 'the killer' stepping over the body and walking towards the bathroom, then said Rachel would have made a sound, alerting 'the killer' to the fact that she was not dead. He said the murderer would have gone back to hit Rachel again, 'to finish her off'. He was lost in his play, fists clenched, jaw tight. Rachel's sister-in-law was shocked by this scene, feeling that it was cruel to do this to Rose and Jim. For their part, the Callalys just wanted to get out of there. Rose said later it was the moment she felt in her heart that her son-in-law had killed her daughter.

Incredibly, Joe re-enacted the murder twice more – once for a press photographer, Kyran O'Brien, and once for Jackie Connor. I've never come across this before or since – this need to replay the crime as a hypothetical 'suggestion' of how it might have happened. I think it showed Joe's deep guilt about his actions.

Jackie was alone with Joe in the house when he walked her through the murder, and it was a singularly upsetting incident for her. Once again, he started to narrate while acting it out physically. Jackie watched as he mimed Rachel receiving two blows to the head. Then he turned and walked towards the en suite, saying the murderer would have gone to wash the blood off. He said that, at this point, the murderer likely heard Rachel make a gurgling noise and went back to deliver another blow. Jackie listened, stunned, as Joe told her that

Rachel had described the whole incident to him in a dream. Jackie asked how Rachel had ended up lying down, and Joe said the murderer had held her down, which explained why there were blood splashes on the skirting boards. Like Rose, Jackie had a horrible sense of foreboding after this unthinkable display by the 'grieving' husband.

By this point we knew that Rachel had been killed between 9 a.m. and 3 p.m., with the likely time of death, based on body temperature, being in the morning. From the evidence accumulated so far, the team had a strong suspicion that Joe O'Reilly was involved in the murder. This was based on several key factors: his boots had shown traces of blood that matched Rachel's DNA; he had lied about his affair with Nikki Pelley; his work laptop contained emails that exhibited a vitriolic hatred towards his wife; and no one could corroborate his presence at Phibsboro bus depot on the morning of the murder. It did all seem to be pointing in one direction.

The investigation team redoubled their efforts, but I had to step away for a few days because the Whelan case required my attention. I flew to Spain on 18 October with DI Dominic Hayes in order to investigate Whelan's life there, question his friends, girlfriend and co-workers, and also to examine the provenance of the false passport he had acquired. We stayed in Spain for almost a week, but about two days after arriving there, I got a phone call from Detective Garda John Clancy telling me that, contrary to all our advice, Joe O'Reilly was appearing on that evening's *Late Late Show*, where he would be giving an interview about Rachel to Pat Kenny. Rose Callaly would be accompanying him.

I was very surprised by this and a little annoyed, because this type of exposure can harm an investigation. I had no access to Irish TV channels in Spain, so I had to rely on the team relaying what was happening as the programme unfolded. What was happening was that Joe gave an interview that became legendary in Ireland and seemed to turn the entire nation against him in just twenty minutes.

It was the body language that spoke louder than any of the words uttered by Rose or Joe. It was commented on afterwards how Rose looked very uncomfortable next to Joe; that she was sort of holding herself tightly, folding in on herself almost. She could not look at her son-in-law, and it seemed like she was trying to create as much space between them as possible. The reaction in the studio, and then in the following days across media and radio, was a widespread belief that Joe was the killer. He had courted publicity shamelessly, and now it was turning on him.

The team were describing it to me over the phone in incredulous tones – unable to believe that Joe couldn't see the face he was presenting and how unconvincing it was. I was later informed by a person working behind the scenes on the show that night that a member of the audience became so distraught after the interview, he had to be removed from the studio. Outside, he told them he was a psychic and he knew that Joe O'Reilly had committed the murder. He wasn't alone in reaching that conclusion.

When I returned to Ireland on 24 October, I asked Rose why she had agreed to appear alongside him. She said that Joe had told her the gardaí had requested that they do the interview together, and it was on that basis she had agreed. It seemed that Joe had seen it as an opportunity to present a united front, which would lend weight to his innocence. If Rose was seen to believe him, how could anyone doubt him?

I went out to the RTÉ studios and spoke to the staff of *The Late Late Show*. Those who were responsible for looking after the guests in the green room remembered it vividly. They described to me how Joe had scoffed all the sandwiches, eating rings round himself, not a bother on him. This had seemed strange to them, given that he was living a hellish nightmare. Rose, they noted, didn't touch a thing. She'd said she couldn't face eating.

They also recalled that Joe had spent much of the time on his phone, talking urgently to someone. After the show, he told Rose and the RTÉ staff that he had to meet with a client, so he wouldn't be availing himself of the hotel room offered to him as part of the station's hospitality. All in all, his behaviour backstage had raised as much suspicion as his performance on camera.

As an investigator, it's at times like these that you have to remain impartial and focus on the logic of what the Garda inquiries are telling you – as opposed to what a TV programme suggests, or indeed what the public thinks or what is appearing in newspapers. We knew the investigation was inching closer to the truth all the while – it was clear Joe's alibi didn't add up, and his behaviour was totally at odds with what had occurred – but we still needed evidence that would convince a jury.

Then, all the digging and painstaking work finally turned up what we needed. As with the Whelan case, the most damning witness would turn out to be an inanimate object: Joe's mobile phone. In 2004, mobile technology was relatively new, and An Garda had never used it in a murder case. The O'Reilly case changed that forever.

We engaged the services of O2 Ireland (now Three), thinking to check Joe's phone records and trace the calls made and received on the day of the murder. We got more than we bargained for, though. There was very little known about pinging at that time, but it turned out that cell site analysis allowed O2 to tell us not only the numbers that contacted Joe or Joe contacted that day, but Joe's own location when he received or made those calls. 'Pinging' was a new word to me then, but it was one I would come to know very well over the subsequent years and was very grateful for, many a time.

When a person sends/receives a text or makes/receives a call on a mobile phone, the signal is picked up in real time by the nearest mast – the phone 'pings' off it, leaving an indelible geographical marker of the phone user. The phone masts don't lie – and so where Joe O'Reilly was concerned, it was all there, in black and white. The first call on the list contradicted the statements of both Joe and Nikki Pelley. Nikki hadn't mentioned being in contact with Joe on 4 October, and he'd stated that he had talked to her around midday, but in fact they'd had several conversations on that day. It started at 5.45 a.m. when Nikki rang Joe, a call that lasted twenty-seven minutes. Then Joe rang Nikki at 7.35 a.m., a call that lasted four minutes. At 8.13 a.m., Nikki rang Joe again and they talked for twenty-six minutes. That list of calls placed a serious question mark over Joe O'Reilly's insistence that he and Nikki were no longer intimate and his marriage had been plain sailing again.

The pinging of Joe's mobile phone allowed O2 to track his movements according to the location of the phone mast his phone was communicating with at any given time. As we went through the records, we saw the real version of his day, and the bald truth of Rachel O'Reilly's murder.

At 8.46 a.m., Nikki Pelley texted Joe. According to his

statement, at that time he was en route to Phibsboro. But the analysis showed that he was on the M50, heading away from the city. His texted reply to Nikki at 8.48 a.m. showed him at Willsborough in Clonshaugh, about seventeen miles from Lambay View. At 8.56 a.m., Derek Quearney rang Joe. They should have been at the depot together, but Joe's phone showed that he was in fact near Richardstown, in north County Dublin, five miles from home. At 9.25 a.m., Derek rang again. This time, Joe's phone pinged off the mast situated at Murphy's quarry, less than half a mile from Lambay View. Joe then received a text at 9.52 a.m., and his phone was still pinging off the Murphy's quarry mast.

At 10.04 a.m., Joe rang Derek and he was back at Richardstown. At 10.07 a.m., Joe texted Rachel, asking her if she and the boys had slept well. That text was also sent at Richardstown, five miles from home and heading in the direction of Dublin city. At 10.30 a.m., Derek rang Joe, who was now on the North Circular Road, Phibsboro. At 11.49 a.m., CCTV footage captured Joe driving back into Viacom after his morning's work.

From all this, we could now piece together what had happened during Rachel's last hours. She dropped her older child at school, then dropped the younger boy at crèche. She drove home with the intention of collecting her gym gear and going for a workout. When she arrived at Lambay View, she entered through the back door and headed to her bedroom. When she stepped into her bedroom, Joe was waiting for her, likely with a dumbbell in his hand. He swung it high and crashed it down on her head, stunning her. Her car keys must have fallen from her hand and landed on the floor, onto which she then fell. What followed was an assault so vicious, it could have had only one outcome: Rachel's death.

Joe's 'dreams' tallied with the post-mortem findings: he hit her until she fell still, bending down to inflict maximum damage. He then got up and went towards the en suite, but Rachel made a noise, which indicated she wasn't dead, and he went back and hit her again, at least once. He made sure this time. Afterwards he cleaned himself up in the bathroom – and he must have changed his clothes as well – left his house, got into his car and drove back to Dublin to resume his day. He then did something extraordinarily cruel: after the phone call from the crèche, he urged Rose Callaly to go to the house, knowing full well what was waiting for her there. He condemned Rose to be haunted by that horrific scene for the rest of her life.

About two weeks or so after I returned from Spain, in early November, I was at the Callalys' house while a journalist was conducting an interview for one of the papers. Joe was in the conservatory, on the arm of the sofa on which Rose and Jim were sitting. I was outside the room, looking in through the glass-panel door, staring at the side of Joe's head – sizing him up, I suppose, because at this stage I believed he had killed his wife. The next thing, Joe turned his head slowly and looked straight at me. We locked eyes, and neither of us looked away.

It was a surreal moment – almost telepathic – in which I knew with absolute certainty that Joe O'Reilly had killed Rachel deliberately and in cold blood. I also knew with absolute certainty that he knew that I knew. And it jolted my brain, this two-way realization. I had to make sure that he didn't get away with murder.

There were two key people who seemed to be in a position to give us more information than they had already, and they were Derek Quearney and Nikki Pelley, who were both on close terms with Joe O'Reilly. In light of the statements they had given and how they differed on some points from the statements made by Joe, it was decided that it was time to bring them in for formal questioning. On 16 November, Nikki Pelley and Derek Quearney were arrested on suspicion of withholding information from the investigation, contrary to Section 9 of the Offences Against the State (Amendment) Act 1998. Quearney was brought in to Balbriggan station for questioning, while Pelley was conveyed to Drogheda Garda Station.

The team was anxious to drill down into Quearney's statement where it pertained to the timings of phone calls that morning. He had essentially backed up Joe's assertion that he was in Phibsboro during the timeframe when the murder was committed. The fact that not a single person in the Phibsboro bus depot had seen the six-foot five-inch Joe in his bright blue jacket, and he wasn't caught on CCTV, meant that the only corroboration for this assertion was Quearney.

So he was brought in to go through it again, in the interview room. He was asked about the phone calls at 8.56 a.m. and 9.25 a.m. – where was Joe talking to him from at those times? Derek couldn't be positive, but he felt Joe had mentioned being around the depot. Quearney was given a break, and some time later he was brought back down for a second interview. During this further questioning, he suddenly jumped up and vomited into a bin in the corner of the room. He was given a fifteen-minute break to collect himself. At that point, he admitted he was feeling frightened and shocked by the whole experience, which was understandable given that he'd never had any dealings with the gardaí before, and certainly not as a detainee.

It was in the fifth interview, having gone through the series of events on the morning of 4 October in detail, that Derek Quearney admitted that he believed his first statement was wrong and that he couldn't have seen Joe in Phibsboro prior to 10.30 a.m. That central plank in Joe O'Reilly's argument had just given way.

Meanwhile, over in Drogheda, another set of detectives was interviewing Nikki Pelley and she had some very interesting information to share. Contrary to Joe's statement that his marriage had been rocky but was now on steady ground, Nikki Pelley described how she and Joe were very much in love and wanted to live together. Joe had told her that he would be leaving Rachel to set up home with Nikki and his two sons. Naturally, she was asked why she had made the relationship sound casual in her statement. She said that Joe had asked her to play it down because if the gardaí knew the extent of the affair, it might come across as a motive. There was also the question of Joe saying that his only contact with Nikki on 4 October was at around midday. The phone records told us a very different story. They had in fact spoken at 5.45 a.m., 7.35 a.m., 8.13 a.m., 11.02 a.m. and 11.05 a.m. There was no way for Nikki Pelley to deny this evidence, and she didn't try to.

The next question was, of course: what had they been talking about? Her answer to this was also very interesting. According to Nikki's recollection of that Monday morning, Joe was calling her because he'd had a huge row with Rachel the night before, during which he'd allegedly told her he was going to leave and take the boys with him. When asked about Joe's antipathy towards his wife, Nikki said that his nickname for

Rachel was 'the Wasp', which he later changed to the very straightforward 'Cunt'. It became clear to us that leaving with full custody was Joe's priority – he wanted to set up house with Nikki and his sons. He clearly hadn't planned to walk out on his family, otherwise he would have been gone a long time ago.

The final piece of interesting information from the interview concerned Joe and Rose's *Late Late Show* appearance. Nikki confirmed that Joe had spent that night with her. That was why he'd had no need for the complimentary hotel stay offered by RTÉ. He had conducted a live interview on the national airwaves, posing as the mourning, grief-stricken husband, then he had gone straight to his lover's house.

The following day, 17 November 2004, both Derek Quearney and Nikki Pelley were released without charge. Their interviews had thrown up further pressing questions, and the only person who could answer those was Joe O'Reilly.

The team now had everything in place to advise the DPP's office of the need to charge Joe O'Reilly, but the DPP directed no charge at this stage. On that same day, I went to Lambay View with a number of colleagues from the investigation team. Our knock on the door was answered by Joe's sister. We advised her of the warrant and what it permitted, and she invited us inside. While my colleagues commenced a search of the premises, I asked where Joe was and his sister directed me to the bedroom. I went down the hallway and was greeted by the sight of a shrine next to the spot where Rachel had died. There was a table set up, and on it was a photo of Rachel with tea lights around it. The curtains were drawn so the candles flickered in a permanent twilight.

It was 10.20 a.m. I went into the bedroom and Joe stood up. He was barefoot. His brother was there too. I put my hand on Joe's shoulder and arrested him on suspicion of the murder of his wife, Rachel O'Reilly. I purposefully made the arrest with Joe standing beside the shrine, exactly where Rachel's body had been found, beaten and bloodied.

Joe took his mobile phone from his pocket and held it out to his brother. I intercepted it quickly and took it from him. I looked at Joe and said, 'Very poignant, Joe, that you're right on the spot.' He said nothing. I let him put on a pair of runners, then I handcuffed him and led him out of the house and into a waiting car that would take him to Drogheda Garda Station. Meanwhile, my colleagues' search turned up a few items that might prove to be of significance – an insurance policy document that was of interest in the light of Rachel's premature death, and a bunch of *Star Wars* costumes in the attic. It felt like all our good work was about to pay off.

We arrived at the station in Drogheda at 10.35 a.m., where the custody record was commenced. This is a crucial document in a trial because it lists exactly what happened to the detainee during their period of detention, what food and drinks were offered and accepted, if a solicitor or family member visited, if a doctor was called or any medication was administered. This ensures that the detainee's rights were respected at all times and that he or she was not under any undue pressure with regard to being interviewed. I am meticulous about custody records because they ensure best practice within the station, and they also support the investigation's methods when they later come under the scrutiny of a defence barrister.

So the custody record was opened for Joe O'Reilly and we did everything by the book. He was interviewed based on our suspicions, but he was largely uncooperative and we gained no further information. His period of detention ended at 10.20 p.m., and at 10.26 p.m. he walked out the front door of Drogheda station, and all we could do was watch him leave.

An investigation must prepare court-worthy evidence, so for now we had to keep going to secure that proof. A murder case requires methodical preparation and rock-solid evidence, which means it also requires Herculean levels of patience. In light of the statement about Joe O'Reilly placing a letter in his wife's coffin, we applied for a warrant to have the coffin exhumed. This was granted and the exhumation took place on 8 March 2005. Unfortunately, the coffin lid had broken some time after the burial, so all of the cards and letters it contained were very wet. They were removed and brought to the forensic laboratory at Garda HQ, where they underwent a special drying procedure. Joe's letter didn't contain an admission of any sort, but there were some striking lines in it. I remember that he described how it was horribly difficult for him to write it for reasons known only to husband and wife. He also asked Rachel to forgive him, although he didn't specify for what.

All that year, the investigation continued, and then on into 2006. On 14 March 2006, Joe was arrested for the second time and brought to Drogheda Garda Station for questioning. There was the matter of his emails to discuss, and also the text messages to Nikki Pelley. The question of how blood got onto his boots was also still outstanding.

Joe was interviewed five times and he remained detached and largely uncooperative throughout, mainly answering 'No comment' to the questions put to him. At the end of the period of detention, we once more had to watch him leave the station. This time, a big crowd had gathered, and cameras flashed as he pushed open the door. Before stepping outside, he turned and looked directly at me, then gave me a brazen thumbs up. I felt he was saying to me, 'You know and you can't do anything about it.' I had to work hard to keep my face impassive as I stared back at him, quelling the urge to run out the door after him and grab him by the scruff of the neck and bring him back in. I thought to myself then: *I'll get to the bottom of this.*

Later that same day, we also rearrested Nikki Pelley. We had received information from a friend of hers who recalled Nikki telling her about Joe and their passionate love affair. She'd mentioned to this friend that Joe had said he would kill Rachel if he could get away with it. That was a serious allegation, and it warranted arrest and questioning. So Nikki was brought in again and this statement was put to her. She had to admit the truth, which was that this conversation had taken place and she had heard Joe say this. Nikki Pelley was released without charge the following day.

In spite of Joe O'Reilly's belief that he had walked free, the investigation team now felt that everything was in place to prove his guilt to the court. For the third time we arrested Joe O'Reilly, this time for the murder of Rachel O'Reilly. When I went out to his mother's house in Dunleer to make the arrest it was with a sense of déjà vu. I stood in his mother's kitchen after finding Joe there in his stockinged feet, and for the second time I put my hand on his shoulder and told him I was arresting him.

I've often heard that expression about blood draining from the face, but this is the only time in my life I've actually seen it happen. His face literally went white from the forehead down. He said six words to me – 'Can I put my shoes on?' – and those were the last words we ever exchanged.

During the preparations for the trial, I kept thinking about

Joe's likely defence, and I had a hunch his team might use the reason of adverse publicity to argue that Joe could not get a fair trial. I wasn't going to let that happen. I enlisted the help of Detective Garda Robert Keogh and the Garda Press Office, and we went through every single word and photo printed about the murder and all that happened afterwards. The final reckoning was that 30 per cent of the coverage had been generated directly by Joe O'Reilly.

I handed our report to the defence team as part of the disclosure process and waited to see what would happen in court.

As is usual, the case took a long time to reach trial, but at 10.30 a.m. on 18 June 2007, Joe O'Reilly stood in the Central Criminal Court and was asked how he pleaded to the accusation of murder. He replied, 'Not guilty.' That meant a full jury trial, with witnesses and the chance to show the extent and breadth of the investigation. It also meant that I was called to the witness stand to give evidence. This is always a daunting task, because the defence will pick over every single word to find a gap – to find any cause for doubt. They want to discredit you as a witness, because that in turn discredits the investigation, which places doubt in the minds of the jurors.

When I was called to the stand, I was confident that all my notes were in order and that I had been honest and transparent in all my dealings, but I still felt a flutter of nerves as I settled into the seat and waited for the highly experienced and respected Patrick Gageby, SC, to question me. He was as thorough as ever, so I spent a considerable length of time in the box.

The main focus was the notes taken on the evening of the day of the murder out at Dunleer, when I spoke to Joe at length for the first time. Gageby was a very adept opponent, but I didn't flinch at any time because I was fully certain that my notes were correct and true. In fact, I had learned them off by heart so I would not forget anything. It's a terrible feeling to come out of the box and realize there were important points you didn't make, and I did everything possible to ensure that didn't happen.

I've had good days and bad days in the witness box, but this was one of the good days, and I fulfilled my role with confidence and clarity. At one point, the junior counsel for the defence put a question to me regarding the phone evidence. Her question was covering a lot of ground and was very detailed, so it went on for a good two minutes before she came up against a question mark. When she paused and looked to me for my answer, I turned to the judge and asked for the question to be repeated as I didn't understand it. The junior counsel jumped to her feet, red-faced with annoyance, and said she would simplify it for me. 'That's grand,' I replied. She asked the question again, very succinctly and quickly this time. I let a few beats go by as I gave the impression of thinking it over carefully. Then I said, 'No.' There was a giggle from the public gallery at this.

The trial lasted for about five weeks and the weight of evidence against Joe O'Reilly was too great to counter, although he never once admitted guilt. I noted with satisfaction that the defence didn't employ the argument of adverse publicity.

On Saturday, 21 July 2007 the jury was due to deliver its verdict. The deliberations had gone on all day Friday and continued on into Saturday, with no end in sight. Eventually, the Callalys decided to go to the nearby Legal Eagle on Chancery Place as there was no way of knowing how long it would take – and I went with them. I had just sat down in front of a pint when the door was flung open and someone shouted that the jury was coming back in. We left our table of full pints and coffees before the steam had even finished rising off the cups, and raced back to the courtroom to sit down and wait. The jury filed back in and took their seats. The judge asked for their verdict. It was unanimous: *Guilty*.

It was like a volcano of tension erupted in the courtroom. All those months of holding steady, swallowing back the rage and the grief, it all exploded into roars and shouts from the Callaly family. I remember looking over at the bench, and the detectives and incident room coordinators were crying. It was an extraordinary sight. It had been such a long and tough road and we had kept at it, step after weary step, and now, finally, came the news everyone had worked towards and hoped to hear for so long. I'm sure those roars sounded very loud in Joe O'Reilly's ears.

The judge banged his gavel for order. At that point, I'm not ashamed to say that I broke down in tears myself. The stress and tension of trailing this killer, of trying to fulfil my promise to Rachel and her parents, were just overwhelming in that moment.

The judge sentenced Joe O'Reilly to life for the murder of Rachel O'Reilly, and he was taken to Mountjoy Prison to start his sentence. He never, throughout all this time, expressed remorse for what he had done, nor did he make any comment or apology to the Callaly family. He showed no emotion in the courtroom. There was a prison officer standing beside him, and when our paths crossed in the corridor outside he said quietly to me, 'Do you want to know what he said to me? Asked what the food is like at Mountjoy.'

Somehow, I wasn't surprised. To this day, the closest Joe

O'Reilly has come to an admission of guilt is those bizarre re-enactments, which showed that he knew the exact sequence of events as evidenced by the blood spatter analysis. Other than that, he has never acknowledged his brutal crime or Rachel's complete innocence. It seems unlikely that he ever will.

Back at Lambay View on the day of the murder, I had said to my superintendent that there would be a reason – a why. In this case, there were a number of different whys, all inter-twined. It wasn't straightforward. The simplest explanation was that Joe had fallen out of love with Rachel and in love with Nikki Pelley. Emails found on his work computer, addressed to a family member, spoke of how Rachel 'repulsed' him, and his anger at her came through loud and clear in his words. His love had been replaced by hate. And that's what we saw at the crime scene – a curdling of love into hatred. This was a crime committed with a dark passion, a twisted commitment.

Added to this was the fact that Joe adored his two sons and wanted to be the one who raised them. His emails called Rachel's abilities as a mother into question. He railed against a social worker who used the term 'primary caregiver' for Rachel and 'secondary caregiver' for Joe. He wrote: *I'm already 'Mr Weekend Custody' in the eyes of the state. Doesn't bode too well, does it?* It's likely this fear he would lose the children to Rachel led to his decision to get rid of her altogether. In his simplis-tic view, he must have thought he could move Rachel out and move Nikki in, and his brand-new family would just take up where the old one had left off. It was a strange and compelling kind of self-delusion.

There was another layer as well, hidden deeper down. As

happens so often in these cases, there was childhood trauma in Joe's past. One day at the Callalys' house, he'd told me that his father was an alcoholic, and although he left the family when Joe was just a young boy, by then he had hung around long enough to make a mark on his children. Young Joe was terrified of his father, whose drunken rages were unpredictable, threatening and deeply stressful. It's hard to foretell how a childhood terror will seep into adulthood, but it always does. These sorts of violent and threatening incidents – as well as living with an alcoholic parent – leave deep mental scars that most people never fully overcome. It could be that those experiences fed into Joe's sense of rage. I think that after his father left, he felt the responsibility of being 'the man of the house'. To him, this meant being tough and unemotional. His desire to take care of his family came from a good place, but it became distorted into a need for control and a level of detachment that made him, in the end, dangerous.

There was a childlike side to him, so maybe a part of him never grew up. He was obsessed with *Star Wars*, as evidenced by the attic full of memorabilia and costumes. The children spoke of how Daddy loved to dress up in the costumes, particularly the Darth Vader one. I'm not a psychologist, but experience tells me there could be something in that. Perhaps Joe O'Reilly's desire to dress up suggested a desire to be someone else – someone stronger, braver, better; someone who was powerful and therefore safe. I've often wondered why we never found the Darth Vader costume anywhere in the house.

When an investigation is over, especially when it ends in a successful conviction, you have to step away and leave it behind. I could spend whatever years I have left to me pondering the whys – teasing them out, coming up with grand theories – but I know the simple truth is that human nature is made up of shades of light and dark. That's just the way it is. In some cases, the dark spills over and cancels out everything else, and that's what happened that October morning in the Naul. For whatever reason, the good in Joe O'Reilly had been overwhelmed and erased by the bad, and he gave vent to it in an extraordinarily violent way. Rachel didn't stand a chance as she went into her home that morning. She had no idea what was waiting for her, and probably had no idea her husband was capable of what he did to her. The Callalys can never have solace, but at least we were able to give them the truth. In the end, that's the most a detective can ever do.

There was still the issue of the headstone to be resolved, and this caused huge distress to the Callaly family. They had applied to erect a gravestone featuring Rachel's maiden name, but were told that Joe had already made an application and was insistent that it feature her married name. He proceeded to have a small cross erected that said *Rachel O'Reilly*, but after the trial this was replaced with a wooden cross that read: *Rachel Callaly Murdered 4 October 2004*. It was very important to Rose and Jim that their daughter's final resting place be marked appropriately and that the O'Reilly name not be included. They fought for this, but Joe fought back, arguing that he was next of kin and had the final say. It wasn't until 2009 that this was finally resolved, after Joe lost his court appeal against his conviction. Finally, the Callalys received permission to erect a permanent headstone to honour their daughter. It stands in Balgriffin Cemetery today and reads as follows:

CALLALY

Cherished Memories Of

RACHEL

Murdered 4th October 2004

Aged 30 Years

Joined By Her Sister

ANN

Who Died 17th September 2010

Aged 32 Years

Sadly Missed By Their Loving Parents Jim And Rose
Brothers Declan, Paul & Anthony

4. The Frustrating Puzzle of a Meticulous Crime

In August 1978, a scrawny seventeen-year-old lad walked into Navan Garda Station and declared that he wanted to join An Garda Síochána. I had thought about it as long and as hard as you do at that age, and I was sure that the life of a garda was for me. So in I went and announced myself to the member on duty, expecting to be welcomed with open arms. The beefy desk sergeant looked me up and down, grabbed me by the shoulder, gave me a brisk shake that rattled my teeth and told me to go off and put some meat on my bones first. I walked out of the station feeling dejected and rejected. It would be decades before I'd come to understand and appreciate that his refusal made me a better detective.

As a result of that door being closed, I had to go and find another one to open. I spent a year or so as a painter and decorator but knew every second of every day that it wasn't for me. Next came a spell with Navan Carpets, in the computer room, which would be unrecognizable to the IT staff of today. Those computers were massive old machines that had disks so big, a grown man had to use two hands and have a strong back to lift and move them. When that company began to nosedive, I bailed and got a job with Union Camp in Ashbourne, County Meath. It was a corrugated packaging company, headquartered in the USA. I was put in the sales department, with a phone, a notepad and a narrow cubicle in which to waste away the hours of my young life. I hated it. So when Navan Carpets came knocking with an offer to return to their fold, I was only too happy to leave the claustrophobic cubicle behind. However, when Union Camp heard of this development, they made a counter-offer I couldn't refuse: more money, and a position in the design department.

The decision to stay with Union Camp turned out to be a very important one because it moulded my whole way of thinking and my approach to problem-solving. My role involved listening to and understanding a client's needs in detail, then designing a millimetre-perfect packaging solution for their specific logistics problem. One of my clients was Tayto, the crisps manufacturer, and I designed the box with the perforated opening that allows easy retrieval of the packets inside. It's a design that Union Camp trademarked and is now standard, but someone had to think it up in the first place and in that case it was me.

I had no idea of my future career as a detective back then, but the problem-solving skills that I honed in the private sector formed the bedrock of my approach in solving cases. The key to my design work was to keep the solutions as simple as possible, and that was an approach that served me well when tracking murderers or deciphering a body of evidence. It was my constant mantra when addressing my teams: *Keep it simple*. The jury, the DPP, the prosecution – all of them have to understand the logic and rationale behind every step of the investigation. Keeping it simple is the best way to achieve this.

The other important takeaway from my pre-Garda years was the work ethic. At Union Camp, management gave the staff the freedom to do things our own way, to take full responsibility for our work and to practise self-discipline. They trusted their staff to get the work done, which meant they didn't chase us or hover over us or monitor us in an intrusive way. When I finally got my wish and joined An Garda, I quickly realized that wasn't the management style at all, and that I was going to have to learn to operate within a very different environment. It was much more stifling, much less trusting. It was, in many ways, dysfunctional. That was a difficult transition, but when I made my way up the ladder and got to manage my own teams, I brought the Union Camp style to bear. It proved to be just as effective as it had in the private sector, and contributed to many solves.

So while I cooled my heels in those other jobs, dreaming of donning that uniform, I didn't realize that I was in fact acquiring the key skills of a detective. With the benefit of hindsight, I would define those skills as follows: the ability to focus, compartmentalize, order and organize; knowing how to keep it simple – people tend to complicate things by making assumptions or jumping to conclusions, but a simple, straightforward assessment of the evidence is always the best method; the ability to build a good team, with respect and trust between team members; and being able to communicate your expectations to your team, brief them well and delegate to them. When a team is headed by a senior investigating officer with these qualities, it bodes well for an investigation's outcome. So when that desk sergeant laughed at my skinny frame and wide ambition, he did me a great favour. I went out into the world and brought those skills back with me.

Solving a premeditated crime demands high-level problem-solving skills. When someone has thought through the ways in which they are going to commit a crime and the ways in which they might get caught, that's a real challenge for an investigation. The perpetrators are already a few steps ahead, and making up ground can be very difficult. And there are different levels of premeditation, from the loosely planned and recklessly executed to the careful planning of, say, a bank robbery. I've dealt with cases on all levels, some with successful outcomes, some that have ended in frustration and the need to find another way around the problem.

The following case provides a good example of the kind of loose planning and reckless execution that can lead to chaos. On 5 February 2009, a car driving down Shop Street in Drogheda swerved off the road and ploughed straight through the display window of Victor Dwyer's shoe shop. Miraculously, no one was injured or killed. The driver of the car was Seamus Cudden, and he had planned to kill Victor Dwyer because he believed him to be the Devil incarnate. The reasons behind this belief remain a mystery; the two men had never met before. Twenty minutes after crashing the car and walking away, Cudden strolled into Drogheda Garda Station and informed the garda on duty that they were probably looking for him. When the needle walks out of the haystack, you put it away safely and give thanks for the stroke of good fortune.

Obviously, this wasn't the action of a sensible person, and in order to detain someone for questioning under Section 4 of the Criminal Justice Act 1984, they must be over twelve years of age and of sound mind. So I had to obtain an expert opinion on Cudden's soundness of mind before proceeding to question him. He was brought, involuntarily, to St Brigid's Hospital in Ardee, where a psychiatrist assessed him. It was found that Cudden was capable of understanding the difference between right and wrong, and therefore he could be interviewed by An Garda. We proceeded as was usual in such a case, putting together the easily available evidence that confirmed his guilt.

The case came to trial in May 2010, and Cudden pleaded guilty to reckless endangerment. That October the judge handed down a two-and-a-half-year suspended sentence for what he called an 'absolutely bizarre' incident. It was bizarre, but it was also easy to secure a conviction because there was nothing sophisticated about its planning or execution.

In terms of planned crimes, there is a criminal who is far out ahead of the pack, and that is the kind of criminal mind that plans and executes a tiger kidnapping, which involves targeting an employee of a bank or other such institution, kidnapping their family and then forcing them to take money and deliver it to the kidnappers. It's a high-risk but high-reward crime. As I often said to my team, give me an old-fashioned murder case any day over a tiger kidnapping. I worked three such cases in my time in Louth Division: the kidnapping of the Hoyne family in Monasterboice in 2010; the kidnapping of the Nawn family in Drogheda in 2011; and the attempted kidnap of a family in Drogheda in 2013. They were all incredibly challenging investigations because of the level of preparation involved on the part of the criminals who carried them out. These were horrible crimes that involved invading a home and terrorizing a family, and I condemn them for that reason – but if I'm honest, there is also a grudging admiration for the meticulous planning behind them. If these criminals decided to use their powers for good, they'd likely have made great detectives.

The Hoyne family kidnapping is an excellent illustration of this type of crime, and why it is so difficult to solve. The term 'tiger kidnapping' refers to how the 'prey' is stalked and tracked before the attack is launched, which very much sums up the modus operandi of the well-known crime boss who I believe was the mastermind behind the Hoynes' ordeal. He'd been learning his trade from the time he was in short pants, and it showed in his thinking. For the purposes of discussing it here, I will simply refer to him as Mr A (the letter does not form part of his initials).

The only small comfort for a targeted family is that the aim of a tiger kidnapping is money – that is always the end point of the crime – so a professional hit team is not out to hurt or maim the family. They just want them scared enough to comply in full and without hesitation.

Bill Hoyne was a senior executive at Brinks Allied, a cash-in-transit security company. The crime boss Mr A located Hoyne online and researched him, discovering his address. He then began to trail him in real life, and Hoyne's home turned out to be a gift: located in its own grounds, set back from the road, with no security alarm and no CCTV. The small team of four men assembled by Mr A set up surveillance on the Hoynes, tracking their movements and figuring out their routines. Bill and his wife, Shirley, were totally unaware of this presence, but it was shadowing them daily as they went about their lives. Mr A was thinking through every detail, assessing every risk, covering every angle.

The Brinks Allied depot had proved rich hunting ground before, most notably in 1995, when a criminal gang lifted almost £3 million from it in a raid that never ended in a conviction. Mr A was aware that financial institutions and An Garda had upped their game since then and established strict protocols to avert and manage kidnappings of staff, but he obviously reckoned that with enough information and clever plotting, he could pull off a heist to make himself rich in one fell swoop – and remain a free man.

I dreaded these types of investigations. As the investigator, you come to the table very late, when the criminal is already ten steps ahead of you. They are usually tech-savvy, very smart and risk-averse, so they put huge resources into ensuring they will not be caught. In addition, the kidnapping will likely involve numerous participants and multiple crime scenes, all of which have to be forensically examined and the resulting mountain of evidence combed through in minute detail. The cars used in carrying out the kidnapping also constitute crime scenes, and must receive the same attention. There could be prepaid mobile phones – lots of them – topped up months in advance and disposed of the moment the raid is completed. It all adds up to a hugely challenging network of scenes and interconnected evidence, and a back-breaking amount of work for the investigating team.

The first indication that a tiger kidnapping was under way was a call from my chief superintendent, who told me a kidnapping was in progress and to go straight to Drogheda Garda Station. That's all the information I was given, so I hightailed it there. When I arrived, the incident room had already been set up; as it was within Louth Division, I was appointed SIO (this role having been created in 2008). The incident room was monitoring all incoming information, ready and waiting to launch into action once events had been confirmed. The news trickling in was worrying – an employee was under orders from a criminal gang, who had his wife and had made threats against her safety if he failed to comply. It was an ongoing situation until about midday, when we heard that the man and his wife were now safe.

The Hoynes' house was preserved as a crime scene, as were his workplace and their cars as we learned more details about the raid. Once we had the all-clear, the technical team made their way to Monasterboice to examine the house. It was a shock when the word came back that nothing had been found. This was a first for me, and I was sure there must be some error. So I went out there and had a look for myself. But there was no mistake. It was the cleanest crime scene I'd ever seen, and it remains the cleanest scene I've ever encountered. There was absolutely nothing to suggest what had happened there the night before. The Garda Technical Bureau team went over every inch of the house and the outside areas in minute detail, but there wasn't a scrap of forensic evidence in the whole place. It was a chilling moment when we realized we had to proceed in the investigation on our own, like a tightrope walk without the net.

This was followed by another shock when the team assigned to identify, retrieve and view any CCTV footage reported back that there wasn't any available. Again, we couldn't believe this could be true. The distance travelled by Mr Hoyne from his home to his workplace to the drop-off point for the cash meant there was a huge area to trawl for CCTV units, but once again we came up empty-handed. The raiders had obviously planned their routes meticulously, because they had avoided the many CCTV cameras that should have caught them out. This was obviously a robbery at the highest level of planning and execution, which really put the investigation team on the back foot.

The Hoynes were able to piece together the order of events for us when we spoke with them the next day, 7 November. Their cooperation was remarkable given the ordeal they had just endured, which had left them upset and traumatized. When speaking to Mrs Hoyne, who was an excellent witness, I got the impression that she had lost her faith in humanity, such was the effect on her of this horrible crime. Nonetheless, they were very decent people and they endeavoured to help us as much as possible. To this end, they gave us as many details about the incident as they could, which was hugely helpful given that we were drawing blanks with forensics and CCTV.

Their version of events was as unsettling as it was straightforward. On Friday 5 November, at about 9 p.m., Shirley Hoyne went outside the house to the adjacent stables to check on her horses. While she was in there, a man in a balaclava stepped out of the darkness and pointed a handgun at her. Two other men appeared, and Shirley was ordered back into the house. The men wore white dust suits, and when they reached the back door, all three of them bent down and took off their shoes, leaving them neatly on the step.

Once inside the house, they quickly apprehended Bill Hoyne and bound the couple's hands with black cable ties. They made it clear that the Brinks depot was their target and that they were intimate with the couple's home and lives. One of the men remarked to Shirley that he liked a particular nightdress she wore. They were letting the Hoynes know that there was no point trying to fool them or work against them.

With the couple securely detained, the next part of the plan was due to kick off at 6 a.m., so they all settled down to wait. No doubt the following nine hours felt interminable to the Hoynes. For their part, the raiders were utterly professional throughout, never removing their masks, never letting names or details slip. They clearly had a well-thought-out plan and were sticking rigidly to it.

In the morning, the raiders conducted a thorough deep clean of the house. They had brought their own bleach in canisters, and they proceeded to spray every surface in the house that might betray DNA evidence – including the door handles, countertops and lightbulbs. It would sound daft to the average person to clean the lightbulbs like this, but it was an indication of the level of preparation that went into this raid. This gang obviously knew that it had become possible to swab for DNA from a person's breath. For example, if a gloves-wearing burglar breaks in through a window, leaving no fingerprints, a forensics team can still swab the glass for DNA resulting from him breathing on it. It sounds like science fiction, but it's true. The fact that the lightbulbs were sparkling and free of any contamination whatsoever showed how well they had done their research. They also vacuumed the whole house, then removed the vacuum bag and burned it in the fireplace. They were definitely on top of the trace evidence side of things, which is why we found nothing. This was where Mr A's careful planning served him well – his team worked efficiently and with focus, and within an hour there was no sign whatsoever that they had ever been there.

At 6 a.m., Shirley Hoyne was lifted, hands still bound, into the boot of her husband's car. She was driven south to a derelict house on Howth Road. A fourth man was waiting there, and he helped her out of the boot and locked her in a garden shed, tied to a wheelie bin weighted down with concrete blocks. Outside on the street, he set the car on fire. He didn't tell anyone where she was – there was no anonymous tip-off – he just walked off and left her to her fate.

The other three raiders had the leverage of Shirley's life to ensure Bill Hoyne's full cooperation. He'd had to endure the sight of his wife being taken away to God knows where, then was told to drive Shirley's jeep to his workplace, the Brinks Allied depot in Clonshaugh Industrial Estate, where he would fill six holdall bags with cash. He drove down the M1, and one of the raiders got out of the car at Balbriggan. The other travelled on to Clonshaugh, getting out just before the depot to allow Bill to go to work as usual. He arrived at the depot at 7.56 a.m., which was caught on CCTV, and informed his colleagues what was happening. The new protocols were enacted and the gardaí were informed.

The gang had given Bill Hoyne a mobile phone and now he used it to inform them that he was permitted to carry only one bag out of the depot. They agreed to this change in the plan. Bill Hoyne then worked quickly, stuffing five of the bags into the sixth one, making it feel full, then adding bundles of cash on top. As a result, the amount in the bag was just €170,000, far short of what the gang would have been expecting to get out of the job. He drove the bag along a route dictated by the raiders, finally stopping at Whitehall Church on Griffith Avenue, where he got out and left the jeep to be collected. As it happened, he spotted a garda on patrol duty and informed him of what was under way. While this was happening, a man got into the jeep and drove it to Ashbourne in County Meath, where the money was removed and the vehicle burned out, thus erasing the evidence. It had been a good outcome for the raiders – except for the fact that their haul was much smaller than anticipated. Still, they had stuck to the plan, executed it efficiently and got away with a large-scale robbery.

This gave us four crime scenes, excluding the car and jeep: the Hoyne family home, the Brinks Allied depot, the derelict property on Howth Road and the final point at Ashbourne. All four were preserved and forensically examined, but there was no evidence to suggest the likely identities of the suspects. So we had no forensic evidence, no CCTV evidence and precious little witness evidence, thanks to the precautions taken by the raiders.

In short, we had no real evidence. There was lots of information from the Hoynes, lots of dots we could connect by virtue of prior experience of other, similar crime scenes, but we had nothing that would stand up in court and secure a prosecution.

The investigation stalled for some time, but then a piece of confidential information opened up an alternative avenue, one that might just bridge the gaps in the case and still get Mr A off the streets. I knew that Mr A was behind the kidnapping and robbery because of this new information, in conjunction with the description of the men's demeanour given by the Hoynes and also the MO of the crime. Mr A was a clever and disciplined man who planned and executed clever and disciplined crimes. Even though he'd made sure he hadn't left an actual fingerprint, in my gut I knew that this one had his fingerprints all over it. As a result, it was essential that we investigate and interview him.

Obviously, I can't divulge anything about the information I received concerning Mr A, but being able to sound out reliable sources is a key part of being a detective. As a DI at that time, you accumulated a huge amount of knowledge about criminals and other people, and made contacts across the board. It was understood implicitly that you had to build up an informal network of eyes and ears, and I had done this over my almost thirty years on the force. As a result, sometimes I'd get a call with a snippet of valuable information – or I might put in a call to a source to find out if they could give me any kind of steer when one was needed. It was just such a source that gave me a tip-off about Mr A.

This has all changed nowadays, replaced by a formal liaison network for sources. The Covert Human Intelligence

Sources (CHIS) system is a dedicated agency with highly trained officers. If any member of An Garda receives information via a source, or any kind of overture from a source, it must be passed on to CHIS for a trained agent to conduct the liaison. This new method undoubtedly has benefits of its own, but in my day it was down to the detective to build up their own network and use it with discretion and care. That's what I did, and it proved effective in the case of Mr A.

The information I had received from my source was sufficient to request a search warrant for Mr A's home and the homes of the other suspected raiders. This was granted, and the necessary warrants were obtained from the District Court. On Friday 10 December at 6 a.m., a team of gardaí knocked on Mr A's front door. They presented the warrant, then fanned out and searched thoroughly. In the master bedroom, a black handgun was found. It was shown to Mr A, who immediately stated: 'It's mine. I got a lend of it. It's for my protection. It's loaded.' It was a small handgun with an orange tip and a scratch down the barrel. This matched the description the Hoynes had given of the handgun that was trained on them during the raid.

That link was enough to bring him in. At 6.20 a.m., Mr A was arrested for the false imprisonment of Bill and Shirley Hoyne. By 8 a.m., he was sitting in Drogheda Garda Station, waiting to be questioned.

Mr A was detained for six hours at first, which was extended by a further six hours and then by twelve hours, bringing us up to the permitted detention time of twenty-four hours. He was photographed, fingerprinted and had buccal swabs taken during this time. He was interviewed nine times over the course of his detention, and throughout every one he maintained that he had no hand or part in the Hoyne kidnapping, and that while he did have a handgun in his possession, it was solely for his own protection. While the gun concerned did match the description given by Mr and Mrs Hoyne, that by itself wasn't enough to connect Mr A to the kidnapping for the purposes of a jury trial and conviction.

I kept the DPP fully informed throughout the interview process, and received instruction that Mr A should be charged with unlawful possession of a firearm and ammunition. He was arrested and charged and later appeared before the Central Criminal Court, where he was given an eight-year sentence with two years suspended. While this was a welcome outcome, it was still a bad day at the office given that we couldn't get justice for the Hoynes, who deserved no less.

One important change worth noting here is the creation of the senior investigating officer position, which was put in place about two years before the Hoyne kidnapping. Prior to 2008, each investigation was overseen by the superintendent, who appointed people to specific roles within the investigation. The drawback with this was that a super might never have been in plain clothes or investigated a case in his career. This would make him, in effect, useless in terms of solving the crime, and reliant on others to investigate and solve it. It's every detective's nightmare to have a district officer who thinks he knows better than the DI and who relies on people with less experience to progress matters.

As the workload continually increased – and investigations became more complex and intricate, with the advance of forensics, technical analysis, phone analysis, IT analysis, etc. – it became clear that it would work much better to have a single detective overseeing the whole investigation. In addition, the Morris tribunal included in its reports a recommendation that this change be brought in, following its inquiry into members of An Garda in Donegal Division. Finally, in 2008, the change was made and was widely welcomed across the force. Tasks were still parcelled out to other detectives and detective teams, but the SIO brought a sense of coherence and joined-up thinking to the whole operation.

There is now specific training in place for SIOs, formerly comprising a FETAC Level 8 course and now an accredited degree course under the School of Law at the University of Limerick. Once qualified, the SIO's responsibilities in an investigation are many and varied, but just to give an overview, they include: setting up the investigation team and assigning jobs in the incident room; visiting the crime scene and making all decisions regarding scene preservation; managing the incident room; chairing all murder conferences; liaising with forensics and the technical teams; planning the direction of the investigation; safeguarding the rights of all suspects, prisoners and witnesses; ensuring all procedures are strictly adhered to with regard to exhibits, witness statements, etc.; leading the team, and keeping them motivated and focused on the end result. The SIO is also the lead officer in court, and is usually the one who is called to the witness box to present and explain the evidence collected and collated by the team.

So it's a huge amount of responsibility, and of course it needs to be replicated across each case that lands on your desk. It's definitely a challenge, but the benefit is that the framework of the investigation rests with one person, who has the ability to draw all the strands together and has the power to keep everything moving along in the right direction – towards the courtroom, and, hopefully, a successful conviction.

While it was demanding, being SIO was a role I really enjoyed because it was intricate and involved, which suited my problem-solving brain. It required meticulous organization, which I was good at and enjoyed, and I also felt I could make a real difference by using my skills to lead the investigation positively and effectively. A good, organized, intelligent SIO can make a huge difference to an investigation because so much depends on the decision-making in the initial stages of the case. If those decisions are sensible and solid, the investigation is grounded in professionalism, accountability and honesty – which were always my guiding protocols. The SIO can also protect the investigation and the team from pressure coming from within the organization; this shouldn't have to be part of the job, but sometimes it is. As a result, the SIO must be confident enough and bullish enough to stick to their decisions regardless of what others think, even when those others occupy higher ranks. There might be a price to pay for this, by being ignored for future progression in the force, but for me, honesty and solving the case were a greater priority than my personal advancement.

In 2010 I was SIO on a case that shared some characteristics with the Hoyne case, namely that we had to deal with a 'clean' crime scene that had all the hallmarks of a professional hit. It posed a huge challenge, and it took a massive team effort to rise to that challenge.

Everyone is familiar with the detective's hunch – that point in the book or film where a lightbulb moment of inspiration provides the crucial clue or link needed to solve the crime. In fiction, it's usually wrapped up neatly and leads directly to the crime being solved, but that's not always the way in real life. It is the case, though, that the hunch – that spark of creative thinking – can flood the investigator's brain with light and make something obvious that was previously hidden. When it happens, it's a glorious feeling, and when that glorious feeling does lead to a crucial link that solves the case, it's a complete high – and an addictive one, at that. I've experienced it a few times in my career, but one of the best involved the solving of a double murder with a professionally managed crime scene. It was a meticulous plan, and it demanded a meticulous investigation.

It was 7 March 2012, and I got a call saying that an unusual crime scene had been found. Chief Superintendent Pat McGee also informed me that I was SIO. I remember he said, 'Good luck. This is one you won't solve.'

The fire brigade had been called to the beauty spot of Ravensdale Forest Park near Dundalk, County Louth, because there was a car in flames. They reached the scene at about 11 p.m. The crew put out the fire, and through the smoke they could discern something inside the car. They went closer to see what it was and were astounded to see a human skull and ribcage sitting on the driver's seat. They noted that the skull was cracked and broken. At this point, the senior firefighter present told everyone to step back because he recognized that this was now a crime scene. They put in a call to the Control Room at Dundalk Garda Station and reported their disturbing find.

The first gardaí on the scene used flashlights to examine the car's interior. The beam of the torch lit up the skull and ribcage the firefighters had described and also revealed a second skull, lying on the floor between the driver's and passenger seats. The bodies of two adult men had fallen together in the blaze and fused, with one lying across the other. So what we had was a car burned to a crisp – and all the evidence along with it – and the skeletal remains of two people who would have to be identified from teeth or bone. That was it. There was precious little to go on in terms of figuring out what had happened and why.

The assistant state pathologist, Dr Khalid Jaber, arrived at the scene around 10 a.m. the next morning and examined it. He found that an accelerant had been used: petrol. This suggested a deliberate act of murder. The bodies were removed for an autopsy at Our Lady of Lourdes Hospital in Drogheda, which was carried out on 8 March. Fragments retrieved from the two men's skulls showed that both had been shot in the head before being burned in the car. This pointed to a professional hit – a bullet through the back of the head and the successful erasing of the evidence. We had a double murder investigation on our hands. It would go down as the only double murder I investigated in my thirty-three years with the force.

An incident room was set up at Dundalk Garda Station. This was a cross-border operation because the crime scene was located south of the border, but only by a mile. So I was working closely with my Police Service of Northern Ireland (PSNI) counterparts, sharing information and setting up lines of inquiry. At this point, we still had no idea who the victims were, but when we heard that two small-time criminals, Joseph Redmond and Anthony Burnett, had been reported missing, it seemed possible that we had a match. Redmond and Burnett were regarded as petty thieves, existing far down the food chain where they picked over the scraps thrown by the big boys. They certainly knew the kind of people who would put a bullet in your head, but why had they been singled out and murdered in this blatant manner when they seemed irrelevant?

The information that was coming in suggested they had stolen a Volkswagen car in Dublin and had been heading north to meet a buyer, who was named as Jason O'Driscoll.

That sent a shockwave through the incident room. O'Driscoll was well known to gardaí as an extremely dangerous man.

We quickly established that the car found in Ravensdale was indeed a VW Golf stolen from the Sandymount area of Dublin in the early hours of 7 March. This supported the hypothesis that Redmond and Burnett were the unfortunate victims in the car. In order to prove this conclusively, we went to the two men's mothers and requested buccal swabs in order to generate DNA profiles. Forensics tested the women's DNA against the DNA retrieved from the victims: a definite match.

Working on the assumption that if Redmond and Burnett had arrived at the out-of-the-way spot by car then the assailant had probably arrived by car as well, our first step was to examine any CCTV footage available in an attempt to identify the likely getaway vehicle. There was footage available from a private residence located about one hundred metres away from the crime scene, and it showed a large silver car in convoy with the victims' car before the time the killings took place. The silver car looked like a Mercedes.

The PSNI informed us that some of their officers had chased a car that same night because it had failed to stop when directed to do so. The car they gave chase to, and noted the registration number of, was a silver Mercedes. Following on from this valuable coincidence, we unearthed footage that showed a large silver car parked at the rear of a premises in Meigh village, just north of the border. In the video, two males could be identified – and one of them was Jason O'Driscoll. The problem was, how could we prove conclusively that the car seen with the VW just before the murder was the same vehicle these two men got out of later that night?

The following day, the PSNI found an abandoned car on

Foughilletra Road in Jonesboro, just a couple of miles away from Ravensdale but on the northern side of the border. It was a silver Mercedes. It had no plates, but it was a similar model to the car we were interested in – a Mercedes S-Class W221. Then we had a stroke of luck: there was false documentation on the windscreen, and this turned out to have the same registration number as the car chased by the PSNI on the night of the murders. It was one and the same vehicle.

The PSNI ordered a forensic examination of the Mercedes, and we were hugely disappointed when the report came back saying that no DNA trace evidence had been found. The car was handed over to An Garda Síochána, and – working on gut instinct – I requested that the Garda Technical Bureau conduct their own examination. But, once again, I received word that there was no DNA evidence.

I didn't accept it. I had a hunch, and that hunch was telling me there was something to be found in that car. I wasn't going to let it go.

It was an unprecedented move when I asked the Forensic Science Laboratory to examine the vehicle for a third time. It was so unusual, in fact, that the state forensic scientist, Dr Emily Jordan, told me she would have to seek permission from her superiors because my request was outside the bounds of protocol. I insisted it was worth doing. Dr Jordan said, 'Well, Pat, if you want it done, you normally know what you're about. And you wouldn't ask unless it was important.' So she went off and argued my case, and permission was granted. The lab got to work examining the Mercedes in forensic detail yet again.

This was the third report on the same vehicle, but it didn't provide the same answer. I smiled to myself when I read Dr Jordan's description of the findings: traces of several DNA profiles, indicating a mixture of three people's DNA. Was one of these our killer? It was a very sweet moment to know that I had vindicated Dr Jordan's faith in me, and proven that sometimes gut feeling deserves to be placed above technical science. Now we had the car and the DNA, it was the breakthrough we hadn't even dared hope for.

The suspect we had in our sights was still Jason O'Driscoll. He was thought to be linked to a number of assassination-type murders committed in Ireland, but so far no evidence had been found to link him definitively to any of those crime scenes. And I had no hope of getting a voluntary DNA sample from him to compare with those found in the Mercedes. My other problem was that I couldn't prove in a court of law that the Mercedes was involved in the crime. I tackled this issue first, hoping something would change with regard to the suspect and we might be able to make a move on him somehow.

I researched vehicle analysis and the new technologies available to assist investigations, and through this I discovered a Bristol-based company called Acuity. They performed highly specialized work in car recognition and movements, being able to identify a car caught on CCTV and match it across all footage on which it is found. This might sound like something that could be done in the incident room, but if we were to turn up in court with CCTV images of a car and point the finger at the accused on this basis, the defence would rip us apart. How do you prove conclusively that the car in the footage is the car driven by the defendant, and that it's the same car on all the various CCTV units that recorded it? That's what Acuity are able to do. Their analysts are highly qualified, using state-of-the-art systems, therefore they can stand as expert witnesses and prove their findings. And in this case, we needed that level of certainty.

When I contacted Acuity about the case, the first thing they said was: 'Don't tell us anything. Nothing at all. We need to be impartial. Just let us look at the footage and we'll tell you if we can help.'

So I told them nothing whatsoever about the case and sent over the footage taken from Meigh village and from the crime scene. They got back to confirm it was suitable for analysis, but they would need a reconstruction carried out for comparison purposes. They asked that we film ten different cars travelling the same routes as in the CCTV footage supplied, at the same time of day/night and recorded by the same CCTV units that had captured the original footage. I agreed to organize this exactly as requested. I didn't tell them that I had the actual car we suspected had been used in the crime, and I never did tell them. But I put the Mercedes into the mix of ten cars and it was filmed, like the rest, under the conditions specified by Acuity.

Their conclusion delivered another sweet moment for the investigation: out of the ten cars used to reconstruct the scene, they identified the silver Mercedes as the one matching the car in the footage. Acuity's report confirmed that the silver Mercedes was at the scene of the crime, and the same car was at a second location forty-five minutes after the killings – caught on camera with the suspect getting out of it. The crime scene may not have yielded any decent evidence, but with a bit of persistence, we now had some solid information to work with.

There was another line of inquiry that proved valuable too. A mobile phone was found in the car, melted between the two bodies, suggesting it had been in a breast pocket. This meant the victims had used mobiles – and therefore there could be mobile phone data. We talked to the families, who were very happy to cooperate, and learned that one of the men had owned one phone while the other man owned two phones. His family gave us both of his mobile numbers.

The phone we'd found in the burnt-out vehicle was an iPhone, and we were able to reconstruct it enough to discover that it had been used for photos and social media content. We surmised that this possibly meant that the second number belonged to his 'business' phone. It also seemed likely that the two phones we hadn't found at the scene had been taken from the men prior to the murders.

We tracked the call data from both numbers, and it made for interesting reading. Just minutes before he was shot dead, Anthony Burnett had used his business phone to make four calls to the same mobile number, and that same number had called him. Whoever owned that mobile number was definitely someone we would want to talk to about the crime. We dug into it and found out that it was the number of a Ready To Go phone. We were able to retrieve the phone's prepay details and discovered that it had been topped up a number of times in Newry. So I contacted the PSNI, who were extraordinarily helpful and granted permission for An Garda to continue our investigation north of the border.

We listed out all the dates on which the phone was topped up in Newry, and noted that one of them was the day after the murder. So we isolated the shop at which it had been carried out. When we looked at the CCTV footage from the shop on that day, we found ourselves looking at Jason O'Driscoll.

At this stage, we also had witness statements telling us that O'Driscoll had had a sum of €1,500 stolen from him and he believed Burnett and Redmond were the culprits. We also had witnesses who named O'Driscoll as the man the two victims had been in contact with prior to the murder with the intention of selling him the VW Golf. Our contention that he was the prime suspect was holding up under scrutiny, because every lead was taking us straight to him.

At this point in the investigation, an incident occurred that greatly aggravated me and which highlighted how much damage can be wrought by media intrusion on sensitive cases. The media are a necessary part of our work, and every garda has to learn how to handle that aspect of the job, but at times it can be very difficult to be understanding of the behaviour of journalists and photographers. I know that they have to make a living and I know they want that all-important scoop, but they must also observe protocols and use plain old common sense so as not to compromise an investigation. The Ravensdale case was an example of the failure to do this.

A journalist wrote a sensational article about the double murder, and it was accompanied by a photograph of the shop in Newry where O'Driscoll had topped up his Ready To Go phone. This came as a big shock to us, because the photograph in question was a still from video footage and should never have been outside the incident room. It was a photo that we'd intended to use at trial.

I was absolutely furious when I saw it out there in the public domain, but I had no way of finding out how exactly it had got there. Nonetheless, I sent a strongly worded letter of complaint to my super, declaring my intention to arrest the journalist for interfering with the running of an investigation. That was a power within my remit, and I wanted everyone to know I could and would use it. What this journalist had done was completely unacceptable, especially when we were so close to concluding the case.

The letter put the proverbial cat among the pigeons, and fur and feathers were flying everywhere. I remained impervious, knowing that I was doing the right thing for my team – and, indeed, for all teams. I knew I had annoyed a lot of people with that move, but you have to step up and protect the integrity of your work and your cases. It would have been remiss of me if I'd done otherwise.

In the end, the incident was investigated but it was all smoothed over and there were no arrests. Once that unwelcome distraction was out of the way, I was able to refocus again on the murders. When you're working a case intensively, it infiltrates your every waking moment – and sometimes your sleeping ones as well. It becomes part of the daily traffic in your head and you can't shut it out. I often lay awake at night, turning a problem or a piece of evidence over and over in my mind, trying to work the angles, trying to see whatever it was I couldn't see. This time, my subconscious proved to be a very effective ally. One night, about ten months after the murders, I was asleep in bed when I suddenly woke up with a jolt, blinking into the darkness. It was a perfect lightbulb moment, the kind of inspiration you can never force or design – it has to come from the lower reaches of your mind when you're not even paying attention. And that's how it was that night. I sat up and had one thought in my head: what if our suspect had been hospitalized during the course of his life and there was a blood sample lying in a fridge somewhere? I had a feeling I was onto something, and that there would be something out there, just waiting for me to come looking for it.

The next morning, I went straight into the office and immediately made an application, under Section 8 of the

Data Protection Act, to the Health Service Executive (HSE), to inquire if this suspect had ever been admitted to an Irish hospital. I got back a promising answer: yes, in 2009, but an application had to be made directly to the hospital concerned if I wished to receive more information. I most certainly did wish to receive more information, so I sent the second application in quickly and waited impatiently.

The next day, a call came through for me from the hospital in question, asking what information I was hoping to learn about this person who had been there in 2009. 'Well,' I said, 'I was kind of hoping you might have a blood sample knocking about somewhere?' There was a pause, and then the reply was priceless: 'We can do better than that. We have a piece of his colon in cold storage.' When a hunch pays off, it really pays off.

I applied to the District Court to obtain a Section 10 warrant to search for potential evidence in the hospital – as O'Driscoll was the legal owner of his body parts, I had to obtain a warrant to take possession of them. I delivered the explanation to the court, setting out my reasons for wanting to examine the slice of colon, and I remember watching the judge as he read it, hoping he would agree. When he looked up from the document, he said, 'Detective Inspector, I love your thinking and here is your warrant.'

Dr Emily Jordan and I went to the hospital, armed with the warrant, and took possession of the piece of colon and brought it to the lab for analysis. After waiting a few days for Dr Jordan to be ready to give her verdict, she rang me and confirmed that the DNA profile from the colon was a 96 per cent match to the DNA retrieved from the silver Mercedes. This is the kind of moment that keeps you doing this tough work, day in, day out. *Got you*, I thought.

The next step was to arrest O'Driscoll and question him. I prepared an extradition warrant because he was resident in Northern Ireland at that time. However, just as I was ready to pounce, I got word from the PSNI that he was on a flight to Spain and would land in about two hours. I remember looking at my watch and thinking, *Right, gotta move now.* I wanted to get him at the airport, before he could disappear into the backarse of Spain, which was a move he'd pulled a number of times before.

I contacted the Guardia Civil and told them about the crime and the extradition warrant. Spanish police officers greeted the plane on its arrival on Spanish soil, and O'Driscoll was detained at the airport. He was brought before a judge there and given two options: remain in custody in Spain on foot of the extradition warrant, or go home and fight the accusation. O'Driscoll indicated that he wanted to go home and deal with An Garda on this particular matter. I'd say he did that because he reckoned we had nothing to go on and he thought he'd walk out of the station a free man after the period of detention had elapsed.

I sent three reliable detectives out to Spain to bring him back, and soon he was sitting in Dundalk Garda Station. I've no doubt he was surprised when we arrested him for the murders of Anthony Burnett and Joseph Redmond, but he never spoke a single word to us. He didn't acknowledge any of us in any way.

Jason O'Driscoll was finally brought to court in October 2017, eighteen months after being brought back from Spain, and was asked how he pleaded. 'I'm innocent, Your Honour,' he replied, before stating: 'Not guilty.' We went through the full rigours of an eight-week jury trial, but when it came time to deliver a verdict, after eleven and a half hours of deliberation, it was revealed that the jury was split: they could deliver neither a unanimous nor a majority verdict. When this happens, the DPP must decide if it's wise to proceed to a retrial or simply drop the charges. The senior counsel argued strongly that it was worth retrying the case, and it went forward for trial again.

It's very hard when a case you've laboured over falls down because of a split jury, especially as there's nothing you can do about it. All the work and circumstantial evidence was put on ice while we waited for a new trial date.

It took until 2018 to reach the final chapter in this case. On 25 June, six years after Joseph Redmond and Anthony Burnett were shot through the head and burned, the suspected killer stood trial for the second time at the Central Criminal Court in Dublin. Jason O'Driscoll stood before Mr Justice Michael White and once again entered a not-guilty plea. Five weeks later, the jury retired. They spent more than seven hours discussing the evidence, then returned to court and delivered a ten-to-two majority decision of 'guilty'. At that point, O'Driscoll stood up and shouted, 'Guilty of fucking what?'

In the end, we didn't have to prove that he pulled the trigger; it was sufficient to prove that he had participated in the murders and was complicit in them. The evidence supported and proved this contention. The planning of this crime had been careful and the execution of the plan disciplined and thorough, but a bit of dogged persistence had broken through those well-laid plans and unmasked a double killer. A good detective is tenacious, willing to see things through right to the very end. This is a crucial trait, because every case presents obstacles that will derail or delay the investigation at some point. It's a matter of thinking over, under, around and outside the box – of pushing continually for the answers and having confidence in your own gut instinct. It can be a lonely road at times, and you can make as many enemies as friends along the way, but that's the price you have to be willing to pay. To my mind, it's worth it.

5. Assault Causing Harm: The Paradox of Cause and Effect

As a detective working in Ireland, assaults are one of the most frequently encountered types of crime. More than 19,000 assaults or related offences were reported between March 2017 and March 2018, and it's a continually rising figure. These can be difficult crimes to investigate, because so many instances of assault involve alcohol – which makes people unusually reckless and impulsive – or they are spur-of-the-moment incidents, the result of a flashing anger and heightened emotion. This 'out of the blue' element can make it hard to pinpoint motive and actions – and criminal intent. So, as an investigator, you have to tread very carefully and ensure that every scrap of evidence is tracked down and examined. That's the only way to find out what exactly happened – then you can work on the why.

The other potential pitfall in such cases is that quite often an assault looks like one thing but is actually something quite different – a phenomenon I've experienced a number of times in my career. If an investigator isn't alive to this possibility, it could result in wrongful accusation and arrest. I've dealt with hundreds of assaults over the years, but there are five cases that stand out for me because in each one there was an alternative conclusion that could have been drawn – and could have been supported by circumstantial evidence – but which turned out to be false. It's a strange feeling as a detective when you realize you almost made the wrong call. It's very sobering, and reminds you just how much you owe to each case: an investigator must do every single thing in their power to arrive at the truth.

My very first day as a detective inspector was 13 October 2010, and my last task as a uniform inspector was to present court proceedings on behalf of the State at Drogheda District Court. As a uniform inspector, you attend the court and represent the State in multiple cases – as many as one hundred at a time. There's no training provided for this – you just have to turn up at court, read the case files, cart them all into the courtroom, and be prepared to present the evidence for the various cases being heard that day. If ever a garda is driven to drink, it's after a day in court grappling with defence solicitors, disgruntled members of the public, absent gardaí and an unsympathetic judge. It's extremely tough work, and when I'd get home from court, I'd be so exhausted from the mental stress I'd collapse onto the sofa, in my uniform, and conk out.

So there was a great sense of relief in knowing that I would not have to engage in court-presenting again – it's a distinct perk of being a DI that you are no longer required to prosecute cases. As I replaced my uniform with my new suit and tie that mid-October day, I felt I had finally got to where I'd wanted to be all along. It had taken twenty-four years of solid hard work, but now I was DI Pat Marry, at last.

I was only on the job a few hours when news of a serious incident came through. I had spent most of the day in court, doing my final stint and finishing up at 4 p.m. I then took a break, changed clothes and commenced the role of DI. I barely had time to sharpen my pencil before a serious incident landed on my desk. At 9.06 p.m., a sudden flurry of emergency calls from members of the public reported a number of men involved in a violent fracas on Castle Road in Dundalk. Gardaí on mobile patrol not far from there made their way to the scene, and as they neared Castle Road they were flagged down by a couple who stated they had witnessed up to ten men fighting and that one young man was lying motionless on the footpath. On reaching the scene, the gardaí found a quiet street. They looked around, and there – half hidden by a parked car – was a topless young man lying on the ground, alive but unresponsive, his right shoulder slightly under the car. They immediately had him removed by ambulance to Our Lady of Lourdes Hospital in Drogheda, where he was placed on life support. They sent a T-shirt and jacket that were found nearby with him in the ambulance.

The injured man was identified as Niall Dorr, an eighteen-year-old local. There was no sign of the gang of men reported and a search of the local area proved fruitless, so attention turned to securing the scene for technical examination. At that time, it was the only means of figuring out who had been involved. Fortunately it was a dry, cold night – good conditions for preserving any evidence. The gardaí on the scene sealed off the area.

The scenes of crime investigators arrived the next morning and carried out a thorough examination. One of the items found was an unlit cigarette, which was lying very close to where Niall Dorr had lain, putting it within the frame of the crime scene. There were some empty cans and other street rubbish, all of which was bagged and tagged. And, of course, there was also his T-shirt and jacket, which were now in a patient's property bag at the Lourdes.

We got word that Niall Dorr had been moved from Drogheda to Beaumont Hospital in Dublin, which usually indicates a serious head injury. Beaumont subsequently returned him to the Lourdes, which I knew from experience was a very bad sign, suggesting there was nothing further that medicine could do to help him. This proved to be true. We received word on 14 October that Niall Dorr had died of his injuries at 2.45 p.m. Those injuries were consistent with violent assault.

Informing family members of the death of their loved one never gets any easier, not from the first time to the last. David Dorr was informed of his son's death by a detective sergeant who knew the family, and he was asked to identify Niall's body. He did so at Our Lady of Lourdes Hospital, and I can only imagine the sense of pain, loss and anger and the raw devastation that accompanied this nightmare task. In every investigation I conducted, I always aimed to keep the grieving family front and centre in the team's mind, because it acts as a motivation to do the work properly and see it all the way through to conviction. For that reason, getting to know the deceased through their family and friends is also important. We got to know Niall through his parents, David and Veronica. They described him as an ambitious young man, well liked and with big plans for his future and his career. The very morning of his attack, he had been interviewed at Cathal Brugha Barracks in Dublin for a position with the Defence Forces. He had already passed a fitness test and was well on the way to fulfilling his dream. I could really relate to that, and it saddened me that he would never get to achieve his aspirations. I wanted to deliver a solid case that would identify and convict the people responsible for the savage death of one so young. I wanted that for Niall, for his parents, and for his only sibling, Shane.

The following day, 15 October, State Pathologist Dr Marie Cassidy carried out the post-mortem at Louth County Hospital. Dr Cassidy's findings were chilling, and underlined the vicious nature of the attack. There were cuts and bruises on

1. Here I am (*front row, far right*) with my graduating class from Templemore in 1986.

2. As a twenty-four-year-old garda I had no idea what direction my life would take.

3. (*right*) In retirement in 2018.

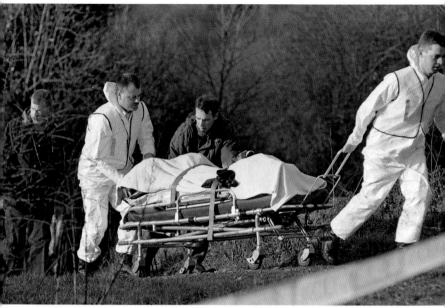

4. Marilyn Rynn's body is removed from the place where she was murdered on 6 January 1996. She had been reported missing on 26 December. It was the first murder case I worked on.

5. David Lawler pleaded guilty to the rape and murder of Marilyn Rynn in January 1998.

6. Colin Whelan. Whelan called the emergency services to say that his wife, Mary Gough, had fallen down the stairs. She later died of her injuries.

7. Colin Whelan was the first person I arrested for murder. I have always seen it as my first meaningful arrest.

8. (*below*) Mary's mother leaves the Central Criminal Court after Colin Whelan was given a life sentence for the murder of her only daughter and best friend.

9. In October 2004, I was called to the scene of an apparent burglary-gone-wrong at Lambay View, the home of Joe and Rachel O'Reilly.

10. Rachel O'Reilly, née Callaly, was thirty years old and a mother of two when she was murdered.

11. State Pathologist Dr Marie Cassidy performed the post-mortem on Rachel O'Reilly.

12. Despite our best efforts to prevent this, the press got a photo of me bringing in Joe O'Reilly after arresting him for the murder of his wife.

13. Rachel's sister, Ann, and parents, Jim and Rose, on 21 July 2007, the day Joe O'Reilly was found guilty of her murder. To the right behind Jim is Tom Gallagher, my superintendent on this case.

14 & 15. Veronica and David Dorr were devastated by the death of their eighteen-year-old son Niall in October 2010. Douglas Ward (*inset*) pleaded guilty to manslaughter after a long investigation into the horrific assault.

16. Shahzad Hussain was convicted of stabbing his ex-wife Rashida Bibi Haider and their friend Muhammad Arif on 6 January 2011. Arif later died from his injuries.

17 & 18. The funeral procession of Jacqueline McDonagh in 2012 after her husband, Michael McDonagh (*inset*), murdered her at their home in Dundalk.

19. Nicola Kavanagh was convicted of arson and manslaughter in 2014 for her involvement in the death of Eva Berrill, a seventy-three-year-old woman who died when her house was set on fire.

20. Ciara Breen. Ciara went missing from her Dundalk home in 1997, when she was seventeen.

21. Seventeen years after Ciara's disappearance, I was appointed senior investigating officer of a renewed investigation.

22. Based on new information, we searched for Ciara's body in four acres of reed swamp in 2015 but we found nothing. It is one of my greatest regrets that her case remains unsolved.

Niall's face, neck, arms and legs, as well as patterned bruises on the forehead and behind the left ear – she concluded that these were from the sole or heel of a shoe. There was actually a footprint on Niall's face, showing the force of the stamps on his head. It had resulted in two fractures of the skull and a brain haemorrhage, which caused bleeding into the skull cavity. The cause of death was therefore given as blunt force trauma to the head leading to fracture and haemorrhage.

This unwelcome news meant that I was dealing with my first murder case as a detective inspector. The incident room was set up at Dundalk Garda Station and I was the SIO in charge. Strangely enough, I had never set foot in Dundalk station before that day, and as a result I didn't even know the detectives on my team. Dundalk was known as 'Fort Apache', and it was seen as a tough posting. As a border town, it had its own atmosphere and culture – and, unfortunately, a lot of crime to go with it. There is always tension in border areas between locals and the police, and Dundalk was no different. The local people were wonderful – a really decent community – but a paramilitary presence creates a fearful environment and that affects people deeply. All in all, it was the kind of station that could make or break a garda.

So, heading up to Dundalk to chair my first murder conference was daunting, to say the least. But my senior officer handed me a lifeline: 'Look for Garda James Doherty, he'll sort you out.' When I walked into the packed incident room, I turned to the person nearest to me and asked him to point out James Doherty. 'That's me,' he said. We shook hands.

James was the incident room coordinator, and he helped me to settle in and get the investigation under way. In fact, he was to become a reliable and trusted friend and colleague over the next eight years. He was, and remains, a truly excellent detective – clever, perceptive and always quick with a good idea.

As the conference chair, I had to structure the investigation by assigning jobs and tasks. I assembled the team into five groups of two detectives each. Because I didn't know anyone, it was difficult for me to match people to tasks such as exhibits officer, but James Doherty was close at hand, advising and helping out. I was very conscious that this would form my new colleagues' first impression of me, so I was anxious to get things right. As DI in Louth Division, Dundalk was now my new base, although I had autonomy in every station in the division. I was going to be spending a lot of time at Dundalk station, so I wanted to get off on the right foot.

The key lead we needed to follow was the witnesses to the incident – to get their statements and dig into the information they provided. We quickly established that Niall had been with two friends when the attack took place, and that up to seven people had attacked them. The friends told us that they had gone to the off-licence and were walking up Castle Road when they were confronted by a group of five men – two of whom they recognized. While Niall attempted to appeal to common sense and keep the peace, his frightened friends sprinted off to avoid the gang, and it was at this point they lost contact with Niall. He had been cornered, alone.

The names of the two men they had recognized were our starting point, and were already known to the detectives in the room. As evidence was thin on the ground, I decided that a review of CCTV would be a prudent first step, before going out to make arrests and interview suspects. I had learned the value of CCTV evidence early on in my career, and knew it could provide information that would help to uncover the truth of an incident. We checked the CCTV in the area of the crime scene first, but soon found that there was no footage of either the crime or the scene. Working on the assumption that the men involved had probably been around the town centre earlier, we canvassed businesses in order to view their CCTV footage. It proved to be a good approach, because we found images of the two men whose names we had, in the company of three other men and two women. We soon had the identities of all seven we believed to have been present – if not involved – when Niall Dorr was beaten to death.

One week to the day after the murder, we set up a questionnaire investigation at the scene of the crime at 9 p.m. The idea was to talk to drivers and pedestrians who commonly passed that way, at that time, on that day. This turned up statements from other people who had been in the vicinity on the night in question, but we still weren't anywhere near having enough evidence to prove who had beaten Niall Dorr.

In total, we had statements from thirteen eyewitnesses, who between them had observed different facets of the encounter. That may sound like the case should have been easy to solve, with all this first-hand evidence to draw on. But, as I learned the hard way, there can be serious flaws in eyewitness statements. I had first seen that on the Marilyn Rynn case, and it had been proven to me again and again over the years. Their willingness to help is never in doubt, but their ability to do so can be compromised by their limited powers of observation and recall. It is an established fact that a victim will remember a perpetrator's face more clearly than a witness to a crime, and that a witness begins to lose memory of the culprit within twenty-four hours of the crime. Plus a witness can be influenced by media articles and others' false reporting of events, and they may recall an image differently from what they actually saw. So while we take witness statements very seriously and are extremely grateful to have them, it's also necessary to be aware of those limitations and to cross-check as much as possible.

In this case, we had the couple out walking who saw the fight quite close up and were deeply disturbed by what they witnessed. We also had a man who was in his upstairs bedroom when he heard the commotion and looked out the window. He described a group of men who started to argue, then he saw one man being chased by a number of people from the group. He looked at where the confrontation had started and saw one man standing over Niall Dorr and 'this man was banging [Niall's] head off the ground'. The man shouted out the window at all of them to disperse. His recollection of the event was helpful, but he could not give a detailed description of the assailant because he was at a distance and had to crane to see out the window.

Of the other ten witnesses, most of them had driven past the incident when leaving the St Gerard novena held in the nearby St Joseph's Redemptorist Church. One told us that 'the fella on the ground looked like he was dead, he was completely lifeless. The fella was kicking him and stomping on his head.' This same witness described the culprit grabbing Niall Dorr by the shoulders and dragging him off the road, which caused his T-shirt to come off over his head. (No one mentioned Niall's jacket, so we didn't know if he was wearing it or carrying it, or when it was removed.) The assailant continued to 'bang his head off the wheel of a car'. When asked to give a description of the man attacking Niall, he could not describe him in any great detail, but he did recall one small thing: the culprit was wearing a shirt, not a T-shirt.

This was also backed up by another witness, who said the culprit was wearing a shirt and a grey hoodie.

That's the other thing you learn about eyewitness statements – it can be the tiniest detail that ends up being the most useful. So the interviewer must be able to notice and remember this sort of minutiae, even if it seems insignificant at the time.

We also conducted house-to-house inquiries, which resulted in some information – but not as much as we hoped. There weren't many people coming forward to cooperate with the investigation, so progress was slow. Fort Apache had pulled up the drawbridge, it seemed.

It was time to bring in the two men identified by Niall's friends. At the station, they admitted to being at the scene and in the company of the five others, but denied any involvement in the assault. We knew from eyewitnesses that the two women identified as being part of the group had hung back and not participated in the attack, so it had to be one of the five men who had delivered the fatal blow. We also had the couple who had flagged down the patrol car, who felt they could identify the culprit.

The interviews with the two men did deliver a key detail: the group of five men had been due in court that morning on charges of assault and public disorder. The judge had postponed the hearing and so they had all gone on a drinking session to celebrate.

I assigned a detective to go back and review all CCTV footage, starting at the courthouse on Crowe Street and tracking the men's movements throughout the day. This game of cat and mouse eventually revealed video evidence of the men going from one pub to the next, from 11 a.m. to 8.30 p.m. One of the men was wearing not a T-shirt, but a shirt.

Half an hour before the assault, the men could be seen leaving the last pub. On the way out, the man wearing the shirt picked up a grey hoodie top and put it on. As is so often the case, the small details connected and suddenly we had a picture. The man in the shirt and hoodie was identified as Douglas Ward, and he was now a suspect in the murder of Niall Dorr.

Our suspicions about Ward were given the opportunity to be proved thanks to witness statements and some dogged police work. We were told that Ward had been given a lift later that night, and that his nose was bleeding. He had grabbed some tissues that were in the car and used them to staunch the flow of blood. He then threw the tissues out of the car window while in a car park. I knew it was a long shot, but nonetheless I dispatched officers to the car park with instructions to search for bloody tissues. They found them, bagged them and brought them back for forensic examination. We now had a DNA profile for Douglas Ward, thanks to his blood on the discarded and forgotten-about tissues.

I had Ward arrested on 17 October 2010 and detained under Section 4 of the Criminal Justice Act 1984. Over the next twenty-three hours, he was questioned about his involvement in the murder of Niall Dorr. We also took his fingerprints and palm prints, photographed him, and took buccal swabs to generate a DNA profile that could be compared against that provided by the discarded tissues. He was then asked to take part in a formal identification parade, but he refused. Any suspect has the right to refuse, but naturally it's noted with interest when they do.

During his period of detention he was interviewed seven times. The interview is, of course, the lynchpin of any investigation – and, as such, officers must be adept at conducting them. We attend training courses in interview techniques, to learn international best practice and helpful methods of questioning. I find the process of interviewing fascinating, and I'm very glad that it has been standardized and structured because it means the detainee spends less time in custody and the questioning is more focused and effective. There's no banging on the desk, roaring and shouting – not any more. That was a waste of time and energy, anyway. Now, everything is kept calm and focused and the interviewer never loses sight of their key aims. It's a fair process that doesn't put undue stress or pressure on the interviewee, and that's a welcome development. It's very much a skill, and you get better at it over time as you become more practised and experienced.

All seven interviews conducted with Douglas Ward were recorded and therefore could be used in evidence. Ward described his day around Dundalk, mentioning the pubs we already knew he had visited. He told us that at 8 p.m. he had contacted a man who owned an apartment near Castle Road, with a view to organizing a party there. The group then made its way to this man's apartment, but he shouted down from the window that he wasn't letting them in. According to Ward, the group then walked away to the right, towards Seatown Place – namely, in the opposite direction to the scene of the crime. We checked the CCTV again, searching for Ward in or around Seatown Place. There was no sign of him. So we went to visit the unwilling party host, and he told us that when he told the group he wasn't letting them into his place, they walked away to the left, which put Douglas Ward on Castle Road at the time of the incident. What Ward was saying did not add up to a convincing alibi when set against the other information we were gathering.

As the SIO, I now had a decision to make. Was the best

solution to continue to hold and question Ward, or was it to try to get an eyewitness to identify him? I weighed it up and decided to release him from custody without charge, in order to allow the team to conduct an informal ID parade and continue gathering evidence.

Ward walked out of Dundalk Garda Station and back to his old life. One week later, we set up the informal ID parade. This involved having the witness sitting in his car on Dublin Street in Dundalk at a time we knew Ward would be there. If the witness saw the man who had attacked Niall Dorr, a prearranged signal was to be given. We filmed the informal ID parade from a number of different vantage points so that there could be no accusation of manipulating the process and it could be shown to be impartial.

Ward arrived in a small black car, got out and went into a premises, then came back out, got back into the car and drove off. There was no signal from the witness, so the operation was stood down. It was only at this point that the witness told us there was a 'strong possibility' that the man who got out of the small black car was the attacker. Given that around 1,500 people had passed through the area during the timeframe of the ID parade, this was a significant statement. The problem was, without the signal, it couldn't be used as evidence. So now I faced another difficult decision: forget about identifying Ward in this way, or hold a second informal ID parade? I was very aware that in a trial in court, the defence could use the fact of a second ID parade to argue that the witness wasn't reliable. On the other hand, it was my duty to seek out and preserve all evidence to prove the innocence or guilt of the suspect. I considered it and decided to press ahead again, although at a different location and time.

The second ID parade took place inside a government

building when we knew Ward would be present. We put the witness in situ, and when Ward came along he was in the company of his brother, who bore a remarkably close resemblance to Ward. The witness did not pick out the suspect.

At this point, we had witness statements putting Ward at the scene; we had a witness identifying Ward as the man who attacked Niall Dorr; and we had Ward's DNA. What we didn't have was conclusive evidence putting Ward at the scene and physically attacking Niall Dorr. In order to generate more information and hopefully more evidence, it was decided to feature the case on *Crimecall*. The programme aired on 25 January 2011, three months after the murder, and I made an appeal live on air for people to come forward and talk to the investigation team. It was a deeply affecting programme, with a photo shown of the baby-faced Niall Dorr. His parents and his kickboxing team were also filmed describing him as cheerful, always smiling, sporty and 'a very gentle person'. He had achieved the level of black belt in kickboxing, and had travelled Europe representing his country. His father David recounted how Niall had filled out an organ donor card that July, three months before his death, and handed it to his mother for safekeeping. After his death, five people benefitted from his organ donation and can thank him for their lives.

We were very clear on the twin aims of the *Crimecall* appeal: first, to ask the local community to come forward and talk to us; and second, to ask those eyewitnesses who were refusing to cooperate to examine their consciences and do the right thing. Niall's mother Veronica made a heartfelt plea, saying she would 'like to see justice done for him'. She urged people not to be afraid, and asked them to come forward with any information. It was a message that went straight to the heart of the community in Dundalk: help us to help one of your own.

After the *Crimecall* appeal aired, there was a good response to the case and a number of people contacted the studio with information. This added more lines of inquiry and allowed us to add to the picture we had already compiled of the days before the attack and the attack itself. But we still needed something definitive.

My own instinct was that this was one case where forensics was going to be the key that would unlock the prosecution. The cigarette had proved to be a match to Ward's DNA. This put him at the crime scene, but it didn't prove he'd laid a finger on Niall Dorr – so we had to look elsewhere. One of the witnesses had mentioned Niall being dragged by the shoulders, causing his top to come off over his head. Based on this small detail we sent the T-shirt for forensic examination, and I asked that the shoulders of the garment be studied closely. This was done, and it was a big moment when we got back the results: Ward's DNA had been found on the shoulders of Niall's T-shirt.

This matched the witness accounts of how Dorr was assaulted, and it put Ward at the scene and physically engaging with Dorr. At this point, we had been investigating for months, so this was a huge breakthrough. I had a niggling worry, though. What if – in a trial situation – a defence barrister argued that Ward's DNA could have found its way onto the T-shirt some other way? For example, what if he'd picked it up in a shop, then decided not to buy it and put it back, then Niall Dorr had walked into the shop and bought it? So we researched the history of the T-shirt. We found out that it had been bought north of the border in Newry, for starters. We checked with Niall's parents, and Veronica told us that she had washed and ironed the T-shirt and Niall had taken it out of the hot press before heading out for the night.

We were satisfied that this meant Ward's DNA could not have got onto the T-shirt before the night of the murder.

But now I had another niggling worry. What if the defence barrister argued that the DNA could have come from saliva – that Ward had spat at Niall, and that was the cause of the DNA match? I went back to the forensics team and put the question to them: could it have come from saliva? This turned out to be a very tough question to answer. The team had to investigate new processes and conduct in-depth research in order to find a way to isolate the source of the DNA evidence. In the end, they developed a process never before used in Ireland. And when they applied this new test to the T-shirt, we got back the result we had been hoping for: the DNA match was definitely linked to skin cells from Douglas Ward, which had been transferred onto the T-shirt worn by Niall Dorr. That put Ward at the scene and in physical contact with the victim.

Our methodical investigation was one to be proud of – we had covered every single angle without exception, and now the forensics had come to our aid by providing the final piece of the puzzle. The team knew the end was in sight now.

We had to seek a court order to allow us to arrest Ward for a second time, and this was granted on foot of the new evidence – namely the T-shirt DNA. On 18 April 2011, Douglas Ward was rearrested for involvement in the murder of Niall Dorr. He was brought to Dundalk Garda Station, and the questions started rolling once again. We asked Ward if he'd ever been in Newry. He said he'd never been to that town in his life. He was asked to recall that day and night in detail, and asked to explain the cigarette and T-shirt with his DNA. Again and again, he told us that he had no idea how his DNA had come to be at the crime scene and on the victim's clothing. But his 'No comment' approach wasn't going to save him now. The evidence had been amassed slowly and carefully, and it was incriminating.

On 30 October 2012, the case came to trial. Ward pleaded guilty to the manslaughter of Niall Dorr and received a sentence of sixteen years, with the last three years suspended. For the investigation team, it was a deeply satisfying outcome because we'd had to work from so little and build up the case bit by bit. There was a slight sting in the tail when Ward appealed the case from prison, citing alcoholism as a disease and therefore a mitigating factor. His sentence was reduced by three years – to thirteen years with the final three suspended. Niall Dorr's family were deeply upset by this reduction in his prison term. However, on 8 May 2015, Ward died in prison. He was only thirty-eight, but he died in his cell after drinking 'hooch', a home-made alcohol. The inquest into his death pronounced a verdict of death by misadventure.

I was very proud of the whole team and their dedication to evidence-gathering over the long months of the investigation. For me personally, it was my first murder case as DI and it ended in a successful conviction – and that was very important to me. I felt I had laid down a marker; that I had started as I meant to go on.

I encountered a similar sort of crime scene in Drogheda in July 2013 – it also involved a man who was beaten and left for dead.

The victim's name was Gerard 'Wobbler' Reynolds, and he was found on a grass area near a housing estate with almost every bone in his body broken. He had been assaulted with cement blocks, which were dropped onto his back and legs as he lay face down on the ground. The attack took place in the early hours of 26 July, but Reynolds wasn't discovered until about 8.30 a.m. by a local resident. The emergency services were alerted and he was removed to Our Lady of Lourdes Hospital, where he would remain in intensive care for fourteen days. He spent a further month in the hospital, undergoing various surgeries and recovering slowly from his ordeal.

As with the Dorr investigation, I knew it was important to examine any CCTV footage we could find between the town and the crime scene – again working on the assumption that the perpetrators had likely been around during the day. Alongside this, I ordered a widespread door-to-door campaign, calling in on householders in the local area to see if anyone could give us a clue – no matter how small – as to who might have carried out the vicious assault.

In a house not far from the scene, the occupant told the door-to-door uniforms that he had installed an audio-visual system in his window box, to keep an eye on his car. So we asked to view the footage of the night in question. Imagine our surprise and delight when it turned up an incredible piece of evidence. The AV unit had caught three people walking away from the crime scene and then stopping near the window box, where they talked about the unfortunate victim and how they had kicked him and dropped concrete blocks on him. It was a ready-made confession.

The three men in the footage were known to us already, so it was a simple matter to track them down and arrest them on suspicion of assault. In due course, they all pleaded guilty and received prison sentences. The householder was pleased that his crime-busting AV unit had helped solve the case. He told us that he only got it because it was going cheap in Aldi, never thinking it would witness a major incident. As with the Dorr case, eyewitnesses were crucial – even if, in this case, that eyewitness was a machine.

*

On 27 November 2010, at about 10.30 p.m., emergency services were called to a house in Dundalk. The ambulance crew couldn't respond immediately, so they contacted the local fire service, who are fully trained first responders and often cover for the paramedics when there is the threat of a delay. Arriving at the house, the fire crew found a distraught seventy-year-old man and an unresponsive woman lying on her back at the bottom of the stairs. The man told them it was his house, that the woman, Sharon McKey, was a close friend, and that he had come back to find her like this and had guessed she had fallen down the stairs. Then the ambulance crew arrived and the scene filled up with people. The paramedics carried out CPR, but they could not get a pulse and the woman was not breathing. So a doctor was called, as were the gardaí.

The doctor arrived, examined the body and pronounced the woman dead, stating the cause to be a heart attack. The uniform gardaí then spoke with the paramedics, the doctor and the friend, and concluded that there was nothing suspicious about this death – that it was an unfortunate case of sudden death by heart attack. Accordingly, the scene was not preserved, all the emergency staff went on their way and it was case closed – though the circumstances did require the body to be removed to Louth County Hospital for a post-mortem.

The autopsy was carried out on 29 November and found the cause of death to be a brain haemorrhage, which meant it was natural causes and we weren't looking at a murder investigation. However, a Garda scenes of crime photographer was in attendance to take photographs of the deceased, and he noticed a mark on the woman's face that had not been there when she was first found in her home. He reported this mark to his superintendent, who in turn requested that the State Pathologist's Office conduct a second post-mortem examination. This was carried out by Dr Khalid Jaber on 30 November. When Dr Jaber pulled out the cold drawer on which the deceased lay, a large footprint was clearly visible across her cheek. He informed the superintendent, who called me and told me to get straight down to the morgue and observe proceedings because we could have a case of foul play rather than a straightforward sudden death. In my head, I was seeing Colin Whelan and his wife, Mary Gough. Was it another case of a woman being killed by someone she trusted and the death made to look like a fall down the stairs?

I reached the morgue half an hour later. I knew Dr Jaber well and had great faith in his work and his opinion. He carried out the post-mortem, which showed that the deceased's blood alcohol level was very high and that there was a sub-arachnoid haemorrhage. Normally, this would lead to a conclusion of natural sudden death. In this case, however, there was the footprint to factor into the equation. Dr Jaber gently cut and lifted the skin to determine the striking force involved. He found that the injury was superficial and not in the facial muscle, which meant there was no pressure applied by the boot-wearer. However, the jaw was broken in two places and there was also a mark on the neck. The question was: did the haemorrhage cause the fall, or did a push down the stairs and the resultant impact lead to the haemorrhage? My superintendent charged me with finding the answer.

I went to the crime scene, but of course it hadn't been designated as such and so it had been cleaned and tidied after the removal of the body from the house. It was just a normal hallway again, so I had to imagine what it would have looked like using the descriptions in the uniforms' notes. It was a tall order, to investigate a potential crime without a crime scene.

There was a table in the hallway, at the end of the stairs, which had been mentioned in the report. Sharon McKey's body had been found lying at the foot of the stairs, near the table. It seemed likely that hitting the table as she fell had caused the broken jaw. There was nothing else to be gleaned from the scene, so I turned my attention to gathering evidence that might solve the mystery of the boot print on her cheek.

The first step was to check the shoe soles of every person who was present at the scene – this meant the paramedics, the gardaí and the family members who had turned up as news spread of an accident at the house. I checked with the fire crew, but it turned out they hadn't actually entered the house, so we didn't need to check their shoes. We obtained impressions of every shoe that had walked through the house that day, but none matched – including the shoes of the friend who had found her. So that was a dead end.

Next we tracked down all the CCTV footage we could find, and through that we built up an exact picture of Sharon's last hours. She had been drinking and socializing in a pub until about 9.30 p.m., when she left with her friend and got into a taxi outside. The taxi drove them to his house. She went inside, while her friend went out for about twenty minutes to get a Chinese takeaway and some cigarettes. We could confirm his movements via CCTV and statements from staff in the premises where he'd bought the food and cigarettes. Nothing suspicious there.

When he got home with the takeaway, the front door wouldn't push open properly. That's when he discovered Sharon lying at the foot of the stairs and called for help. Everything we found out corroborated his version of events, and we had no reason to suspect him of lying.

The other angle on the sudden death was the subarachnoid

haemorrhage she had suffered. I researched the phenomenon of haemorrhages and found that symptoms typically
present in the days prior to death – for example, vomiting,
headaches, irritability and coldness. I set about tracing Sharon's movements in the days before her death and found a
witness who described her sitting at the bar in a pub a few
days before her death, dry-heaving. Her close friend also
remembered her having a headache the day she died – plus
she had pulled a duvet around herself in the house when he
stepped out to buy the food and cigarettes, presumably in
an attempt to stay warm. Again, this all pointed to natural
causes. The only fly in the ointment was that boot print, and
try as we might, we couldn't locate its owner or its reason for
appearing on Sharon McKey's cheek. I filed my report, rec-
ommending that it was a case of natural death and the Louth
County Coroner should be allowed to deal with it, as it was
not a crime.

That was all well and good, but my detective's brain was itch-
ing to find out what had actually happened to cause that boot
print. The not-knowing was driving me insane. I kept thinking
it through from every angle, puzzling over why we hadn't found
a match to the shoe. It was keeping me from my sleep.

Two weeks later, I received an unexpected call from Dr
Jaber. It was 11 p.m. and I was in bed, drowsily thinking about
the unsolved 'crime', when my mobile started to buzz. I
answered and Dr Jaber asked for my email address. I recited it
and he said, 'Ring me back when you get the photo' and then
he hung up. Well, now I was wide awake. What photo?

I stared at the phone, willing it to make a noise. Finally –
ping! – an email dropped into my inbox. I clicked on it and a
photo opened up: the muddy sole of a boot that had the exact
pattern I had been staring at for so long – the same pattern

as the boot print on Sharon McKey's face. I smiled to myself and thought, *Good old Jaber.*

I scrabbled to locate Dr Jaber's name in my contacts and pressed Call. He answered immediately. 'Where did you find it?' I asked. He laughed and said, 'You won't believe this . . .' He described how he had been in his office at the state pathologist's in Marino, standing by the window, looking out at the Fire Service training grounds next door. There was a bevy of recruits doing manoeuvres out in the field, and he watched them being put through their paces. When the training ended, the recruits made their way back to their building – leaving an empty field with a rash of boot prints. In a moment of inspiration, Dr Jaber grabbed his camera and ran over to the field, where he photographed the freshly made prints. He compared them to the one that had been driving us all crazy, and lo and behold, it was an exact match. Dr Jaber had missed his calling – he should have been a detective, because this was *Columbo* levels of brilliance.

The next morning, I went to the fire station that had sent the crew to the scene of Sharon McKey's death. I spoke to the crew members who had attended that night. Initially, they were evasive, heads down, not meeting my eye, and I realized that they were scared they were in trouble. I explained that the mark on Sharon McKey's face had in no way caused or contributed to her death – that we knew she had died from a brain haemorrhage – but we wanted to solve the mystery of the boot print. Then I stayed quiet, because silence can be far more helpful than words at moments like this. Sure enough, a head was raised, and one member said that he had gone into the house to help move the body, and while doing so it was possible that his foot had slipped off the stair and touched the deceased's face for a moment.

Finally, the niggling mystery was solved. As we had hoped and suspected, there was no foul play involved in Sharon McKey's untimely death. It was a relief to everyone that she had not suffered any ill-treatment. We will never know if the fall or the haemorrhage came first, but at least we could be certain that she died of natural causes. I was indebted to Dr Jaber's quick thinking for the answer. Indeed, without it, I'm not sure the cause of the boot print would ever have been found. His lateral thinking sparked the clue that gave us the missing piece of the puzzle. It was an exemplary lesson in the art of creative problem-solving.

There were two cases I worked on in which the potential cause of death and the occurrence of death were separated in time: the assault on Deepak Abbi in Drogheda, and the assault on Michael McGeown in Dundalk. In both cases, the delay between cause and effect made it more difficult to trace an evidential path from one to the other. And, as with other assaults, there were alternative explanations that could have been put forward. Both of these investigations required careful, step-by-step detective work to move from the obvious and easy conclusion to the truth. I was lucky I came to these cases as a more seasoned detective, because I already had experience of looks being deceiving. As a result, I was well placed to question the evidence before us and push the investigation in the right direction.

Deepak Abbi was an architect who lived and worked in Drogheda. His family-run practice was situated on Bessexwell Lane, a narrow and unlovely laneway running from Shop Street to Mayoralty Street. It was the kind of place where young people with little to do might loiter; the kind of place that always seems to smell of urine. Mr Abbi had experienced trouble with loiterers in the months before the incident that preceded his death, and things came to a head on 19 July 2012. It started when Abbi came down from his upstairs office and spotted a youth on the ground floor of the building. Hood up to cover his face, the boy had forced open the front door and stepped into the premises. Abbi told him to leave immediately. He then tried to snap a photo of the boy on his phone, at which point the boy turned hostile and aggressive.

The altercation spilled out into the laneway, attracting a crowd. It was about two o'clock on a bright summer's afternoon, and the town was busy with the normal lunchtime traffic. But in Bessexwell Lane, the situation facing Abbi was spiralling out of control. The boy shouted at him, 'Come on, hit me!' Abbi did not engage in any physical action, but the boy pushed him in the chest, slamming his back into the wall. Abbi cracked his head, then slumped to the ground. The boy kicked and thumped him where he lay, until passers-by intervened, at which point the boy wriggled away and sprinted off, shouting racist obscenities over his shoulder as he went.

The witnesses helped Abbi to his feet, but he declined any further help. He had a large lump on the back of his head and bruising on his left shoulder and his leg. But he decided not to seek medical attention. I can only imagine that he feared reprisals against his family.

Three days later, on Sunday, Abbi told his wife he had a headache and felt unwell. At about 5 p.m., he was sitting at his kitchen table, holding his aching head in his hands, when he collapsed. An ambulance was called and transported him to Our Lady of Lourdes Hospital. The medical team quickly ascertained that he had suffered a bleed to the brain and transferred him to Dublin's Beaumont Hospital, which specializes in head injury. Abbi's family told them about the bang to the head he had received during the altercation. Two days after he collapsed at home, Deepak Abbi passed away.

I received a call from the hospital, outlining their concerns about this particular death, given that it was preceded by an assault. It is relatively common for an assault to lead to death at a later date, so a full investigation team was set up to examine the incident prior to Abbi's death. As SIO, I set it up as a full murder investigation, but my brief to the team was to establish whether or not it was a murder. I was thinking at that point we would probably discover that the blow to the head on the 19th had caused Abbi's death on the 24th. It seemed a strong likelihood. However, we had to proceed with an open mind and put assumptions aside in order to conduct an accurate investigation. I had seen other serious incidents being mishandled in the past, when a lack of decision-making or delayed decision-making hampered the solving of the case. I knew that if I was complacent in assessing the incident, there was a danger that the investigation would be complacent and therefore sloppy. As SIO, it's essential to be decisive and accountable. Another person might have seen this as an open-and-shut case of murder or manslaughter through assault, but I had learned enough by now to know that nothing is ever quite that simple.

I set up a team at Drogheda Garda Station and we began to compile the evidence. There was some pressure to come up with an answer because the case had featured on Pat Kenny's radio show and in the national newspapers, so there was widespread public interest in the outcome. The team got started on CCTV and interviewing all those who had witnessed the altercation on Bessexwell Lane. I attended the post-mortem, which took place on 25 July under the direction of Dr Marie Cassidy. Her examination, as well as a subsequent examination of the brain by an expert neuropathologist,

confirmed that Abbi had died of natural causes. Their conclusion was that the haemorrhage would have occurred,
regardless of the incident on the 19th. His death was in no
way connected to the bang to the head he had received when
pushed by the youth in the laneway.

If we had allowed assumptions to direct our work, we
would have been setting ourselves up for a fall. It was a lesson I had learned time and time again, and it was confirmed
yet again now. We continued to gather evidence and conduct
a thorough inquiry, and we arrested the youth involved in
the altercation. He was questioned about the assault on Abbi
and also the attempted burglary at the premises. The investigation had turned up enough evidence to prosecute on these
grounds, and the case duly came to the District Court. The
youth received a custodial sentence (of which details cannot
be divulged as he was a juvenile at the time), but he was
rightly spared the charge of manslaughter or murder.

The incident that preceded the death of Michael McGeown
echoed that of Deepak Abbi: he was assaulted by a young
man, thirty years his junior, who delivered a blow to his
head. He fell down as a result, but got back to his feet and
carried on with his normal life. Six days later, on 6 March
2014, McGeown collapsed and died. The same question was
posed again: was it murder or was it natural causes, with the
assault being just a coincidence? The difference this time was
the results of the post-mortem, as the pathologist's findings
made this a murder investigation.

I got the call on 3 March, three days after the assault. On
that day, Michael McGeown was found unconscious in his
bed. An ambulance was called and took him to Our Lady of
Lourdes Hospital, and he was moved to the intensive care

unit. At this point, we knew that McGeown had been struck during an incident in a pub on 28 February. We knew this because McGeown's boss at Pa's Bar in Dundalk had taken him to hospital after the incident and had also called the ECAS emergency line and reported the assault. The Emergency Call Answering Service (ECAS) is a centralized call centre for all 999 calls that puts callers through to the appropriate emergency service. On this night, it put McGeown's boss through to Drogheda Garda Station, and the garda on duty took down the details of the alleged assault. McGeown had been seen at the Lourdes after the assault, so the hospital had full knowledge of the incident and its aftermath. When he turned up unconscious and unresponsive, the medical team suspected immediately that there was a connection between the two events.

I was appointed SIO, with the incident room at Dundalk station. I had a team of three detectives, and we got to work piecing together McGeown's movements on 28 February and trying to discover what had led to the assault – and who had assaulted him. While we were doing this, Michael McGeown, who had never regained consciousness, passed away on 6 March. The following day, Dr Marie Cassidy carried out a post-mortem at the morgue at the Lourdes. The conclusion of the examination was stark: subdural haemorrhage caused by a blunt force trauma to the head. In the incident room, I informed the team that we were now working on a murder case.

We quickly established that McGeown had been out for a few pints in a pub near his house on 28 February. He worked at Pa's Bar, but on this particular night he had gone into Fagan's Pub on Castletown Road because it was raining and the pub was on his way home. Unfortunately, there was no CCTV system inside or outside Fagan's, so we couldn't review footage to confirm his movements. We did, however, have a number of eyewitness statements that gave us a very clear picture of what happened that night.

The barman was well placed to observe the events that unfolded. He was dealing with a big, beefy customer who was drunk and becoming aggressive, a man he knew to be Charlie Hutchinson. As Hutchinson argued loudly with the barman, McGeown – who had been by himself, enjoying a quiet pint – came over to help calm the situation. He knew the drunk man, because his nephew was seeing the man's sister. And as a barman himself, McGeown would have been used to dealing with the drinkers in town; used to quelling situations that were threatening to escalate. So he went over to the arguing men and spoke some soothing words, and this seemed to mollify Hutchinson. McGeown then returned to his stool at the bar and his pint. Hutchinson apparently still wasn't in the state of mind to be reasonable, however. He went over to McGeown, words were exchanged, and then the barman saw Hutchinson deliver a punch to McGeown's right temple, which caused the older man to pitch off his stool and onto the floor. Other customers saw the aftermath – the angry young man, face twisted in anger, and the injured older man, lying flat out on the floor.

The barman ordered Hutchinson to leave, which he did. McGeown was bleeding from the head where he'd been struck, and the barman fetched a towel to staunch the flow. McGeown rang his own boss to tell him he had been assaulted by Hutchinson. Later, at 11 p.m., he rang his boss again and asked him to bring him to hospital as he felt the wound needed medical attention. At Louth County Hospital in Dundalk, McGeown received stitches to close the wound and was then transferred to the Lourdes for further care.

There, he was X-rayed, prescribed painkillers and antibiotics, and then released with some information about head injuries and warning symptoms.

For two days, McGeown went about his life as normal, socializing with family and friends and working behind the bar at Pa's. But on 2 March he vomited, and that evening he told his daughter he was feeling unwell. He mentioned calling an ambulance, but then decided just to get some rest. The following morning, his daughter could not contact him by phone and became very worried. She rang a friend who lived close by and asked him to check on her father. When the friend did so, he found McGeown lying on his bed, clothed – breathing but unresponsive.

We learned all this very quickly, thanks to the customers present in Fagan's that night, and we also learned, through a confidential informant, that Charlie Hutchinson was planning to leave the jurisdiction to avoid our inquiries. We had to move fast to ensure we didn't lose the prime suspect. On 5 March, the day before McGeown died, we arrested Hutchinson for assault causing harm and brought him to Dundalk Garda Station. At this stage, I was satisfied that we had the right man, given the number of people who had identified him. It was very helpful too that McGeown had told his boss all about the incident, and that his boss had reported it to the police. It meant we had a paper trail, from the hospital and from our own files, leading from McGeown's wounded head to Charlie Hutchinson's fist. It wasn't open-and-shut, though, because we still had to prove that the punch that had felled McGeown was directly responsible for his death. There was still a lot of work to be done.

When McGeown was discovered at his home unresponsive, what was happening in his brain was the cause. A subdural haematoma is an area of bleeding between the skull and the brain surface. In layman's terms, there are three layers protecting the central nervous system: the dura mater, the arachnoid mater and the pia mater. A subdural bleed occurs between the dura and the next layer – the arachnoid – and it happens when the blood vessels have been damaged. One of the ways those vessels can be damaged is a head injury – like, for example, an injury caused by a punch. I've been glad to see the proliferation of the 'One Punch' campaign, highlighting the danger of even a single blow to the head. It's crucial that people understand just how easily they can cause irreparable damage by punching someone in the head, right up to causing death.

When I looked into subdural haematomas, I learned that there are two factors that can make survival an outside chance: advanced age and excessive alcohol intake. McGeown was in his early sixties and had been a heavy drinker for years, which put him in the bracket of high vulnerability. (Incredibly, excessive drinking over a long period of time can shrink the brain, which in turn can make the blood vessels more prone to damage. That's a hell of a thought next time you're nursing a hangover.)

The post-mortem findings backed up my own research – a blunt force trauma to the head had caused subdural bleeding, which had eventually led to haemorrhage and death. To the best of our knowledge, the only incident of blunt force trauma suffered by McGeown prior to his death was that punch in Fagan's. That put Charlie Hutchinson squarely in the frame.

Once arrested, Hutchinson was questioned about the incident a number of times but refused to comment, other than to confirm that he was in the pub that night. So we had no confession, but we did have independent witness statements all agreeing that the man who threw the punch was Charlie Hutchinson. Without his cooperation, the next step was to back up the statements by asking a witness to identify him.

Hutchinson refused to participate in a formal identity parade, which didn't surprise me, so we opted for another tack: the informal ID parade. I brought the barman from Fagan's to the station for this purpose, but Hutchinson was wise to it and covered his face. A week later, when he was out on bail, we tried again, this time by bringing the barman to the Castletown Road area, where Hutchinson was going about his business. The barman had clear sight of him when he came walking down the road and entered the post office, and he identified him as the man who had punched McGeown. That was a key piece of evidence – enough to forward a file to the DPP, which directed that a charge of manslaughter should be brought against Hutchinson. Taken together with the witness statements, forensic evidence from the pub, the report of the assault to the Garda, the hospital's records and the post-mortem's clear, undisputed findings, it was enough to build a solid case against Hutchinson.

When it came to trial in Dundalk Circuit Court in November 2014, Hutchinson pleaded not guilty, so it was a jury trial. It was a short one, though, lasting only a week. During that time, one of the jurors fell ill, so the trial proceeded with eleven jurors. Dr Cassidy's evidence was vital. She was able to explain the bleeding on the brain very clearly for the jury. She noted that when a punch is inflicted on one side, the brain shudders in the skull cavity and it is the opposite side that suffers the damage. The jury listened to her attentively and they understood. The verdict was a ten-to-one majority: guilty. Charlie Hutchinson wasn't there when Michael

McGeown died, but he was the direct cause of his death none-theless. Hutchinson received a custodial sentence of seven years, with the final year suspended.

These cases were demanding and complex, and I learned a huge amount in unravelling them – as much about human nature as about how to conduct a successful investigation. It's the baby-steps approach that delivers a good result – taking each piece of the story and each bit of evidence in turn, examining it methodically and then slotting it into the bigger picture. I was really struck by all the ways in which these investigations could have got it wrong, and I mulled over that for a long time after each case, relieved that I hadn't fallen into the trap of assumption or lazy thinking.

As a detective, you're dealing with people's lives. If I make a mistake, someone could have their whole life turned upside down – or, worst of all, an innocent person could go to prison. As there are so many assault cases coming down the track all the time, it would be all too easy to get complacent. These incidents confirmed the need to be on the ball each and every time – to bring the same level of energy and commitment to every single case, no matter how straightforward it might initially seem. That's a golden rule for any investigator.

6. The Devil is in the Detail

Attending a crime scene is an unnerving and unforgettable experience. I've stood amidst the remnants of the violent end of a life so many times over the past thirty years, but I can still vividly remember each and every one. Each was unique, and uniquely horrible. It's a necessary part of being a detective, but really, you wouldn't wish the experience on anyone.

The immense sadness that pervades a crime scene is stifling, and it clings to your skin as much as the stench of death. You can scrub away the smell, but you can't scrub away that sadness. It attaches itself to you, and you have no choice but to live with it. That's the way it was for me with the scene of the murder of Jacqueline McDonagh – it was a chilling image that I'll never be able to erase.

There are many ways of tackling an investigation, but one of the hallmarks of those that I conducted was the use of experts from outside the ranks of An Garda Síochána. I was always open to engaging the help of an expert in any field that might help the investigating team. I felt it was a strength to know when to ask for help and to be able to seek out the right person to give that help. This approach enabled my teams to secure evidence and solve the riddle posed by many a crime scene – and it was absolutely essential to us in solving the murder of Jacqueline McDonagh.

Before describing that case, however, I want to mention an earlier murder investigation that required lateral thinking and outside help to allow us to piece together the confusing evidence presented by the crime scene. It remains one of the most fascinating expert collaborations I have ever been involved in, and it confirmed for me that investigating teams can be made stronger and better with expert outside backup.

On Friday, 29 October 2010 at 11 p.m., four men went to a house in Ardee, County Louth, to kidnap a suspected drug dealer in order to extract money from him. This four-man team had been put together by other criminals, who were owed money and had decided it was paying-up time.

The house was a terraced property on a council estate, standing opposite a communal green area with a dipped hollow in the centre of it. Two of the men broke in through the back window, then went and opened the front door to allow their two colleagues to enter the house. All four then ran up the curved staircase, which had a little landing halfway up. As they charged up the stairs, two shots were fired at them: one hit the first man to go up the stairs in the arm; the second shot hit the third man just above the heart, going past his collarbone and lodging down at his waist.

All four intruders retreated quickly down the stairs and out of the house. The man who had sustained the chest wound made it about three hundred metres from the house, then fell into the hollow area on the green. He died in that hollow from his gunshot wound and the resulting blood loss. His name was Stephen Hanaphy, and he had just handed us a complex puzzle to solve.

Hanaphy's body lay in the hollow until about 4.30 a.m., when a man a bit worse the wear for drink stumbled across it on his way home. That's when the Garda were informed, and we became aware that we had a murder to investigate. The incident room was set up that morning at Ardee Garda

Station, and I was appointed SIO. After the 10 a.m. murder conference, I went out to the scene to assess it for myself.

The cordoned-off area of investigation followed the intruders' path from the house as they'd sprinted away towards a hedged area. I stood and stared at the white-and-blue tape, mentally reconstructing the scene in my mind based on what I knew so far. I was remembering the Marilyn Rynn crime scene too, where the boundaries hadn't been wide enough and evidence was missed. I'd always promised to try to avoid that mistake myself.

The area of investigation struck me as being too narrow, so I went with my gut and insisted it be extended to take in the area beyond the hedge. I was glad I did that because we found evidential items under the hedge, including clothing and phone SIMs, that might otherwise have been missed.

It didn't take long for us to figure out who Hanaphy's teammates were. The other man who'd sustained a bullet injury turned up at a hospital seeking treatment, which alerted us to his presence. And in the end, the three men came to us voluntarily, turning up at Ardee station to give their side of the story.

The three intruders were interviewed separately, at Coolock and Balbriggan stations. The result of this was three different versions of what had happened, and no way of knowing which version was correct. One of them said that the resident of the house had pulled a gun on them, then chased them outside, continuing to shoot all the while. He remembered seeing sparks ricocheting off the ground at their feet as they pelted away. Another one said that the resident had pulled a gun and shot at them out through the upstairs landing window. The third version we were told was the least helpful of all – this one claimed that he'd run and hid in a hedge and seen nothing, blinded as he was by fear and leaves.

The ballistics team went into the house to do a forensic investigation, to see if they could give us some provable answers. They found firearms residue on the window on the landing upstairs. As it was almost Halloween, I asked that they perform extra tests on the residue to prove that it definitely came from a firearm and not from a banger or a firework. The result came back and it was conclusive: the residue was from a firearm and no other source. This told us that shots had been fired upstairs, but from where exactly? And was it the shot fired near the landing window that had penetrated Hanaphy's chest and killed him? Somehow, we had to find a way to show the exact spot from which the shots were fired – and, crucially, the exact spot from where the fatal bullet was fired.

The post-mortem was helpful in showing us the trajectory of the bullet. To do this, Deputy State Pathologist Dr Jaber threaded a thin metal rod through the body to follow the path of the bullet from collarbone down to waist, where it had become lodged inside the body. I was curious to know how Hanaphy had managed to become a dead man running – how had he made it three hundred metres with a bullet lodged inside that was causing massive internal bleeding? Dr Jaber explained that his body would have been pumped with adrenaline from the break-in and the confrontation, and that and the shock of being shot would have carried him along. Once he stopped running, he would have been dead before his body hit the ground.

We had a lot of information now, but we were still missing some crucial pieces of the puzzle. Through the ever-resourceful Dr Jaber, I learned about Michael Gilchrist, Senior Professor of Mechanical Engineering and Head of the UCD School of

Mechanical and Materials Engineering. That's a mouthful, but put simply it meant he was an expert in blunt force trauma, which made him just the person I needed to consult. I set up a meeting with him and talked him through our crime scene and the difficulty of ascertaining the location of the gunman in the house when the fatal shot was fired. We discussed the problem and came up with an innovative solution: we would perform a 3D reconstruction of the crime scene. This was a first in Ireland, so we were heading into uncharted territory, but Dr Gilchrist was confident it would prove useful.

On the appointed day for the reconstruction, a team of five people arrived at the house in Ardee: myself (as SIO), a detective garda, Dr Gilchrist, Dr Jaber and the ballistics sergeant on the case. I had bought a draper's dummy from a shop in Ardee, and I took it out of the boot of my car and carried it over my shoulder into the house, much to the amusement of my colleagues, who laughed at the sight of me. The mannequin could be moved up and down to change the height, a feature that was essential for our purposes. The dummy was well travelled by this stage, because I had taken it first to the State Pathologist's Office. There, Dr Jaber had drilled a hole in the chest, replicating the exact point at which the bullet had entered Hanaphy's body.

At the house in Ardee, we re-created the crime scene, re-enacting how the four men entered the house and ran up towards the first floor. The Garda ballistics sergeant took up various positions, holding a laser pointer that he aimed towards the approaching dummy. We went up and down the stairs again and again, with the sergeant continually changing his location. Then, finally, we got it. As we moved the dummy up the stairs, we reached a point where the beam of light penetrated straight into the 'bullet hole'. That was it – the exact location. The gunman had been standing on the top step of the stairs, adjacent to the landing window, when he fired the fatal shot at Stephen Hanaphy.

The investigation team worked hard to piece together the rest of the scene. They could establish that two people were in the house when the four men burst through the front door: one downstairs and the gunman upstairs. They also ruled out the version whereby the gunman was shooting out the window. This in turn confirmed that Hanaphy couldn't have been hit as he ran away from the house. As for the sparks so vividly recalled, that was also a piece of fanciful thinking. Ballistics showed that the bullets were lead-tipped, while the path the intruders raced along was tarmacadam – which meant there could have been no sparks. No, only two shots were fired in total during the attempted raid, and they were fired inside the house.

After all our work to solve it, unfortunately that case never made it as far as a courtroom. The DPP decided not to proceed, so that was the end of that. The two residents of the house have since died of natural causes, so there is no one left to prosecute, anyway. That's a disappointment, but I'm still proud of the way that investigation was conducted and how we utilized creative thinking to find out the truth. It proved yet again that seeking out the right experts and listening to their contributions can be the difference between a successful outcome and a dead-ended investigation.

In 2012, I was faced with a murder scene that posed many questions, and answering them required the investigation team to move very carefully and cautiously in order to arrive at the truth. It was definitely one of those cases with a few twists along the way, and we had to have our wits about us to stay one step ahead.

It was the early hours of 29 August 2012, about 4.30 a.m. When the phone started to ring, my brain brought the noise into my dream. It took a good few moments before I woke up enough to disentangle the two worlds and I realized the sound was my mobile. A glance at the clock told me it had to be bad news.

'Are you awake?' said the voice at the other end. 'Sorry to bother you, but we have a murder. It could be a domestic, but we're not sure.'

I had to push sleep away and focus, and get the brain working properly.

'What's happened?'

The garda told me he was at the scene, with the body of a badly beaten woman. She was lying in the hallway of her own home, and her three children had been removed from the house. The eldest child, a fourteen-year-old girl, had made the call to the emergency services, telling them that two men had broken into the house and attacked her mother, but her father had run them off. 'What's the demeanour of the husband?' I asked. The garda described him as being in bare feet, with blood spatters on his legs, and that he was saying the same thing: men broke in and attacked his wife and he ran down the stairs and scared them off. He seemed distressed. The garda went on to say that the woman was undressed apart from her underwear and her clothes were strewn about the floor, and that there was an almighty amount of blood spattering on the walls. His question was simple: 'Will we arrest the husband?'

It's a key decision in any murder investigation: when to

arrest a suspect. My advice to my team was always to make an arrest only when they had reasonable grounds for suspicion, and good cause to suspect that the person in question was responsible. An arrest made too early can hamper an investigation by erring on the side of assumption, which is often lazy thinking, and can let the suspect see your cards prematurely, giving them a good eyeful of what you do and don't know. In addition, a rearrest requires a court order based on new evidence, so you could be making more work for yourself. The moment of arrest must be chosen very carefully.

So this was a crucial question, and I had to get it right, no matter that I'd just been woken up. I had to make the call based on four facts: 1. the husband had blood on his person; 2. he did not appear to have any defensive wounds; 3. his description of what had occurred was vague; and 4. the deceased was almost naked, with her clothes strewn about the hallway. I quickly evaluated what I knew of the scene and made my decision: don't arrest the husband, but take a full witness statement from him, seize his clothing and let him go.

Another detective might have considered some of those facts reasonable grounds and proceeded with the arrest, but I was trying to think through the angles. My reasoning for holding off on arrest was fourfold. First, the husband's version of events was backed up by the child's call to the emergency services, so that was two witnesses saying the same thing. Second, if the blood on his clothing was substantial, it could hold key evidence in the form of the attackers' DNA. Yes, it could be his wife's blood because he was involved, but it was also the case that he had legitimate access to the crime scene and could have acquired blood from his wife's body as a result of this: benefit of the doubt, in other words. Third, while his description of the intruders was vague, that could be down to shock rather than guilt. Fourth, it was possible that the intruders hadn't expected the husband to be present and had fled at the sight of him, without any physical inter-action between them and him. On this basis I decided to proceed with caution, and not jump to the assumption that the husband did it.

Once I had given instructions to the garda at the scene, I lay down again and slipped back into my dreams. I knew it might be the last decent rest I'd get for a while, and there was nothing to be done for now. I'd have to be at the murder conference at 10 a.m., focused and ready for action, so I set the alarm clock for 7 a.m. in order to grab a couple more hours of sleep. When it blared at me to get up, I was awake, dressed and out the door quickly, headed straight for the crime scene. I wanted to see it for myself before the murder conference. It was important to get a very clear picture of what we were dealing with so I could report back to my col-leagues and get the investigation in gear immediately.

The house was a three-bedroom, two-storey, semi-detached home on an estate in Dundalk. Identikit housing – normal, ordinary – which made the scene inside all the more surreal. While the residents of the homes all around us slept soundly behind closed curtains, we were looking at a shocking scene of brutality.

I reached the house at 8 a.m. It was quiet by then – the emergency services had left, the doctor had pronounced the death at 4.25 a.m. and the family had been removed. The only one left was Jacqueline McDonagh, the deceased. She was lying just inside the front door, in a narrow, wooden-floored hallway, and her body indicated a terrible death. It had been left in situ so the scene could be forensically examined and viewed by the state pathologist, and therefore it was being preserved by two uniformed gardaí.

I pulled on all the protective gear, including overshoes and gown, and went inside and into the hallway, stepping slowly and carefully. I stood near the body, just silently taking in everything I could see, every detail of what the scene was trying to tell me. The deceased was lying on her back, feet towards the front door. Her body was very badly bruised all over and there was a lot of blood. Just beneath her was a white telephone, an old landline model, and it too was smeared red with blood. There were bloodstains along the walls that looked like someone had staggered along, using the wall for support, leaving the red marks on the white paint as they went. I could also see blood spatter on the floor and ceiling. The pattern suggested the possibility of a weapon of some sort because it looked like impact spattering, possibly from spraying off a repeatedly raised weapon. It made me think of the Rachel O'Reilly murder scene, because this spoke of hatred and anger that had erupted into manic violence. It was hard to believe that one human being could do that to another.

It is a very powerful experience to see a life extinguished, to see the amount of blood that a violent murder involves. I've noticed that there is a particular silence at a murder scene, one you don't hear anywhere else in your life. It's the silence of goneness, of someone suddenly ripped out of the world when they didn't want to go. Standing there in the silence, you're witnessing the struggle to live versus the intent to kill, and it creates a sadness that coats the whole scene – and you along with it.

I studied the scene carefully, contemplating what the blood patterns suggested about how this woman had died. Then I went to talk to the uniform garda who had attended the scene last night and was still there, watching over the body. 'So what do we know?' I asked. He took out his notebook and recited the facts as they stood. The first call to the emergency services had been made at 3.18 a.m., when the eldest daughter had called on her mobile and reported that her mother was not breathing. At 3.25 a.m., the emergency operator rang Dundalk Garda Station to inform them of the incident. The ambulance crew arrived at 3.33 a.m. The first paramedic on the scene found the front door open but no sign of forced entry, the porch light on and a body visible through the doorway. He carried out CPR with a defibrillator, but the victim was non-responsive. He noted the blood on the walls and floor, the man standing there with blood on his legs, the children crying upstairs. When the first uniforms arrived on the scene at 3.38 a.m., the paramedic quietly told them the injuries and that the scene looked suspicious. The uniforms noted the blood spatter, the blood-smeared phone and the husband in his bare feet, wearing shorts, with blood spots visible on his legs. They, too, felt that this didn't look right.

The uniforms could hear the distraught children upstairs, so they took the husband up with them to tend to the children. There they noted half of a pair of garden shears on the floor. They established that the deceased was Jacqueline McDonagh, and that her husband was Michael McDonagh. When he tried to go back downstairs, the uniforms insisted he remain with them. They talked gently to the children, trying to reassure them. One of the uniforms noticed McDonagh picking up the half-shears and wiping it with a towel. When he realized the garda was watching him, he dropped it and threw the towel into the children's bedroom.

The first step was to remove the children from the scene,

for their own safety and well-being. But it presented a difficult task, because the only way out of the house was past the crime scene, which the children obviously had to be protected from seeing. All gardaí are extremely sensitive when it comes to dealing with children, doing everything possible not to add to the trauma they have already endured. In this case, a female garda stayed with the children to reassure them. It's usually the case that a woman's presence can calm a distressed child, so whenever possible, a female colleague will be present.

The other gardaí formed a chain from the stairs to beyond the front door, and they swiftly passed each child from one to the next, telling the children to keep their eyes shut tight. The whole operation was completed as quickly as possible, so they were out of the house and away from the scene. They were then brought to the home of a family friend, to be comforted.

The doctor arrived at the scene at 4.10 a.m., donning full protective gear before going inside to check the victim. He pronounced the death at 4.25 a.m., at which point the house could be sealed off and the scene preserved. During that early-morning phone call I had ordered that once the doctor left, no person was to be allowed to enter the scene until the Garda Technical Bureau arrived. The garda assured me now that this order had been upheld.

I could tell already that blood spatter analysis would be key to solving this crime, so I rang the lab and asked specifically for a blood specialist to be sent with the GTB team. I talked to the technical team and also to the forensic lab, which would be carrying out the forensic examination. I was very clear in my instructions, because clear communication is essential both to the investigation and to the presentation of evidence at a trial. I had learned that it was important to give the examination teams the 'what' and the 'why': what I wanted studied, and why I wanted it studied. Being explicit in this way benefits everyone because it focuses the examination and ensures it ticks all the necessary boxes, and it also benefits the members of the team who later have to sit in a witness box and explain what they did, why they did it and what the results were. This clear and focused approach is the best start you can give any investigation.

I then left the crime scene and drove to Dundalk Garda Station to chair the murder conference. The incident room had already been set up and a number of detectives had gathered to hear about the case. I talked them through the facts as we knew them so far, my own thoughts, the nature of the crime scene and what information it might yield to us, as well as briefing them on the various examinations of the scene that were due to take place that day. We divvied up the jobs, and I started them immediately on a review of CCTV footage, house-to-house inquiries and background searches on the family. I asked what we knew about the husband, Michael McDonagh, and it turned out he was already known to local officers. He was a bare-knuckle boxer, known in the ring as Michael 'Mad Dog' McDonagh, and he had even featured in a documentary called *Knuckle*. A team began scouring the details of his life, building up a comprehensive portrait of who McDonagh was and where he came from.

At the same time as the murder conference got under way, the team from the lab arrived at the McDonagh house and commenced their examination. They erected blue tents around the front door, to protect the hallway from the view of residents and journalists. Beyond the blue tents, they had a lot of work to do to examine and catalogue the whole scene. It took six hours to complete their task. They rang me at about 4 p.m. to follow the protocol of telling the SIO the examination was complete, and to talk me through the initial findings. The lead forensic scientist, Mr John Hoade, a blood pattern analysis expert, performed this task. He had found a variety of patterns at the scene – impact spattering, cast-off staining on the ceiling and clotted airborne blood that had been sprayed onto the walls, and contact staining and hair transfer patterns. He interpreted this to mean that the attack on the victim had been both violent and sustained. The DNA profile of a sample of the blood matched that of Jacqueline McDonagh, and a bloody fingerprint on the phone was found to be hers as well. He also noted that there wasn't as much blood on the victim as would be expected, but he believed this was because she had washed much of it off. He noted that there was blood in the basin of the understairs toilet, suggesting that she had been attacked, then made her way to the loo where she'd washed herself in the sink, and then was attacked again. I took particular note of his use of the word 'sustained' – that didn't exactly suggest intruders racing in and then out of the house in short order. The idea that she had been attacked, got away and washed off the blood, presumably thinking it was over, and then been attacked again was chilling. I couldn't begin to imagine what Jacqueline had gone through that night.

Just inside the hall door, the forensics team found a half-section of a pair of garden shears. They discovered the handle in the living room and the other half-section upstairs, where the uniforms had left it in situ. They concluded this would once have been a single item. They took samples from blood found on the pieces of the shears. In the team's opinion, it was likely the shears had been used as a weapon and had been swung repeatedly and with great force. When describing all this to me,

Mr Hoade made an off-the-cuff remark, saying that the shears looked 'newish'. The use of that word stuck with me too.

Once I had received the forensics team's verbal report, I gave the go-ahead for the rest of the Garda Technical Bureau to go in and do their examination. I also requested that the Louth Divisional Search Team conduct another, separate examination once the technical team had concluded theirs. This was a bit of a belt-and-braces approach, but I had high regard for the Divisional Search Team and always found it worthwhile to get their input on any investigation.

There is some overlap between the three examination teams, which are the Divisional Search Team (DST), Garda Technical Bureau (GTB) and Scenes of Crime Unit (SCU). There are local SCU teams in each division, and their officers are trained specifically to examine and catalogue a crime scene. The GTB, based at HQ in the Phoenix Park, does the same work but also draws on analysts who are experts in fields such as fingerprints, ballistics, photography, forensics and blood spatter. The choice to use either the GTB or SCU is made by the SIO – they never work the same scene.

When the GTB get called in to conduct an examination, they put together a team based on what the scene requires and also appoint a crime scene manager to oversee and collate the various strands. The DST, by comparison, is made up of four sergeants and forty-eight gardaí, all ordinary members who undergo specialized training and make themselves available when a call goes out for an examination to be conducted. I had great faith in this team and promoted their work in every way I could. They were under my remit, so any investigation requesting them to do a search had to go through me in the first instance. They never let me down, and I was always confident in their ability to do an excellent job.

Every crime scene is different, but each one is the starting point for an investigation. As such, it is absolutely crucial that intelligent and informed decisions are made at the outset regarding the extent of the preserved area, the examination requirements, and which teams or independent experts should be called in to interrogate the scene and locate potential evidence. That is the responsibility of the SIO, who must assess the particulars of the scene and then plot out how it will be examined – and *why* it will be examined this way. This task requires extensive experience in order for it to be performed correctly. The decisions made in these initial hours can help or hinder the entire investigation, and a successful outcome often hinges on them. As SIO, you get one chance to gather all the evidence that's there, otherwise it will be lost and unusable.

By the time I was assessing the McDonagh crime scene, I had the requisite experience to size up the circumstances accurately and make good decisions. Based on what I had learned on the O'Reilly case, I decided to call in the GTB to ensure that every millimetre of the scene was examined thoroughly and by a number of different experts. I had requested that the blood spatter analyst survey the scene first, to assess the information provided by the blood patterns in the house. Then I gave the go-ahead for the full GTB team to examine the scene.

After that, the state pathologist conducted an on-site examination of the body, prior to it being removed for the postmortem. When all the technical work had been completed, I called in the DTS to do a full search of the whole house. The DTS operates from a different angle than the technical teams, moving beyond the scene itself to search for documents that might be of evidential value, or to look for a weapon if it's not evident at the scene. They don't read the story of the crime itself – they are searching for the 'why' behind the murder, and that makes their work incredibly important to an investigation. The DST help us to try to explain the crime, which in turn directs us to the person responsible.

The GTB conducted an extremely detailed search, as always. They discovered a CCTV unit in the McDonaghs' house, set up to record the area just outside the front door. The internal unit was located upstairs and it had been smashed, but it was taken away for analysis nonetheless. If it had recorded anything, it could provide key evidence. Their search also turned up some interesting finds. They, too, noted the pieces of the garden shears and took samples from them. They also found a knife on top of a cupboard and took samples from that. Jacqueline's clothing was strewn about the hallway, but her jeans were just outside the front door. They had bloodstains on them and a slash through the fabric, which meant something sharp had cut through the denim. The fact that the halves of the shears were found upstairs and downstairs pointed to the attack commencing upstairs, in the bedroom. The team found a dent in the plasterwork over the marital bed that matched the shape of the shears' blade, and of course the CCTV unit was smashed as well. It suggested that Jacqueline had been attacked in the bedroom first, then made her way downstairs and tried to clean up the blood in the understairs toilet, and then was attacked again in the hallway, where she desperately tried to ring for help. As the teams' investigations pieced together the likely chain of events that led to Jacqueline's death, a picture emerged of a truly shocking murder.

Everything was photographed, mapped and catalogued, ready for the investigation team. The DST performed their search, giving us three separate reports detailing every scrap of information that could be lifted from the scene, including the finding of vials of steroids and associated equipment. Once all of this had been completed, Jacqueline could finally be removed from the house where she had been killed. The local funeral directors performed this task with great respect and dignity and brought her to the mortuary at Our Lady of Lourdes Hospital, where the post-mortem would be carried out.

I brought the findings of the searches back to the incident room and we pooled the information unearthed so far. The CCTV footage had been recovered from the damaged unit, but it had only recorded until 1.40 a.m. It showed the family arriving home just after midnight, after a day socializing with members of their extended family. It was clear from the images that Michael McDonagh was happily drunk when they arrived home, as he could be seen dancing and smiling as Jacqueline unlocked the front door and opened it. There was nothing whatsoever to suggest that a few hours later the same woman would lie dead on her hallway floor. However, the house-to-house inquiries had revealed that a number of neighbours had heard shouts in the early hours. Some said they'd heard a woman's voice screaming 'No, no, no' and 'Michael' and 'Help me'. Unfortunately, they also said it wasn't unusual to hear shouting and arguments from the house, so they hadn't responded to the noises.

What really interested me about these statements, though, was what they didn't say. If two men in balaclavas had kicked in the front door of the house, beaten the occupant, then been roared at and chased away by her husband, wouldn't someone have heard or seen something of that? It was the absent words in their accounts that spoke the loudest.

I drove to Drogheda that afternoon to attend the post-mortem, which was conducted by the deputy state pathologist,

Dr Michael Curtis. I have attended several post-mortem examinations of women who have died as a result of assault and domestic violence, but I had never before – and have never since – witnessed such serious injuries as those that were evident on Jacqueline McDonagh. Her body lay on a crisply clean white sheet, and against that stark whiteness the huge purple patches of bruising were lurid. They didn't look like bruises – they were so extensive, it looked like someone had daubed purple paint in blotches across her body and particularly down her arms and hands. The gold of her wedding band glinted from her bruised, swollen fingers. Her hair was matted with blood. Her face was covered in yellowish-purple bruising. Even her eyelids were bruised. I felt deeply sorry for this woman, who was so young – still in her thirties – and who had been beaten into her very last breath.

Dr Curtis was also struck by the severe bruising arising from the assault. He was an experienced pathologist, but this was a highly unusual sight. He catalogued all of the bruising, which stretched across much of the body's surface area. He also found that there was bleeding on the brain, and three very deep gashes in the scalp. The shape of these wounds was consistent with the shape of the broken-apart shears found at the house. This would later be confirmed when Jacqueline's DNA was found in the blood samples taken from the shears. There were also deep wounds on the left forearm, and similarly deep gashes on each shin. Dr Curtis reiterated his original finding: this was a brutal, sustained assault, resulting in injuries from head to toe. He also noted that death might not have been immediate. This was borne out by the fact that Jacqueline had staggered to the downstairs loo to try to clean off the blood, and it would also be later confirmed by the phone record analysis.

The post-mortem left us in no doubt that this was a murder investigation. I knew it was essential that we cover every single angle and not jump to any conclusions, because that could lead to slipshod investigating. We had to be sure that our efforts resulted in evidence that would hold up in court and bring the perpetrator to justice. Jacqueline had suffered terribly at the hands of her killer, and we wanted to ensure that the person who did this paid the price. Jacqueline deserved that, as did her distraught family.

The investigation team trawled the phone records of the landline in the house to establish if there was anything evidential there. The phone had been found under Jacqueline's body and was covered in blood, which suggested she had tried to use it. This proved correct. The call data showed that Jacqueline had desperately tried to get help as she lay dying. She had called her father's mobile several times and had also dialled 999, but was unable to speak. In fact, she'd attempted to ring various numbers over an eighty-minute period, but her body was failing and she was too weak to dial correctly and speak.

I was anxious to listen to the call to the emergency services made by Jacqueline's daughter. I got the recording and sat in a quiet office, listening intently as the girl said that two men had burst into the house and attacked her mother. I listened to it again and again and was satisfied with what I had picked up on. I asked several colleagues to come in and listen to the recording, then asked each one individually what they had heard on the tape. They all reported hearing what I heard: a mumbling voice in the background, prompting her. It was reasonable to assume that her ten- and eight-year-old siblings weren't the prompters.

It was very early days in the investigation, but the combination of available evidence at the scene and detailed examinations had already thrown up convincing evidence that this wasn't a case of intruders breaking in and harming Jacqueline. The facts we had established so far were pointing in one direction – Michael McDonagh.

It was a very persuasive hypothesis: we could not establish any comings or goings to or from the house before, during or after the murder; the 999 call clearly showed that the young girl was being prompted; the murder weapon had been proven to be the garden shears; the CCTV unit had been deliberately smashed; Michael McDonagh's bloody palm prints were found on the wall directly over where the body lay; we knew Jacqueline had tried to call for help; from interviews with family members, we knew there was a history of domestic violence and that it was bad enough that Jacqueline had taken her children to a women's refuge on a number of occasions. We were building up a clear picture and I felt that another few days – a week at most – would see us ready to arrest McDonagh on suspicion of murder.

That's when I got an entirely unexpected call from McDonagh's solicitor, saying he wanted to talk to us the following day, 30 August. He indicated that his client wanted to make a confession. Well, this was a surprise. I had my own theory as to why he was doing this, but I kept it to myself until I'd heard what he had to say.

The next day, I and two of my team met with Michael McDonagh and his solicitor at Store Street Garda Station. It meant a drive down to the city, but McDonagh's solicitor was Dublin-based and Store Street was near his office, so that was the place chosen. There, McDonagh admitted to being responsible for the death of his wife, alleging that Jacqueline 'goaded him' into a fit of anger that made him unrecognizable to himself. By doing so, he forced our hand because we had to arrest him on foot of these verbal admissions. We performed the arrest and brought him to Dundalk station, where we took fingerprints, palm prints, photographs and buccal swabs. The following day we took swabs of blood, urine, and samples from beneath the fingernails and between his toes (because he was barefoot at the crime scene), as well as a foot impression. He was interviewed on six separate occasions, and each time he refused to sign the memo, which was the written record of the questions asked and the answers given. He just kept repeating that he didn't intend to kill her. He told us that the CCTV at the house was fake, but of course we knew it was real and had been recording until 1.40 a.m.

I kept the DPP informed all throughout his questioning, and that night we were given the direction that Michael McDonagh was be charged with murder. He was released from the previous charge and immediately rearrested for the murder of Jacqueline McDonagh. The team now had to build a court case that would secure a conviction, but the question remained: why had he come to us and confessed? I told the team my theory – he was angling for a manslaughter conviction – and they agreed that this was the likeliest motive for his actions.

It was easy to see why: a conviction for manslaughter carries a sentence of zero years to life; a conviction for murder carries a mandatory life sentence. Manslaughter is an unlawful killing that is not murder and it has two categories: voluntary and involuntary manslaughter. Voluntary manslaughter implies an excusing circumstance, such as provocation. Involuntary manslaughter can be the result of an unlawful and dangerous act, or a negligent act or omission. Given that McDonagh had referred to his wife's 'goading', it seemed plausible that he was angling for voluntary manslaughter. We all agreed that this made sense, but what we didn't know was the exact 'excusing circumstance' he was going to argue. Whatever that trump card was, we would have to be able to prove conclusively otherwise.

I was still mulling over the forensic scientist's comment that the shears looked 'newish'. It kept tugging at the edge of my mind and I realized it could lead to potential evidence. I asked one of the investigation team, Garda Freda McCague, to research the shears – the manufacturer, where they were made, the distributor and where they were sold. She got onto it immediately and quickly discovered that the shears were made in Germany and the main distributor was Aldi. We discussed this and agreed that the next step was for her to view all the footage from the checkouts at the Aldi outlet in Dundalk and match up all receipts relating to the sale of shears in August 2012. Working quickly and methodically, she was soon back to me with good news: she had identified Michael McDonagh purchasing a pair of shears on 25 August. Another piece of the puzzle had fallen into place.

In September, I was enjoying a night out with friends, catching up. The work of a detective is unpredictable and can easily take over your whole life, so every now and then I had to stop and do something civilian, just to feel like I also had a normal existence outside An Garda Síochána. It gives you some perspective to step away every now and then.

On this night, I was receiving the usual interrogation about the cases I was working on, and I was giving my usual answer: 'No comment.' I never discussed my work, not even with my closest friends, because I felt that would be disrespectful to the victims and their families. I might not have discussed it, but that didn't stop my friends guessing and giving opinions. So, on this night, one friend was asking if I was involved in 'that case in the papers' – the murder of Jacque-line McDonagh. No comment. 'The husband is a bare-knuckle fighter, he'd know how to throw a punch.' No comment. 'I'd say he's half mad on steroids, a man that size.' No comment, but now my brain is ticking because I remembered the Divisional Search Team found the paraphernalia of steroid-taking at the house. I listened intently as my friend went on to tell a story about a cyclist he knew who was taking steroids and it had led to angry outbursts that were out of character. *Interesting*, I thought.

The next day, I contacted the pathologist and asked him if there was any known connection between steroid use and anger issues. He told me there were studies concluding there was a connection, and an equal number of studies conclud-ing there wasn't. He said it was called ''roid rage' and that I should look it up.

That was a new expression to me, but I set about finding out everything I could about 'roid rage. I learned that it was a defined condition whereby users of regular and high doses of anabolic steroids can act aggressively as a result of taking the drug. In fact, there were some murders and assaults in the previous few years that had been attributed to steroid use. I sat back in my chair as it dawned on me: I was staring at Michael McDonagh's trump card.

I read accounts of men who had taken steroids, which are used to build muscle through increased testosterone, and then beaten their wives or girlfriends to death and later described how the steroids made them irritable and aggressive. The research showed that some users became aggressive, violent and antisocial, but others did not.

A blood sample had been taken from McDonagh while in custody, about fifty-two hours after the murder, and I requested the lab test it for anabolic steroids. The answer came back: we cannot perform that test. Another round of research and phone calls led to the answer: only the French authorities could help us. So the sample was sent to a lab in Paris and the results came back: DHEA 340 ng/ml, testosterone 1 ng/ml, testosterone enanthate 10 ng/ml. Now, that was gobbledegook to me, but I was determined to badger every expert I could find until someone translated those measurements into the effects of steroid use on Michael McDonagh on 29 August 2012.

I worked my way through every expert in Ireland, but was eventually told that the UK-based experts had the most up-to-date knowledge and systems. I was advised to seek out a consultant forensic toxicologist and I went straight to the top – Dr Simon Elliott, an eminent consultant based in London. He informed me that normally he could help, but that my request was very specialized and his branch of forensics didn't get involved in anabolic steroid analysis.

I turned the problem round and round in my head, then I remembered something. The Olympic Games had been held in London that year, from July to August, and there had been some sort of scandal about the Russian athletes and doping. Who had tested those athletes, I wondered? I made some inquiries and was directed to the Drug Control Centre at King's College London. I put in a call and was passed from person to person until I was finally put through to the director, Professor David Cowan. I explained to him that I needed a specialist, expert opinion on the steroids in McDonagh's blood sample and whether they could cause him to kill his wife. I also explained that while McDonagh was in Garda custody, and before any blood sample was taken, he had been visited by a doctor who prescribed and gave him Dalmane for anxiety. I advised him of this in case this drug showed up in the sample.

As we discussed it, I felt that Dr Cowan fully understood my problem and my reasoning. After that phone call, I looked him up and found that he was regarded as a world expert on ana-bolic steroids and related compounds. He held a BSc and a PhD in Pharmacy, was a Fellow of the Royal Pharmaceutical Society of Great Britain and a professor of pharmaceutical tox-icology at King's College London, and had spent the last thirty-five years analysing hormones and anabolic steroids and studying their adverse effects. Finally, I had the right expert.

I sent the sample to Professor Cowan and asked him to trace back the fifty-two hours from the time the blood sam-ple was taken to the time of the murder, in order to find out if a substantial amount of steroids had been in McDonagh's system at that time – enough to lead him to 'roid rage and to killing his wife. It was a tall order, but if anyone could do it, this was the man. Then I had to sit back and wait.

After several weeks I received Dr Cowan's report, which was comprehensive and precise. He stated that the information relayed to him about Michael McDonagh – the fact that he was a bare-knuckle fighter and bodybuilder – was consistent with the three empty vials taken from the crime scene. The vials had contained substances commonly used by bodybuilders and which contained growth-promoting agents, including ana-bolic steroids. He commented on each of the three steroids found in McDonagh's blood sample. Firstly, DHEA – an abbre-viation of dehydroepiandrosterone, an anabolic steroid that is produced naturally in the human body. Secondly, testosterone – one of the most important anabolic steroids produced naturally in the human body. Thirdly, and most interesting to the case, testosterone enanthate – a substance foreign to the human body. It is usually administered by injection as a source of testosterone, because it is converted to testosterone in the body. As such, it is used medically to treat individuals with a deficiency of natural testosterone.

Dr Cowan's conclusion was the key finding for me: 'I can find no evidence that Mr McDonagh took large doses of anabolic steroids. In particular, I can find no evidence that the concentration of anabolic steroids in his body at the time of the crime was large. This leads me to the opinion that it is unlikely that anabolic steroids caused him to kill his wife.'

Those sentences scuppered any notions McDonagh might have had of using 'roid rage as a defence in court. It had taken a hell of a lot of persistence and legwork to arrive at that conclusion, but it was absolutely worth it.

The report was served on Michael McDonagh and his legal team three weeks before the trial was due to commence. That was a very good moment for me. I felt deeply satisfied that the investigation had covered every single angle, even the ones the defence didn't want us to know about. It was a fantastic piece of investigative work by the team, and I was very proud to be a part of it. The next step for me as SIO would be to present this intricate and carefully built-up case to the court during the trial.

It took more than two years to come to court, but on 9 February 2015 the case was heard by Mr Justice Paul Carney at the Central Criminal Court. The court was expecting a jury trial, but there was another twist when McDonagh's counsel stood up to tell the judge that their instructions had changed in the previous few minutes. They wished to submit a plea of guilty.

A guilty plea to the charge of murder is rare, because it is always perceived that there might be some chance in the course of a jury trial to wangle a manslaughter verdict. There's always the possibility that the Garda investigation may be flawed, which makes it worth a gamble. But not in this case.

I gave evidence in the case, and Jacqueline's family also asked me to read to the court their victim impact statement. It was a heartbreaking statement, full of love for the daughter, sister and mother they had lost. I was very glad that they got the opportunity to present Jacqueline to the court – not as a body, a victim or a case, but as a woman with a big heart, who was full of laughter and utterly devoted to her family. I felt it was important that everyone got to know that Jacqueline. I read the words: 'We died when Jacqueline died, we now have the guilt that our life will never move on.'

Michael McDonagh hadn't just killed Jacqueline – he had murdered so much of their children's future, he had deprived her of her own future, and he had left a legacy of grief and sorrow for all those who had loved Jacqueline.

The investigation team uncovered a life that was lived in fear and dread. Jacqueline had married Michael McDonagh when she was only nineteen, and friends and family guessed that the abuse had started just a few months after their wedding day. I think most detectives would agree that domestic violence cases are distressing and terribly sad. There are usually the same markers: the woman's spirit is broken and her self-belief destroyed, making her unable to see a way out; people guess or know that it's happening, but they don't know what to say or do; and the woman never speaks of it because she doesn't want to cause family tensions, and wants first and foremost to protect her children. So those around her turn a blind eye to the regular bruises and scrapes, and the woman does flee and seek refuge and help – but each time she returns to the house and her husband, the dangerous cycle starts all over again. I'm not a psychologist, so I can't explain why this occurs in so many marriages, but it does.

According to family and friends, it was thought that Jacqueline McDonagh had lived in fear for fifteen years, suffering regular beatings and emotional and verbal abuse, but when I checked, there wasn't a single Garda record of it. She had never reported her husband.

That's the terrible truth at the heart of domestic violence cases – the abused person doesn't reach out to those who could really help. And in many cases, that inability to protect herself or to condemn her abuser leads to a woman being injured, maimed or killed. It's a harrowing thing to encounter, and a very difficult thing to understand.

Both of these cases – Stephen Hanaphy and Jacqueline McDonagh – were important in confirming for me that my approach to running an investigation was working. There are always different ideas in the room as to how it should be done, but these two big solves gave me belief in my own way of setting up and conducting an investigation team. This was important, because the confidence it gave me was transferred to the teams I worked with and ensured everyone gave it their best. These cases had required persistence and strategic thinking, and they proved that those traits are crucial in a good detective. It was clear to me that it doesn't serve justice well to simply put all faith in technology – there must be an inquisitive human brain behind it all, pushing for answers, questioning everything and making the links that lead from murder to murderer.

The other crucial thing that I was well aware of by now was the need to consider at all times the trial, and the potential questions and arguments that could be used to cast doubt on the investigation. I had done this in the O'Reilly case, where I'd had a hunch that the defence would go for media interference compromising a fair trial. And now I had anticipated the defence's leading argument in the McDonagh case – so much so that the plea was changed at the last minute, which was very satisfying.

After the McDonagh investigation, I really understood that the defence barrister must feature in my thinking and strategy at all times. He or she had to be a shadow sparring partner, countering the investigation at every turn, ensuring I could anticipate and handle every parry that could be thrust at us in court. I have huge respect for defence barristers, because they are very clever people and dedicated to their job of defending their client. There is nothing personal in the attacks they launch on the witness box, and I've often had them come over to say that to me. *No hard feelings, Pat.* There never are, but that doesn't mean the witness box in the Central Criminal Court isn't the loneliest place in all the world.

To my mind, a detective has to always think of their case in terms of the future court trial and anticipate the framework of the defence's position, in order to ensure that every box is ticked. This sort of forward thinking can ensure that you don't have a garda or SIO sitting up in the witness box stammering, stuttering and red-faced – liable to be brought down by the defence's needling arguments. As an investigator, your credibility and integrity can fall in seconds if you show a weakness that the defence can pounce on, and then it can be made to seem that you didn't do your job correctly, which in turn casts doubt on the investigation's methods and conclusions.

In the early days of my career, I hadn't the experience to understand the court system and how best to fulfil my role within it. As a uniform garda, the District Court is where you have to give evidence – and you have to quickly learn how to do so. I think every garda remembers their first time in the witness box vividly, usually because of how terrified they were beforehand. For my part, I had rehearsed the oath to such an extent that I could have recited it backwards, word for word. The walk up to the box seemed a mile long, and I felt every pair of eyes in the courtroom turn to observe me. Even though you're not the one on trial, you still feel that this is your moment to be tried by the judge, the defence, the prosecution and the accused. Your notebook is like a security blanket, and you clutch it tightly, the sweat of your fingers leaving its mark on those pages forever. Then the defence barrister stands up and the questions start and your mind goes into freefall and it's all over in jig time and you think, *That wasn't so bad*, and you feel a sense of confidence that makes it easier the next time.

That all changes when you step up to the level of senior investigating officer on major crimes. The District Court is left behind and you now have to perform in the daunting atmosphere of the Central Criminal Court, and in cases where people's reputation and liberty are on the line. The defence barristers there are extremely bright and clever and have vast experience of cross-examining gardaí, and their whole aim in court is the total opposite of yours. With experience, you can rise to this challenge very well, but at the outset it's very difficult. I have seen some gardaí being dissected piece by piece by shrewd barristers, leaving their credibility in tatters. I have witnessed gardaí come down from the box with beads of sweat running down their temples, faces bright red after their ordeal. There is nothing as bad as the feeling of walking away from the witness box knowing you were wrong-footed and didn't do well by yourself or by your case. Perhaps you forgot a point you wished to make, or perhaps you hesitated in answering an important question – or perhaps the defence barrister honed in on some detail you hadn't really considered before and it plainly showed. Whatever the cause, when you step away knowing that you didn't give it your best, it's a feeling that haunts you.

I remember watching one young garda in court being called up to the box. He was nervous as hell, but he stood up and walked slowly towards the chair that awaited him. He sat down and then swung the seat around so that he was facing the wall behind the judge, looking directly at neither the court nor the judge. I was sitting along a row of gardaí and there was a lot of under-the-breath muttering going on, generally of the 'WTF?' variety. What was this lad doing, presenting his back to the defence? The judge asked him if he was okay, if he was comfortable, and he replied, 'Ah yeah, grand, Judge.' He didn't budge for the whole cross-examination, but answered all the questions with his back to the court. That was his way of handling it and controlling his nerves, and he was let at it. It was a strange sight, but it just shows how stressful giving evidence is, even for gardaí.

Handling a cross-examination well is a skill that must be learned through bitter experience. One of the things I noticed in my first outings as SIO was that the crime scene mapper was always the first called for the prosecution, followed by the scenes of crime photographer. From watching the defence barristers in various cases, I realized their strategy: undermine the mapper and their work, then undermine the photographer and their work, and you have successfully cast doubt on the quality of the investigation straight out of the traps. Once I cottoned on to this, I countered it by giving very clear instructions to the crime scene mapper and photographer – and also to the forensics and technical teams – telling them what exactly I wanted them to do at the crime scene; and, crucially, why I wanted them to do it. This meant they landed in the witness box with their reasoning and conclusions laid out clearly before them. They couldn't be hounded into not being able to answer why something had been done or not done. It gave them great confidence when called up to give evidence as well, because they knew they had the paper record to back up their actions.

Over time, I expanded this preparation to include a pre-trial conference, which I held about one month before the trial convened. I invited all members involved in the trial to attend, for the purpose of going through the evidential requirements – such as notebooks and exhibits – and to discuss any concerns anyone had about how the questioning might proceed. This proved a welcome innovation, especially by uniform gardaí who didn't have experience giving evidence in the Central Criminal Court. I was always keen to talk to the garda in charge of the custody record in particular, as they inevitably came in for stiff interrogation from the defence. The custody record sets out in detail the treatment of the detainee while in custody, and therefore a defence barrister will drill down into it to find any mistakes or omissions. It's a good tactic, because if anything can be shown to be remiss with the arrest or the period of detention, then the whole thing falls apart and the memos – the record of the interviewee's answers – are deemed inadmissible. That's death to any prosecution and must be avoided at all costs. So by holding a pre-trial conference, I did my best to ensure that everyone was aware of what their role was and was confident that they had carried out their duties correctly.

I had seen some very unprofessional behaviour in my early days, and I made absolutely sure that was never a feature of any of my teams or cases. When I was a uniform giving evidence in court one day, I'd watched with discomfort as the garda in charge of exhibits was asked to produce a particular exhibit by the defence. He headed down the back of the courtroom and started rustling in bags and dropping things and muttering swear words to himself. It was embarrassing, and I felt annoyed at him for letting the side down. Eventually, the defence asked, 'Do you have the exhibit, Garda?' and he replied sheepishly, 'I left it in the back of the car.' He had to leave the court, go outside and retrieve it from his car boot, then come back in and produce it. He left the court waiting and made himself look incompetent in front of the jury, which naturally reflected badly on the whole case. I kept my opinions to myself that day, but I made a private vow that I would be professional at all times and in all settings, and I like to think that I upheld that vow throughout my career. I was always meticulous about checking that my officers had their notebooks ready and in hand going into court, and that the exhibits officer had all exhibits lined up, numbered and in order so that they could put a hand to them immediately. I wasn't going to have Officer Bumbling-the-Feck-About on my team, undoing all our hard work.

Having my own cardinal rules for conducting an investigation was another way of guaranteeing that I – and by extension all members of my team – performed well in court and gave the best account of the case and the evidence possible. My teams could recite these rules in their sleep: be honest, be accountable, be respectful, be professional – and, most of all, keep it simple. If you are honest and present all the evidence simply and clearly, you cannot go wrong. The biggest threat to a court appearance is cutting corners and then not being completely honest. If an SIO is sitting in the witness box trying to bend a straight line, the defence is going to tear them apart – and their case along with them. But if your decision-making every step along the way has been that of an honest person, then any reasonable person will see that and you won't go far wrong. The evidence in a murder case can be very complex, but if you learn to present it in a simple, clear manner that joins the dots one by one, then the jury will come along with you and understand the pertinent facts and their meaning.

By the end of my time as a murder detective, I wasn't being called to the box any more because the defence had realized that I was a strong witness and that I would take any opportunity to add more information to my answers – so that the jury had an even fuller picture of events, as presented by the prosecution. As I said, it's a skill – and like any skill, it requires study and practice to master. But it's worth the time and effort because, as the McDonagh case shows, it can make a huge difference in the successful prosecution of a crime.

7. The Murderous Impulse

When people hear that you solve crimes for a living, it always spikes their interest. And then come the inevitable questions: 'Are you armed?' (It depends); 'Have you ever shot anyone?' (No); 'What was your most interesting case?' (Hard call, but possibly the murder of Mary Gough and the work it took to prove her husband, Colin Whelan, was the culprit); and 'Did you ever deal with someone you thought was evil?'

It's interesting that the question of 'evil' comes up again and again, often in the form of: *Does it actually exist?* That's a very complicated question, and I'm not sure I have a clear answer, but generally speaking I am not inclined to use the word 'evil' for anyone.

In the course of a career in the police, most officers will meet someone who makes them uneasy or even scares them. Given that we see human nature at its worst all the time, and tend to be pretty robust in dealing with it, it is striking when you get that prickly feeling around someone for a reason that's hard to define – it's a gut instinct; a reflexive reaction to their presence, their way of looking at you. The person's energy puts you on edge and makes you wary.

My understanding of evil is that it's a no-holds-barred state of mind that stems from a complete lack of empathy or guilt, arising from some intrinsic quality in the person that's outside of anything to do with their background or any underlying biological issue (such as mental illness) – in other words, they are born that way. That idea of innate evil is something I struggle with, though I came across a few characters in my career that were as close to that definition of evil as it's possible to get. I am not a psychologist or a psychiatrist (or indeed a theologian), so I can't say I have the full picture – only my years of experience and my instincts as a garda and a human being. But when you're looking into someone's eyes and they seem dark and murderous and totally lacking in remorse, it's hard not to believe that evil exists after all.

To explain what I mean about having this uneasy feeling about someone, I'm going to share a few stories here. But – and maybe it's telling that I feel the need to do this for the only time in this book – I am going to change certain identifying details in the first two of these cases simply because I am wary of the people involved who are still alive.

Back when I was a uniform cop on the beat, still new to everything, I was in the patrol car with my partner when we got a call about a robbery in progress at a shop not far from Dublin city centre. Away we sped, and we screeched to a halt outside the shop and ran in. We had just missed the burglars, who had taken off with a sum of money. Thinking fast, I said to my colleague, 'I bet they're going to make a quick escape by the field at the back.' There was a wild green space behind the shop and it seemed an obvious escape route to me.

My colleague agreed and we told the shopkeeper we were going to try to intercept them, and out we went and sped off again. We reached the field quickly. The grass was long, the field neglected, so my colleague suggested that while he went and hid the patrol car, I should hide myself in the grass and wait to see if the young robbers came along. I thought it was a great plan and hopped out of the car.

So he headed off to park the vehicle out of sight, while I

surveyed the field, chose a likely spot and lay myself down flat on the ground, baton at the ready, hidden in the long grass.

Just a few minutes later, I heard some dogs start up a barking nearby and I knew that meant someone was about. Then I heard the rustling sound of grass being pushed through by legs. *There's more than one of them*, I thought to myself. *Right, Pat, here we go.* The sound moved closer and closer, and when it was almost beside me, up I leapt, baton raised, letting out a roar. The four lads I'd surprised let out a roar as well, then scattered in the blink of an eye. I'd recognized all of them in that second and I knew I had the right people. One of them wasn't quick enough, and I let fly with the baton and caught him a wallop on the arm, then launched myself at him and we both fell to the ground, me on top of him. I held him down, and at the same time I grabbed the radio on my shoulder and yelled for my colleague to get there quick. He came running and together we arrested this lad and got him into the patrol car and back to the station.

This lad, I'll call him Mr B (not part of his initials), had an aura about him that would make you very wary and uneasy. The fits of anger he was prone to were frightening and he clearly had no sense of right or wrong. He had black, unreadable eyes and was unpredictable; you wouldn't turn your back on him for a second. He just didn't seem like other people. I remember him looking me dead in the eye and saying, 'I'll get you.' I didn't doubt him.

A few years later, by which time I was a detective, I was called in to investigate a bank robbery on the east coast. The bank's CCTV footage showed a man coming into the bank, masked, holding up his knife and shouting for the money. We were all staring intently at the footage, trying to pick up every detail, when I had a brainwave.

'What if he came in earlier to case the place?' I said. 'Rewind the tape and let's check if anyone came in wearing those same clothes.'

So the tape was rewound, and again we all hunched forward to watch closely. The next thing, onto the screen walks our thief, recognizable by his clothing and build, and guess who it is – only my old friend Mr B. I looked at my colleagues and the bank staff and said, 'I think I've got this one solved. I know exactly who he is, and he is most definitely capable of armed robbery.' He was duly arrested for the crime and sentenced to five years in prison. I was very glad he was off the streets, even for a short time.

Another man that immediately comes to mind when thinking about this concept of 'evil' and whether individuals can be said to be evil is someone who was a hardened criminal – the really hard-core kind – who had his name attached to two unsolved murder cases that I inherited when I became an SIO in 2010. He was on the run abroad because of these murders and other pending charges, and he was busy enjoying his freedom when he got involved in an incident in a bar. A young man took exception to how Mr C (not part of his initials) was treating a waitress and told him so. Thirty minutes later the young man was lying dead in a pool of blood, shot multiple times. It all happened in broad daylight, so inevitably it spelled the end of Mr C's period on the run. He was locked up in a foreign jail when I made an application to interview him regarding the crimes being investigated in Ireland.

The local set-up was different from the Irish and UK systems, in that a judge rather than the police was the investigating authority. This meant that our interview had to be overseen by a judge, who would conduct proceedings in a court setting.

On the day of the interview, my colleague and I waited in the small courtroom, and at the appointed time the door opened and into this small space stepped Mr C, accompanied by a prison officer. He was brought over and seated near the judge's bench.

He looked over at me and my colleague, and slowly, deliberately made a cut-throat gesture at us. This was my first time meeting him, and the hairs on the back of my neck were standing up. The energy coming off him was dark and overpowering. It's hard to explain, but he seemed to fill the whole space with a deadening, suffocating atmosphere, which enveloped us all and made me want to get out of there.

The judge obviously registered it too, because he beckoned the prison officer to his bench and whispered something to him. The officer stood Mr C up and removed him. When they were gone, the judge moved around the courtroom, closing all the windows. He looked over at us and said, 'Not a nice man.' That was an understatement if ever I'd heard one.

Fifteen minutes later, Mr C was brought back into the courtroom, this time flanked by four armed police officers. The judge was taking no chances with this particular man. The rules were explained to Mr C, as was our reason for wishing to speak to him, but he made it clear he had no interest in cooperating. I put our questions to him, but he just stared at us coldly. He declined to give any DNA samples, he declined to sign any court documents, he declined to answer any questions. At the end of the interview, he was removed from the court and taken back to prison, and we had to go home empty-handed. We did complete a file for the DPP on both murders, but no prosecution has occurred in either case to date.

Afterwards, my colleague and I returned to the airport to

catch a flight home. Our liaison in the local police force had remarked to us that he got 'an evil feeling' from Mr C, and as we drank a coffee in the airport lounge we talked about how the judge had reacted so strongly to Mr C's presence. We both admitted that he had given us the creeps, and that this was one of those times that got you thinking that there might actually be something in this concept of evil – and, if it existed, it was present in that room. I don't think there was any amount of money you could have paid either of us to be in a room alone with that man. I had no desire ever to be in his company again.

I knew that I wanted to help put away people like Mr C, simply to safeguard everyone else. To him, putting a bullet in another human being was simple and didn't cost him a thought – a way of thinking the vast majority of people can't begin to fathom. But that's what you've got to hold on to: it's a small minority who are capable of that level of disconnection and violence.

The third man who had this same malign and frightening aura was Christopher Ward. I wasn't SIO on the case relating to him, but I was a DI at the time, supervising the day-to-day running of the investigation. Ward had lived in England for most of his life, where he had racked up ninety-two convictions in his forty-nine years, starting from the age of twelve. He came from a fractured and dysfunctional family. Two of his brothers had taken their own lives – one while awaiting trial for murdering his mother. It wasn't a normal upbringing by any means, and it had curdled Ward's soul and made him a dangerous man.

In 2011, he came to Ireland to visit his father, who lived in Dundalk. One evening he called in on his father's sister, Kathleen Ward, who also lived in Dundalk. She had never met him before, but she welcomed him into her small and tidy home, they shared a cup of tea and he told her about his life, his love of fitness and the gym, and his ambitions. He visited with her for about ninety minutes, then went on his way. There was nothing unusual about his visit, and Kathleen regarded him as a decent-enough chap.

A week later, on Sunday, 13 March 2011, Christopher Ward again visited Kathleen at her home, but this time he wasn't invited or expected. It was 7.05 a.m., and Kathleen had just dressed and was about to boil the kettle. The doorbell rang. Surprised at someone being about at this early hour, she went out to peek through the window, and there on the step stood her nephew. She opened the door and welcomed him in, offering him a cup of tea, which he accepted. Kathleen's house was open-plan, so he sat on the sofa in the sitting room while she walked over to the kitchen to make the tea. As she did so, Ward silently came up behind her, put his hand over her mouth and pressed a knife to her throat, warning her that he would kill her if she made any sound. He pushed her towards the sitting room, knocked her to the ground and pulled off her clothes. All the while, he continued with his threats of killing her, and his elderly aunt was in genuine fear of her life. After pulling off her clothes, he undressed himself and stood before her naked. Still holding the knife, he raped her on the sitting-room floor. The attack in the sitting room lasted about an hour. At that point, he dragged Kathleen by her hair into the bedroom and attacked her again and again, using the knife and his constant threats to terrify her into silence.

Ward finally left his aunt's home at 10.45 a.m. He just calmly got up, got dressed, gave a final warning that she was to tell no one what he had done to her, then left. Kathleen immediately rang her niece in Dublin and told her what had occurred. Her niece made her way to Dundalk, arriving at about 12.45 p.m., at which point she helped Kathleen raise the alarm and inform the gardaí. Once the call came through, two uniforms went straight to the house to assess the situation. They found a highly distressed elderly woman who was very clear in her account of what had happened and who had raped her, plus they could see a knife in the bedroom and a tub of butter on the floor, which Kathleen alleged had been used by Ward during the attack. On that basis, the uniforms called for scenes of crime officers to attend, and they preserved the scene.

The first time I met Ward was in the Central Criminal Court at his trial, which started in April 2014. I had to have him extradited from the UK to Ireland to face the charges. Two detectives had gone over to interview him about the alleged rape while he was serving time at Brixton Prison for another crime, and he surprised us all by agreeing to giving a buccal swab so a DNA profile could be generated. We had thought he'd sit there and say 'No comment', but he answered the questions and gave the sample voluntarily.

When tested, the sample matched one taken from the victim, which strengthened the case and corroborated Kathleen Ward's statement. Thinking back on it, I think he firmly believed that his victim would withdraw her complaint out of fear of him, which is why he had no fear of her. So while he knew there would be a DNA match, he didn't think there would ever be a trial. He had underestimated the strength of character of Kathleen Ward, though. Not only did she go through the rigours of a trial, she waived her right to anonymity so that he could be publicly identified.

When I saw him in the courtroom, I got that same cold

feeling from him – it seemed like he was empty inside and that emptiness was sharp-edged and dangerous. He pleaded not guilty and showed no remorse towards his elderly aunt. Kathleen Ward arrived at the court in a wheelchair and with an oxygen mask. Christopher Ward objected to this and we had to lift the old woman, without her oxygen mask, into the witness box before the jury came out. He had insisted on this because he believed the sight of her with her mask and chair would generate a sympathy vote from the jury. It was cruel to say the least, but he couldn't have cared less about her suffering. I felt raw contempt for the man every time I looked at him, but also that old sense of wariness that came with the presence of pure badness. I remember being struck by the comment of the senior counsel for the prosecution, who remarked that in all his career, Ward was 'the most evil person' he'd ever encountered. It was very hard to see beyond that assessment.

The judge and jury found Christopher Ward guilty of the crime of rape and in May 2014 he received a fourteen-year sentence. In 2015, he lodged an appeal against his conviction, which was scheduled for April. However, less than two weeks before the appeal was due to be heard at the Court of Appeal, Ward had a heart attack in his prison cell and died. To be honest, when I heard the news, the only thing I felt was surprise that he had a heart.

Another vicious rape case that I worked on led me to a very difficult conclusion about the perpetrator. Back in 2004, when I was a detective sergeant working out of Balbriggan station, I encountered a young man who – at just sixteen years old – was already very dangerous because he was totally disengaged from other people and the pain or terror he was causing them. It was deeply unsettling to witness this in someone of his age.

This young man was already in the care of the State, being a resident of St Michael's in Finglas, which was a youth detention centre. On the afternoon of 14 February 2004, he and a fellow resident of the Finglas centre were brought out on a day trip by two care workers. They went to the Omni shopping centre in Santry first, then headed out to Skerries for a walk by the sea. During that walk, the two young men sprinted off before the care workers could do anything about it. The care workers searched for them, but eventually had to report them as missing; they rang it in at 6.45 p.m., informing a senior colleague at St Michael's. At 7.20 p.m., the centre contacted Finglas Garda Station to inform them that the two young men had absconded. The desk sergeant in Finglas immediately rang Balbriggan and alerted the officer on duty to the fact that two young men were out and about who definitely should not be unaccompanied.

When I arrived into work the following morning at 8 a.m., it was clear it had been a busy night. This sixteen-year-old youngster was in a cell, on suspicion of being involved in an alleged rape in Skerries. I quickly got up to speed: a young girl called Nicole Hayes had reported that she was raped the night before; she had been taken to Our Lady of Lourdes Hospital in Drogheda and a search had been conducted for her attacker but to no avail, then at 12.50 a.m. a youth had contacted the station saying he had escaped from St Michael's and wanted to be brought back there. He was picked up in a patrol car and brought to Balbriggan first so his claim could be verified, and once at the station, the officers noticed his clothes and runners were covered in sand. He also had a fresh scrape on his face and a suspicious stain on his T-shirt. Based on this, the young man presented as a suspect in the alleged rape, and for that reason he was arrested at 1.20 a.m. and detained.

I took part in interviewing him that day at the station. When I walked into the room I was struck by his age first, because he was just a lad of sixteen, but also by his attitude, which seemed far beyond his years. He would not admit anything and was well aware of his rights and our limitations. He was well versed in Garda custody matters, and he believed that if he said nothing, we would have to let him go. We put our questions to him, and he denied any involvement in the attack on Nicole. He admitted to being in Skerries but said he hadn't met anyone. He declined to give a blood sample but agreed to give a sample of pubic hair. He was confrontational, telling us he'd hardly have contacted the gardaí after committing a crime, so the fact that he had gone to them asking to be brought back to St Michael's meant he wasn't the one who had raped the young girl. We conducted a second interview a few hours later, but this time he was uncooperative, telling us again and again: 'I am not answering the question.' For a youngster, he was certainly able to stand his ground.

In the meantime, the incident team worked on piecing together what had happened. They had an excellent witness in Nicole, even though she was only a girl of thirteen at the time. She was very clear in her descriptions of what had occurred and when, and her story was backed up by the physical examinations conducted in the hours after the rape.

She had gone into town with her friend to meet up with other young people. It was common for a group to meet up at weekends – to sit on the beach in an area called Red Island or to hang around the pool hall. On this night, Nicole noticed a young man who wasn't known to her, but he was with the group, drinking with them. She asked him his name, and he said he was Michael McDonagh and that he came from Longford. He boasted about being in juvenile detention – for robbing cars, he said – and told her that he'd done a bunk that day with his friend.

The gang of youngsters were standing around outside Bob's Casino, chatting and laughing together, but McDonagh suggested to Nicole that they head off alone, towards Red Island. She said no but he pulled at her, tugging her hand and insisting. She walked off with him and they soon left the group behind, heading into the dark quietness of the empty beach. They reached an area known as 'the Springers', a popular diving spot in summer. They went down the steps and onto the concrete platform and walked the length of it, towards the sea. They reached the steps that led into the water and stepped off to the right, onto the seaweed-speckled rocks. He remarked to her that no one could see them now; Nicole looked around and agreed that they could no longer be seen by anyone. That's when his demeanour changed.

In an instant, he changed from a laidback teenager hanging out to a terrifying attacker, intent on hurting her. He grabbed Nicole by the arm and pushed her onto the ground. She lay on the cold, wet rock, stunned, and instinctively covered her face with her arms because he was standing over her in a threatening manner. Without a word, McDonagh proceeded to kick her repeatedly in the face. He said he would kill her if she said anything, so now she was truly afraid. He bent down and grabbed her by the throat, pressing his two thumbs into the soft flesh either side of her windpipe. He dug into her flesh so hard, she couldn't breathe. Nicole flailed wildly, scratching his face as she tried desperately to breathe and to make him stop. He continued to try to strangle her, as the tide lapped against her body and the seaweed swished to and fro. That turned out to be what saved her, strangely enough. As he tried to choke the life out of her, her body kept slipping away from him on the seaweed, just enough that he couldn't pin her down fully. By now – wet, cold and terrified – Nicole gave up as her strength ebbed away, just like the waves. She blacked out.

When she came to, McDonagh was no longer trying to kill her. Instead, he was on top of her, the weight of him pushing her down into the rocks and the water. It was when she felt seaweed brushing against her legs that she realized she was no longer wearing her trousers. Her underwear was gone too, as were her runners. She knew what he wanted to do, and she fought back with every bit of strength she could muster. She pushed him off and crawled over the rocks towards a sandy area, scraping her knees and legs as she went. But after that burst of effort, she had no energy left. She sank down on the sand, exhausted, and McDonagh came after her and low-ered himself onto her shivering body again. She pleaded with him that it was her first time and he was hurting her, but he was in a different zone, focused only on what he wanted to do, totally disregarding the fact that she was telling him not to, telling him to stop, telling him she was in pain. For Nicole, the attack lasted a lifetime, and it seemed he would never leave her alone. But, finally, he got up and then told her to get up and sit on a rocky ledge while he searched for his trousers. As he hunted about, he told her to call him by a name that she knew was not his. Instead, he gave her the name of the friend he had absconded with, a coldly calculated move to try to plant that name in his victim's head.

Still in shock, physically and mentally, Nicole sat there while he dressed himself and then thanked her for a great Valentine's night. He kissed her cheek, told her he would return in five minutes, then left. It took some time for Nicole to raise the energy to get herself out of the Springers, but eventually she made her way up the steps and walked in the direction she had last seen her friends. She cried out for help, and soon she was surrounded by anxious friends who listened as she told them a boy called Michael McDonagh had raped and beaten her. The truth of the attack was plain to see – her face was very badly bruised and swollen and she could barely open her eyes. She was naked from the waist down, unable to walk properly, and her body was covered in sand and scratches and blood.

Just before midnight, one of Nicole's friends rang Balbriggan station to report the rape. Gardaí were dispatched immediately, and they found Nicole sitting on the grass, dishevelled and distressed, with her equally distressed friends minding her. Her mother had also been informed and she was there too, facing the nightmare task of helping her thirteen-year-old daughter come to terms with a violent sexual assault. The two gardaí who attended the scene took charge and asked Nicole for a description of what happened. She was able to point out the exact location and tell them what she knew about her attacker. The gardaí then removed her from the scene so she could receive hospital treatment.

At 12.40 a.m., two other uniforms arrived to preserve the scene. But time and tide waits for no man, as we know, and the tide was coming in fast at Skerries. The two uniforms were faced with a crime scene that was about to be washed away. They had to think on their feet and act quickly, which thankfully they did. They retrieved items of possible evidential value as quickly as possible, bagging them up for later examination. By torchlight, they searched the area around the Springers and found a white runner and a spot on the sand where there was a lot of blood that looked fresh. They took some of the bloodied rocks and also a blood-covered seashell. The beam of the torch across the encroaching waves showed up a pair of jeans floating in the water about four feet from the shore, which they waded in to retrieve as well. They also found a pair of white underwear, ripped and bloodied. This was good police work under pressure, and provided important evidence to corroborate Nicole's version of events.

At 12.50 a.m. Michael McDonagh made his call to Balbriggan station, asking for a lift back to St Michael's. And now he was here, in a cell, sixteen years old and suspected of a serious sexual crime. It's a difficult day in any station when your ideas of the world are turned on their head and you face the disturbing reality that a life can be shattered in seconds by one bad-meaning person. It's an uncomfortable thing to face – perhaps even more so when you're dealing with minors. They're meant to have their whole lives ahead of them, and yet here we had one boy whose life was going to take a very sharp turn into long-term incarceration if he was proved guilty, and a girl who had been handed a life sentence of hellish memories to live with. When you're a parent yourself, these cases really hit home. I was so sorry that this young girl had suffered such a brutal attack; and I was sorry, too, for her parents, whose lives were also shattered by the events of that night. It wasn't going to be an easy road for any of them, but our job was to ensure that the person who had done this to Nicole faced justice and punishment.

The investigation was a joint task between Ashbourne and Balbriggan stations and I headed up the team at Balbriggan, where the incident room was based. For the next month we worked hard on compiling the evidence, which was all leading towards McDonagh. But on 30 March, I received an unexpected call. It was from St Michael's, informing me that Michael McDonagh wished to talk about the events of

14 February. The following day, we sat down to interview the boy again, and this time he was very cooperative. He had decided that telling the truth was his best option. So he told us the truth. He described what he had done that night exactly as Nicole had described it. I remember him saying he didn't know why he'd flipped and started kicking her and trying to strangle her, that it was 'pure stupid'. He expressed remorse for his actions, telling us that he couldn't stop thinking about it. It was a full confession, which meant the trial would be straightforward with a guilty plea.

The case came to trial on 9 February 2005 before the Central Criminal Court. McDonagh entered a guilty plea, so there was no call for a jury trial. The judge passed a sentence of nine years for two counts of aggravated sexual assault and nine years for three counts of rape, to run concurrently. As the sentence was handed down, Michael McDonagh turned to the gallery and winked at Nicole – the final insult. He was remanded to St Patrick's Institution in Dublin, but was later moved to the Central Mental Hospital in Dundrum after a diagnosis of paranoid schizophrenia. In July 2010, at the age of twenty-one, he was found dead in a seclusion room at the Central Mental Hospital.

You learn a lot about human nature as a detective. As I said earlier, I'll hold my hands up straight away and say that I'm not a psychologist or a criminologist or anything else that gives you a formal qualification to make pronouncements on human beings; but I do have the benefit of decades observing people in the most stressful situations of their lives. I get called in when things have gone terribly wrong, when there is a victim who demands justice and there is a perpetrator who must be tracked and, if necessary, punished. I come in after the event, but I get to study the aftermath and all the many elements that led up to the moment of transgression.

One of the side effects of investigating murders is that you do end up wondering if every one of us is capable of killing – is it a case of 'there but for the grace of God'? The fact that evil and wrongdoing feature in every religion and philosophy humans have generated suggests that we are all capable of criminal actions – that it is part of the human condition. Murders can arise from any number of circumstances, and you can't predict who will be a perpetrator and who will be a victim. I have certainly met people who have committed terrible crimes and can scarcely believe it themselves, because it's so out of character and beyond the bounds of their normal thinking. For many murderers, they never saw themselves as capable of murder prior to the moment when they raised a hand in anger at someone. Those cases are very difficult because, to the victim and the victim's family, the murderer is, understandably, an aberration or pure evil. But to the investigator, who gets to hear the whole story and interact with the suspect, the murderer can be many other things as well: vulnerable, mentally ill, damaged by childhood experiences, an addict, disadvantaged and neglected from the day they were born.

Wrongdoing, impulsive behaviour, irrational decisions, hatred and anger – these are all part of human life and human nature. If we could fix society so that people didn't get damaged in the first place, there'd be very little crime, but that doesn't look like ever being achieved by human beings. Since the dawn of civilization there has always been an unequal and unfair social system, and this creates a vulnerable and exploited class of people. That saying about money being the root of all evil is probably more true than we realize, because really, when it comes down to it, money and economics are the pillars on which inequality is built. And inequality means social disadvantage, means social disillusion, means social disengagement, and that's where you get hopeless people in hopeless situations who cause damage all round.

John Lonergan, the former governor of Mountjoy Prison in Dublin, is a very powerful speaker on this topic. His extensive experience with those incarcerated for crimes has led him to conclude that social and economic disadvantage is a key driver of criminal action. I would be in agreement with him on this. Our prison populations are skewed towards a certain demographic, and that is people born into disadvantaged circumstances – often to young parents who are struggling to cope with their own lives, and with very little in the way of stability or structure and no emphasis placed on education. For a person born into this sort of life, the path to prison is a fairly easy one to fall onto and follow.

In a way, it would be easy to put all serious criminals and murderers under one banner – 'evil' – that separates them from the rest of us, but that would be simplistic. It might be an unsettling truth, but it's true nonetheless that very few of the criminals I've dealt with could be classed as evil in the sense of lacking in remorse or having no moral compass whatsoever. Sixteen-year-old Michael McDonagh was an example: he committed a truly horrific – indeed, a monstrous – crime for which he was deservedly punished, *and* he was a troubled youth who was capable of expressing remorse (albeit the sincerity of that remorse might be up for debate). On the other hand, a man like Mr C, who cold-bloodedly pumped bullets into a man who merely suggested that he stop hassling a waitress, would not have done that. He was of a different order.

I have met murderers who seemed perfectly normal and

decent in conversation – men like Colin Whelan, who murdered his wife deliberately and coldly. Whelan committed an atrocious murder, but on meeting him, you couldn't see any of that in him. It was actually hard to believe that he had killed in cold blood because there was nothing about him that set the radar beeping – no evil aura, no black-eyed stare, no sign that he felt entitled to do anything to anyone. It simply wasn't there.

That's something I've often puzzled over late at night, and really all I can conclude is that everybody is capable of doing wrong, but the vast majority choose not to because they don't want to hurt another person. There is a small minority who do consciously choose to kill or commit crimes because they want to – because it's a high or a form of revenge on society or a release of some kind. Those are the ones you might label 'evil', but, as I've said, I've met precious few of them, so it can't be a common characteristic. Indeed, what I've found is that when you dig into these people's lives, you will very likely uncover that unholy trinity of childhood abuse, parental alcoholism and an unstable home. I've seen those things feature again and again and again in the cases I've worked on over the years. When someone is born into that sort of environment, it can be tremendously difficult to move beyond it in a meaningful way. It seems to be the worst set of cards you can be dealt in life.

As a detective, you are at a remove from the crime because you aren't the victim, which means you can listen to both of the stories behind it – that of the victim and that of the perpetrator. I'm well aware that a victim of crime often doesn't have the luxury of listening and understanding. To them, it's a black-and-white case: the person who hurt them is bad and deserves stern punishment. I do understand that, but I also understand that a detective is in a different position, able – indeed, obliged – to hear both sides. I think that's an important thing for detectives to remember, that listening and hearing are also part of the job. Every crime is complex, and none of us can afford to stand in judgement on someone else; that has to be left to the courts. Around the time of the attack on Nicole, the children's charity Barnardo's had a tagline that I felt was very insightful: 'Every Childhood Lasts a Lifetime'. I've thought exactly that in the interview room many a time.

A final observation stemming from this consideration of what makes people do bad things is the difference between men and women in their reactions to difficult lives or childhood circumstances. It seems to me that men are far more likely to become perpetrators, while women often become victims, in an ongoing cycle that blights their lives. Because it happens relatively rarely, and seems so out of kilter with the normal order of things, I think this is why the idea of a female killer is so fascinating to people. From what I've seen, women tend to internalize their pain and turn it on themselves – for example through self-harming or alcohol abuse – whereas men are more likely to lash out at someone else in order to relieve their inner turmoil. I can't say why this is; it could be social conditioning, different ways of processing emotions, a different sense of one's place in the world – I'm not qualified to call it. But it is a phenomenon that is readily noticeable among the population when you work as a detective. That's why, in my thirty-three years on the force, I dealt with only two cases involving female murderers, although strangely enough they both took place in the same year and in the same town: Drogheda.

The killing of Eva Berrill in August 2014 was one of those

crimes that could be called evil in that it was an utterly sense-less act committed by someone who simply did not care about the consequences of her actions. On the night of 16 August, Eva was in bed in her house on the Chord Road, which lies alongside the River Boyne that bends its way through the town. It was a warm summer's night so the window was open to allow in some air. Eva was a woman of seventy-three, and following a stroke she was confined to a wheelchair, so her bedroom was on the ground floor of the house. Her husband was her devoted carer, and on this night he ensured Eva had everything she needed and was comfortable in bed, then he nipped across the road to their local pub, where he enjoyed a pint and a chat with his neighbours. He went back and forth a couple of times to check on his wife. But in between his visits, a fire broke out in the house and it quickly raced through the rooms, engulfing everything in its path. Eva was defenceless, unable to move quickly, and she sustained serious burns in the fire. She would die of her injuries ninety-six days later, to the devastation of her family.

The incident was investigated because the scene was suspicious. We conducted all the usual forensic and technical examinations, but the real breakthrough came from CCTV footage obtained from a camera outside the pub across the street. We watched in shock as a young woman came walking along the Chord Road in the company of three young men. In the video she stops at the open window, takes some paper and holds her lighter up to it. When the paper catches fire, she pushes it through the open window and into the curtains. The little flame extinguishes as the paper burns up. The young woman patiently lights another piece of paper and reaches in to hold it against the net curtains. The flames take hold, licking the flammable curtains, finding the material and oxygen necessary to become a conflagration, and the young woman walks on down the road.

It was shocking to watch it all happen – so random, so callous. And the video continued on, showing the same young woman and her male friends walking back down the street again, past the house where Eva Berrill was now in mortal danger. It was obvious the fire had truly taken hold, but they just walked on by, doing nothing. Inside the house, a woman was losing her life because of that random act of badness.

The video evidence, along with the forensics, meant that the young woman was easily apprehended and had no choice but to plead guilty. Her name was Nicola Kavanagh and she was twenty-eight years old. When she was brought to Drogheda Garda Station for questioning, detectives from my team interviewed her and I observed her in the station. She had all the hallmarks of an undernourished female, both in terms of body and mental well-being.

It was yet another time when I had to listen to the words 'I didn't mean it to happen'. Sometimes you can get very tired of those words, especially when an act committed is so inevitable in its consequences that a child could have predicted it. The Berrill family were left grieving because of a casual act of badness, and there's no justice in that. But then it was also yet another time when I heard a tale of a young life ruined by parental alcoholism and abandonment. Nicola Kavanagh had been dealt the hard cards, and things had been spiralling out of her grip for some time. It was just terribly sad for both women that her unravelling ended in murder.

Kavanagh stood trial in Dundalk Circuit Criminal Court, where she pleaded guilty to arson and manslaughter. The judge sentenced her to twelve years in prison for each offence, running concurrently. He did offer her a chance at life, though, by suspending the last four years of each sentence on the condition that she enter into a good behaviour bond for a four-year period following her release. Of course, as with all these cases, the victim's family always gets handed a lifetime sentence.

At the start of that same year, I had dealt with a very different murder committed by a woman – one that emphasized the importance of methodical police work in a number of ways. It was about 3 a.m. on 1 January, just a few hours into the new year, when my phone rang and woke me up. Thankfully, I had had a very quiet and sober New Year's, so I was able to focus quickly. The colleague on the other end apologized for robbing me of sleep but told me that a stabbing had occurred some time after midnight and the victim had just died of his injuries. 'The partner did it and she's made admissions,' he said.

My first question was: 'Were notes taken of her admissions?'

'I don't know.'

'Where is the suspect now? Has she been arrested?'

'The suspect? I let her go down to her mother's house. It's in the same estate.'

I bit back a choice swear word and took a deep breath. 'Why did you do that?'

'Well, she was upset and I thought her mother would calm her.'

'And did it not occur to you that her clothes were possibly evidential and she could be changing them as we speak? Or that she might be now concocting a story with others to mitigate her actions?'

Silence.

I waited.

Then: 'No.'

I was going to ask why I was being called now instead of at midnight, but I knew there was no point. This is something that unfortunately occurs in An Garda too often – someone with no investigating experience (as was the case with the person who called me on this night) makes critical calls on the handling of a situation, and their lack of basic knowledge leads to poor decision-making that delays or derails investigations. One of the first things you realize as a detective-in-training is that the initial decisions made with regard to an incident are absolutely crucial to the success or otherwise of the case. On top of that, poor decisions can be scrutinized later at a trial – often to the detriment of the investigation and the evidence. I had encountered this scenario many times before, so I had to swallow my frustration and focus on what I could do to get the case on track.

'I recommend that the suspect be arrested on suspicion of murder and brought to Drogheda station.'

'Okay, Pat, I'll get that done.'

I reached the station about 7 a.m. with the intention of speaking to the gardaí who attended the scene, and then speaking to the suspect to assess her demeanour. But first I stopped to talk to the member who had been assigned the task of maintaining the custody record throughout the period of detention. In the Dublin Metropolitan Area, a sergeant takes charge of this, but outside Dublin a garda will normally be given this role. I made a point of explaining carefully to the garda in question the necessity and importance of adhering to the rights of the detainee at all times and offering her a solicitor. The custody record is an extremely important document. It's like our own Geneva Convention, ensuring every person who is in custody is treated with dignity and respect and accorded their lawful rights. It is crucial that it is fully and accurately maintained because it is also an exhibit if the case reaches court, and as such it will be gone through with a fine-tooth comb by the defence, looking for any gaps or cracks to wedge a doubt or a complaint into. As a result, I was always extremely particular about the custody record and the methodical keeping of it, and this case was to be no exception.

After that conversation, I talked to the gardaí who had attended the scene. I wanted to make sure they had notes taken and that a copy of these had been supplied to the arrested person while in custody. Garda notes are crucial, and it's hard to believe that some still prefer to memorize them instead of writing them down. A garda's notebook is evidential, which means the recorded notes are of huge value, especially when an accused makes a pertinent comment.

Once I had established that they were aware of the importance of the notes, I asked what had happened. They told me they had been called to a house in the town, where a man was reported stabbed. This man turned out to be Wayne McQuillan, the boyfriend of Paula Farrell. They had been in a relationship for about a year, and drinking to excess seemed to be a recurring problem for them. On this night, both had been drinking when a row broke out between them. The row had turned physical. Whatever had occurred, it had ended with McQuillan being stabbed four times, causing his death.

Armed with that information, I went to have a chat with Paula Farrell, but when I met her I realized that wouldn't be happening for a while. She was in a poor way, and a doctor called to the station to assess her fitness to be questioned ruled that she was in no fit state due to being under the influence of alcohol. He recommended a six-hour rest period before we talked to her, and we adhered strictly to that. During those six hours, while the suspect slept off the effects of a New Year's Eve gone very wrong, I dug into her medical history. She had mentioned to the desk sergeant that she had mental health issues and had not taken her medication in some time. That statement concerned me, as it could pose further issues for the interview process. My question was: *Does this woman have enough mental capacity to undergo questioning?* I asked the desk sergeant to call in an independent doctor to conduct a full medical examination to answer this for me. I specified that it should be a female doctor, as I also wanted the suspect to be examined for any bruising or injuries on her person. I did this because I had noticed a bite mark on her face, which led me to think she might have had an altercation with the deceased prior to the stabbing incident.

After six hours had elapsed, the female doctor went in to visit Paula Farrell and conduct her examination. She did a thorough assessment, mental and physical, and delivered a written report to the effect that the suspect was fit to be interviewed. Once she was ready to talk, Farrell was cooperative and readily admitted her part in the incident that evening. Their verbal row had become physical and she alleged that he had bitten her, banged her head and attempted to strangle her. In the midst of this, she got her hand on the knife block in the kitchen, pulled out a knife and stabbed him four times. From our point of view, it was now a straightforward route to arrest, detention and court.

When we spoke to her, it became clear that Paula Farrell was another victim of a damaged childhood, having suffered abuse at a young age. She presented at the time of her arrest in a pitiful state – a woman who suffered from mental problems and who had relied more on alcohol for support than on her medication for weeks prior to the night of the incident. She was charged with murder and later secured bail from the High Court, on the conditions that she would sign in at Drogheda Garda Station once a week and stay well away from the deceased's family, who lived not far from her home. In fairness to her, she did sign in as and when required, and she gave up alcohol and on her own admission did not leave the house for fear of meeting members of the McQuillan family, whom she did not want to upset.

The case came to court in June 2015, with a not-guilty plea lodged at the arraignment. It was brought before a jury in the Central Criminal Court on 24 June. During the course of the trial, I was there to give evidence. The defence tested Paula Farrell's treatment while in custody. If the gardaí involved had slipped up in any way, then any admissions made by their client while in custody could not be entered as evidence. The judge listened, then demanded an original copy of the custody record, saying he would read it during the lunch break. At 2 p.m. we all filed back into court to hear his verdict. I felt a rush of pride and satisfaction when he said to the court: 'I have read the custody record and all I can say is that the level of care the gardaí showed to this lady while in Garda custody was exceptional.' That certainly put a stop to any questioning of Paula Farrell's time in custodial care. Some weeks after the trial, I wrote to each of the members in charge during her detention period and thanked them for their professionalism and their contribution to the investigation. I've no doubt that I have annoyed and irritated many colleagues over the years by being so pernickety about the custody record, and indeed about all documents, but this case vindicated those efforts.

After three and a half hours of deliberations, on 17 July

2015 the jury found Paula Farrell guilty of murder and Mr Justice Patrick McCarthy handed down a mandatory life sentence. There has been a twist in this story, however. In June 2018, the Court of Appeal quashed that conviction on the basis that the trial judge ought to have allowed the jury to consider the partial defence of provocation. Paula Farrell is awaiting a date for a retrial to be heard, so the ultimate outcome remains to be seen.

The death of Wayne McQuillan illustrates how it's scarily possible to be tipped over the edge as the result of a blinding flash of anger that takes over and shuts down a person's rational mind temporarily, albeit aided and abetted by alcohol in Paula Farrell's case. I've seen this happen many times, and these are the killers who are usually in shock in the interview room, unable to comprehend their own actions and filled with remorse for those actions. These are the ones that make you wonder how solid the line is between the innocent and the guilty, and how lucky you are never to have stepped over it. I have heard the words 'I didn't mean it to happen' so many times during my career. I have watched accused after accused shaking their heads, as if trying to reset reality to what it was before, when it made sense. 'I never wanted to kill anyone' – that's what they say, their voices strained with emotion and fear. These people will for evermore be classed as killers, left with the grim realization that what was done in a moment of rage or jealousy or mental pain can never be undone.

The murder of Muhammad Arif in Drogheda in 2011 had these hallmarks – a case where three lives were ruined in one moment of jealous rage, and no amount of remorse would be able to undo that damage. On 6 January at 2.04 p.m., a call was placed to the emergency services. A man reported that a woman had been stabbed and needed assistance, and he gave the address. The operator tried to get more information, but the man stopped talking and the line went dead. The mobile phone from which the call was made was that of Muhammad Arif. He hadn't mentioned his own injuries, but at that moment he was dying from two stab wounds to the abdomen.

At 2.08 p.m., the operator contacted Drogheda Garda Station and reported an incident at Fitzwilliam Court, an apartment block on Dyer Street in the town centre. Two gardaí were at the address by 2.15 p.m., as it's very close to the station. There, they found a woman receiving medical attention in the lobby, while a man was being tended to in apartment number 48. The gardaí recognized the man because he worked as a security guard at Tesco supermarket. That was Muhammad Arif. The woman identified herself as Rashida Bibi Haider and alleged that her ex-husband was the assailant. The gardaí recorded this allegation. The two stabbing victims were then removed by ambulance to Our Lady of Lourdes Hospital.

An investigation was set up at Drogheda station into the unlawful wounding of Arif and Haider, and I was appointed SIO. The scene was preserved and a search undertaken to find the weapon used. That very afternoon, a uniform garda going through the wheelie bins at the apartment complex found a black-handled knife with a bloodstained blade. It was a good start.

We quickly established that the injured parties were cousins and that they had lived together at 48 Fitzwilliam Court, along with Rashida's husband, Shahzad Hussain. Arif had arrived in Ireland from Pakistan in 2004 and had established a good life in Drogheda. His job in Tesco meant he was known around the town, and he was well liked by all who knew him. Rashida had come to live in Ireland in 2008, sharing the apartment with her cousin, and then her husband had joined them in 2010. The living arrangement didn't last long because in November 2010 Rashida moved out due to marital problems. Shahzad subsequently moved out as well, in December, and moved in with friends at the Mosney asylum centre. The reason cited for the marital problems was Shahzad's suspicion that Rashida and Arif had become intimate; this was denied by Rashida.

As the three people involved were Pakistani nationals, I decided to contact the chief imam of the Islamic Centre of Ireland, Shaykh Dr Umar Al-Qadri, to seek his advice. He was extremely helpful, emphasizing that he wished to co-operate fully with the laws of the land. I was grateful to have his support, but little did I realize just how effective his help would be.

It was after midnight when my phone started ringing. I was on the upper floor of the station, still at my desk. The caller was the desk sergeant on the ground floor. He proceeded to tell me, in a voice full of disbelief, that at 11.50 p.m. a man called Shahzad Hussain had walked into the station, looking to be arrested for stabbing Rashida and Arif. He spoke no English, so he'd simply held out his arms, indicating that handcuffs should be applied. I have to admit, that was a first for me. I guessed – rightly, as it turned out – that this was thanks to the persuasive powers of Dr Al-Qadri, who had urged the man to take the moral course of action and admit his wrongdoing. Hussain was arrested at 12.05 a.m. and was now being detained.

Not long after 1 a.m., my phone started ringing again. I was informed that Arif had undergone emergency surgery in

Drogheda and had then been moved to St Vincent's University Hospital in Dublin. His condition had deteriorated, and at 1.02 a.m. he had died of his injuries. Rashida had also undergone emergency surgery in Drogheda, for injuries sustained to her liver, but so far she was stable. As I sat at my desk in the quiet station, I was thinking that it was going to be a very interesting day tomorrow.

The following day, an interpreter arrived to facilitate the questioning of Shahzad Hussain. Given that he had decided to do the right thing, Hussain cooperated fully throughout the detention and interview process. He gave his version of events, which differed from that supplied by Rashida in that she denied any intimate relations between herself and Arif.

Hussain alleged that he had been hurt and angered by the problems in his marriage, which he felt were caused by his wife's feelings towards Arif. On the morning of 6 January, he had called Rashida's workplace but had been informed that she was on a day off. Working on the theory that she might be with Arif, he had boarded a bus from Mosney to Drogheda with the intention of confronting them. When he arrived at the apartment complex, he had to wait until someone was coming out so he could gain admission. He made his way upstairs and let himself into the apartment. He said he found Rashida and Arif naked in bed together, which led to an uncontrollable rage. (Rashida stated that she was coming out of the bathroom when her husband arrived, while Arif was in bed after working his normal nightshift.) Rashida followed him into the kitchen. There was a knife on the table and he grabbed it and threatened his wife with it. (Rashida stated that he hit her at this point, she cried out and Arif came to her aid.) Arif came out of the bedroom and Hussain ordered him to go back in, which Arif refused to do. Hussain held the knife to Rashida's throat. Arif shoved Hussain away from Rashida. In response, Hussain stabbed Arif in the stomach. He described it as a madness that descended on him in that moment. Arif then went over the window and began shouting out for help. He pulled out his phone and dialled 999 and tried to get help that way, but he lost consciousness while talking to the operator. While this was happening, Hussain advanced on Rashida and stabbed her twice in the stomach. On the other end of Arif's phone, the operator could hear the sounds of the attack and a woman crying out in pain.

In common with so many others, Hussain said it was all a terrible accident, that he had never wished to kill Arif or Rashida, that he had lost his mind and done something he deeply regretted.

It was done, of course, and there was no undoing it. Muhammad Arif was dead, leaving a wife and three children in Pakistan. Rashida Bibi Haider survived the attack, but undoubtedly the mental scars took much longer to heal. Both Rashida and Arif, while he was alive, had consistently denied the allegation of an affair, both to Hussain and to their families and various friends. Whatever occurred between the three of them in the apartment that day, whatever his intention, the simple fact was that Shahzad Hussain had taken a knife and plunged it into another man's stomach, killing him. His shock and disbelief at his own actions were familiar to me, but as in all the other cases, they couldn't change the facts. The investigation team put together a watertight case and, when it came to court, Hussain received a life sentence for murder, a seven-year sentence for causing serious harm to Rashida and a concurrent two-year sentence for assault causing harm to Rashida.

That wasn't the end, though. Hussain subsequently appealed the conviction for murder. The Court of Appeal ruled that the trial judge ought to have included the matter of provocation in his summing up, and for that reason a retrial was ordered. When that came to court, Shahzad Hussain lodged a plea of guilty to the charge of manslaughter and the life sentence was reduced on conviction to ten years for the lesser crime.

As a citizen, I can have opinions on the causes of crime and shout about those who commit crimes and detest what they do, but once I have that number on my shoulder, it's different. A good detective must reserve judgement, must listen and hear the story behind the crime, must listen to all that's being said and not said – because that's part of justice. We have to treat people as human beings, even when their actions suggest they don't deserve it. A key part of justice is respect and fair treatment, and that's worth upholding in a civil society. I lived through the bad old days when sometimes those in custody were treated roughly and shouted at, and I'm very glad that type of thing doesn't go on any more. Now it's a clean and monitored system, and that's the way it should be because we have to stay on the right side or else we're not worth our badges.

There's one final case that illustrates the point that a good detective has to be alive to the whole story – no matter what the circumstances – because otherwise they could miss something important. There was a man I arrested in Balbriggan on suspicion of stealing oil from an oil tank in the garden of a private house. He was brought into the station and it was explained to him that he would be put into a cell until we were ready to question him. He became very violent with the desk sergeant who was relaying this information. In the end, it took three of us to escort him to the cell and get him into it, because he was behaving so aggressively. I was not looking forward to the interview as he was obviously going to be extremely difficult to deal with and I felt he was unpredictable and posed a threat. Nonetheless, it had to be done, so a colleague and I sat with him in the interview room and tried to conduct the interview. As expected, he was abusive and aggressive and doing himself no favours in how he was handling the situation.

I was at pains to explain the process to him, including his rights while under detention. I passed a copy of the document setting out his rights across the table to him, as an act of reassurance to try to calm him down. At that moment, my colleague and I exchanged a look as we both realized what was going on. He was looking at the document upside down, and didn't turn it around. I asked him if he was okay with point 8, regarding a certain right. He looked down at the page. I asked him if he could locate point 8. He said he could.

As gently as I could, I said to him, 'You can't read, can you?'

There was a painful silence, then he lowered his head and said quietly, 'No, I can't.'

We told him it was nothing to be ashamed of, that it was never too late to learn. At this, our bullish, macho, aggressive prisoner broke down and cried like a baby right there at the table. Through sobs, he told us how difficult and stressful it was to get through life without the ability to read and how deeply this had affected him. Somehow, the theft of the oil seemed less important now, because this man needed to be informed about adult education and what opportunities were available to him to learn how to read and write. I went off and looked up all this information for him, and he appreciated it and thanked me and my colleague for our understanding. The difference in his demeanour was absolutely astounding.

I didn't let the crime go, of course, and asked him about it.

Straight away he admitted it, saying he needed the stolen oil for his tractor. But the admission was no big deal for him as he felt he might have opened a door to solving his major life difficulty.

This was a story I kept at the forefront of my mind for the rest of my career, and I told it to any colleague who would listen. It was a big lesson for me about the benefit of showing empathy and decency to every person I dealt with, regardless of what side of the law they were on. There's almost always a story behind the crime that contains an explanation, if you care to listen.

8. The Disappointments and the Hopes

My mother pressed a coin into my hand and instructed me to walk to the shop, buy a pound of butter and walk straight back with it – and no dilly-dallying. I was ten years old and liable to flights of distracted fancy, as well she knew. I raced off, the big coin clutched tightly in my palm, going before any of my four siblings could decide to tag along. I shot down Bridge Street in Navan, like a bullet from a gun, and headed straight to Cuff's shop on Railway Street, just as my mother had bid. But as I careered around the corner, the way was blocked by a huge, tall man in full uniform. He was a magnificent sight, and I was forced to halt my gallop in order to step around him. He smiled down at me from his great height and I admired the gleaming silver chain on his tunic. His demeanour, the immaculately turned-out uniform – to me this man looked purposeful, strong and smart.

'How are you, young man?' he said, and we exchanged pleasantries. I was in awe of him.

I got the pound of butter and raced back to Bridge Street again, where my mother was waiting. 'Mammy, I spoke to a guard,' I said, breathless with the excitement of the encounter. She gave me a child's definition of a garda – 'he takes away bad people and locks them up to keep us all safe'. That picture – of the strong, uniformed man, robust in his principles, taking away all the badness – stayed with me. I admired it, and somewhere inside me the seed was sown that I wanted to become that myself. In that chance meeting was the reason behind my whole career – the desire to protect the good.

Every new recruit to the Garda swears an oath that is basically a vision statement for the organization:

> I hereby solemnly and sincerely declare before God that I will faithfully discharge the duties of a member of the Garda Síochána with fairness, integrity, regard for human rights, diligence and impartiality, upholding the Constitution and the laws and according equal respect to all people; while I continue to be a member I will to the best of my skill and knowledge discharge all my duties according to law, and I do not belong to, and will not while I remain a member, form, belong to or subscribe to any political party or secret society whatsoever.

The name An Garda Síochána means 'Guardians of the Peace', and the motto is 'to protect and serve the community'. This is the ambition shared by everyone who joins the force. It doesn't always go to plan, but if you go to Templemore any year and talk to the new recruits, you'll hear a version of 'protect the innocent' from every one of them. There was an old notion that joining An Garda was a vocation, like becoming a nurse or a priest. I think that idea has fallen away now, but there was truth in it – and certainly there was for me personally. The men and women who choose a career in the police force or the Defence Forces tend to share a common sense of decency and of right and wrong. And they are willing to go to the front line to defend those beliefs, so it is vocational in a sense. I think there is a personality type that's attracted to these jobs, and within that there are subsets of personality types that want to become detectives or community police officers or forensics officers or members of the Special Detective Unit.

In terms of detective work, those who lean in this direction tend to be bright, with a lot of empathy and an interest in human nature. Personally, I wanted to become a detective because it seemed to be a very direct way of 'putting away the bad people', as my mother would have said. I knew I had natural problem-solving ability, and my years in the private sector had given me excellent self-discipline and good organizational ability, so I felt I could assist ably in solving crimes and delivering justice for victims. Over a thirty-three-year career, there were many highlights, such as solving the murders of Rachel O'Reilly and Mary Gough, tracking Colin Whelan assiduously in order to bring him to justice, and – my last big case – working on the murder of my colleague and friend Detective Garda Adrian Donohoe. (The trial of his alleged killer is due to happen around the time this book is published.) The interaction with the many families of victims who relied on me and trusted me also meant a huge amount. Those were times when I felt that I was fulfilling my oath as a garda and making a valuable contribution to society. Those were the good days.

Of course, when you believe you've solved a case, correctly identified the perpetrator of a crime and helped to build a watertight case that leads to a guilty verdict, you hope that it will result in a sanction that not only fits the crime but also sends a message about the value we as a society put on people's safety and security – and, most of all, on their lives. While I agree wholeheartedly with promoting a fair and respectful police force and judiciary, it is still necessary that criminal acts, whether intended or unintended, are punished appropriately. If I were in a position to devise a sentencing system, I would categorize premeditated murder as first-degree murder, carrying a mandatory sentence of natural life. In other words, you take a life, you give yours in return. I would classify those cases where a person was an accomplice but didn't pull the trigger as second-degree murder, and this would carry a sentence of thirty-five years before parole. Manslaughter, which is where the killing was unintended, would be classified as third-degree murder and carry a mandatory sentence of ten to twenty-five years, at the discretion of the judge.

I would do all this because I think justice would be served by defining mandatory sentences. It would send out a very clear message to criminals, plus it would give the public confidence in the justice system because it would guarantee that a convicted person would not get out early for good behaviour. These are the changes I would welcome in our justice system, to recognize the seriousness of the crime of murder. It's a crime that ripples out to affect so many people, and those effects carry on for their whole lives. In the previous chapter I explained in detail why I was willing to listen and understand all the elements that led up to the crime, but once the crime of murder has been committed, the response should be severe and consistent. The victims and their families deserve no less.

Inevitably, when I think about the days when I was able to feel satisfaction in a job well done, I remember that there were bad days as well, particularly when I couldn't deliver a well-solved case that was ready for court scrutiny. Those cases stay with you; they are the ones you think of at 3 a.m. when the clock is ticking and the tap is dripping and your mind keeps working and won't let you sleep. You go over the evidence again and again, looking for the crucial detail you missed. Those are the regrets, and regrets run deep.

In terms of unsolved cases, there are a few that bother me still that I would have dearly loved to solve, especially as I got so close to doing so. In October 2010 I took over the murder case of Seamus McMahon, who was shot dead at his apartment in Saltown, Dundalk, on Sunday 21 March that year. When I examined all the files, I could see how to progress the case by taking a different approach. The team instigated that new approach and our work resulted in discovering the reason why McMahon had been killed, the identities of the culprits – including the person who pulled the trigger – and the identification of the car used in the crime. However, it is one thing knowing something and another thing entirely to convert that knowledge into hard evidence that can secure a conviction. By the time I retired in 2018, the case was still filed as 'Unsolved', in spite of great work by the team. I passed on my thoughts as to how it could be solved to my successors, and still hope to hear of an arrest and conviction one day.

One of my greatest regrets is that the disappearance of Ciara Breen remains unsolved. Ciara's mother, Bernadette, was heartbroken by the loss of her only child, and I wanted to give her the comfort of knowing that the person responsible for her daughter's disappearance was behind bars. It haunts me still that this couldn't be achieved, and also that we couldn't locate Ciara's remains so she could be buried by her family.

Ciara disappeared on 13 February 1997, when I was serving as a sergeant at Clones Garda Station in County Monaghan, so I wasn't involved in the investigation. She was seventeen years old and living at home with her mother in Dundalk. That evening, she went out for dinner with her mother, then they returned home and watched TV together before calling it a night at 12.25 a.m. At 1.50 a.m., Bernadette looked into her daughter's bedroom to check on her, and the bed lay neat and empty. She immediately checked the rest of the house, but there was no sign of Ciara. The only sign of her daughter she could find was a partially open window downstairs. There was no money missing, no clothes missing and Ciara's passport was still there, so Bernadette thought she couldn't have gone far. The next morning, Bernadette had to get to Dublin for an appointment. On her return to Dundalk in the afternoon, Ciara still wasn't home. At 6 p.m., Bernadette rang Dundalk station to report her daughter missing. Ciara Breen has never been seen again.

An investigation was set up and quickly established that Ciara had been seeing an older man who lived nearby. Liam Mullen was thirty-five years old, but he had taken a shine to the young woman who lived a few doors down from his house. When the investigation team talked to Ciara's close friends, they insisted that Ciara had a date with Liam Mullen on 13 February and was planning to escape out the window to meet him. The team pieced together as much information as they could, and I upgraded the investigation from missing person to murder – even though we had no body – based on witness testimony that Mullen was in a relationship with Ciara and was due to meet her on the night she disappeared. We arrested Mullen on suspicion of murder on 10 September 1999. He was detained and questioned, but refused to answer any questions and was later released without charge. The investigating officers hit a brick wall, because there was no body and no evidence to suggest she had, in fact, been murdered. She was officially a missing person, even if the officers involved had a strong suspicion that she had been killed.

There was a lengthy gap in proceedings then because the Breen case was taken away from Dundalk station and put under the umbrella of Operation Trace, which connected a number of cases of disappeared women and investigated them as the work of one perpetrator. As a result, the case was no longer being conducted by the Dundalk team and everything came to a halt. Operation Trace was a wide-scale investigation that sought to link the disappearances of six different women, all of whom have become well-known names in Ireland: Fiona Sinnott, Josephine Dullard, Deirdre Jacob, Ciara Breen, Fiona Pender and Annie McCarrick. I always believed Ciara Breen had no place on the list, but the powers that be thought otherwise. I also thought it was daft to think the six disappearances might be linked – that there was a serial killer, in other words – and I still hold to that opinion.

So that's how it came about that almost twenty years later I was appointed SIO of the renewed investigation into Ciara Breen's disappearance. In order to conduct the review, I had to request the file from Trace. A box arrived and I removed the lid and reached in for the file. Nothing. I turned the box upside down: no file on Ciara Breen. I eventually had to go back to the original investigation team and ask them to do a bit of searching. Lo and behold, it turned up in the attic of a retired garda. That sort of slipshod approach always drove me insane, but as ever, I had to put that to one side and get on with reviewing the case.

I went through everything in detail, and decided it was worth revisiting those who gave key statements back in 1997. I also requested that the case be featured on *Crimecall*, to jog people's memories. Enough time had passed that I felt people who might have been reticent to get involved back then just might be ready to talk now.

The *Crimecall* piece aired on 15 December 2014. It featured an appeal to the public for any information regarding the disappearance, with Ciara's mother, Bernadette, making a heartfelt plea for help to end her agony of not knowing what had happened to her only child. In particular, we appealed to the writer of an anonymous letter, received five weeks earlier after a local media appeal. This letter suggested that Liam Mullen had information about Ciara's disappearance and we were hoping whoever wrote it might come forward to talk to us in person. The appeal requested that anyone with information contact me or the incident room at Dundalk.

We didn't receive many calls after *Crimecall*, but there were a few people who contacted us with interesting information – both before and after the programme. In particular, a woman who was dying of cancer had urged her daughter to give a truthful statement about what she saw that night. In June 2014, the daughter contacted me and told me that on the night Ciara disappeared, she had seen her being assaulted and chased by Liam Mullen down by the railway tracks. She had not revealed this to the investigation team the first time round. In December that same year, we received two more anonymous letters, both suggesting that Liam Mullen knew the truth about Ciara's disappearance. As we talked to people in Dundalk, his name came up again and again – that he had definitely been seeing Ciara, that he was regarded as a threatening figure by most women who knew him, that he was possessive, that he had been too old to be having sex with a seventeen-year-old, that she was going to meet him the night she disappeared.

We tracked down some ex-girlfriends of Mullen's and a picture of him began to emerge that was far from flattering. These women described a possessive, controlling man who could fly into jealous rages. They recounted trying to break it off with him and being scared by his reaction. They spoke about the days and months after the break-up that he spent trailing them, taunting and threatening. He fathered a number of children with a number of women, but took responsibility for none of them. He seemed to have left a trail of destruction through many families in the area.

The other very interesting piece of information we received concerned Mullen's reaction to the *Crimecall* programme. He was in a local pub when it was on, and the barman and other customers were watching it avidly. Several different people asserted that when the programme ended, Mullen stood up and said something to the effect that Ciara was gone and was never coming back, then he abruptly walked out of the bar.

We decided it was worth rearresting Mullen so that we could question him about these various allegations. The super had to go to Dundalk District Court and apply for a warrant to arrest him this second time, which was granted. On 21 April 2015, Mullen was arrested and brought to Drogheda Garda Station. He was detained for twenty-four hours and interviewed six times in that period. I remotely monitored the interviews, which were conducted by two detectives from my team. At one point I thought Mullen was going to admit to the crime because he broke down and began to cry, but then he caught a hold of himself and the shutters came down again. Just as in 1999, he declined to answer any questions or cooperate in any way. And just as in 1999, the following day he was released without charge and we found ourselves staring at a brick wall.

There was more to the story though, because after his arrest and release, the Garda Confidential Line received a number of calls, all suggesting that Mullen had told someone in the weeks after her disappearance that Ciara was buried in a bog near the railway tracks, behind McArdle's Brewery. We talked again to people who would have been drinkers at the time, hanging out with Liam Mullen, and found there was a widespread rumour about the bog being the place where Ciara's body was buried. This seemed to be backed up by two men who recalled Mullen talking about a girl he liked, after Ciara, and commenting that she wasn't being cooperative and could end up in the bog, 'like the other one'. In statement after statement, people alluded to the bog, either because Liam Mullen himself had mentioned it to them in some way, or they had heard that he had told a particular friend of his about it. It seemed too important, too emphatic, to dismiss as grapevine gossip.

The team took the major decision to conduct a physical search at the place referred to, which was Balmer's Bog, about a mile from Ciara Breen's home. I had to go to Dundalk District Court to secure five different warrants to allow us to carry out a full search operation there. It was a mammoth joint effort involving the Garda Technical Bureau, the Louth Divisional Search Team, members of the Defence Forces, a specialist cadaver dog and a forensic archaeologist. We also invited the assistance of the Independent Commission for the Location of Victims' Remains (ICLVR). One of the commission's members advised us on the operation, and also conducted a site visit during the excavation work.

We moved onsite on 18 August 2015, and conducted a search of four acres of reed swamp until 9 September. During the search, it was discovered that in the key area, a contractor had deposited hundreds of tonnes of hard fill – as directed by the landowner. The hard fill was made up of rubble and rocks, and it was thought this dumping might be illegal. What I do know is it meant the task of finding human remains was suddenly much more difficult and far more unlikely. There was a barrier between us and what lay beneath, one that hadn't been there in 1999. It was bitterly disappointing. What was noted with interest, though, was the frequency with which Liam Mullen was spotted passing by the entrance to the search site – four times in one day on one occasion. Local gardaí knew this route wasn't part of his very predictable daily routine of drinking and loitering.

On 9 September, the search equipment was packed up and the effort to locate Ciara Breen's remains was stood down. After so long on the case, I felt I knew what had happened on the night of 13 February, but there was simply no way to prove it. We couldn't even prove that Ciara was dead.

So she remained a missing person, with no further leads, no lightbulb moments of clarity, a trail gone resolutely cold. I felt awful that I had to give that news to Bernadette Breen. After all that waiting and hoping that the answer might finally be found, I had to tell her that we had drawn a blank. She deserved the truth but I couldn't give it to her. That was, and is, a huge personal and professional regret.

There was another addendum to the story in July 2017. The now fifty-five-year-old Liam Mullen was stopped by gardaí in Dundalk on suspicion of drink-driving. It appears that he quickly swallowed a substance he had on his person before the officers arrested him. He was brought to Dundalk Garda Station, where he complained of feeling unwell. A doctor was called in, but despite the doctor's efforts, Liam Mullen died in the station. Bernadette was distraught when the news was relayed to her, because with him died the best chance of discovering what had happened to Ciara, or where her body might lie. If he knew the real story, Liam Mullen had taken that knowledge with him to the grave.

So I think if I had to nominate my single greatest regret in my thirty-three years on the force, the case of Ciara Breen would be it. We knew so much, we'd gathered so much information, we'd pieced together so many hours of Ciara's life, but ultimately we couldn't source the evidence to corroborate our belief as to what had happened to her. Personally, I believe there is one person left alive who possibly knows and could tell us where Ciara's body lies, but the identity of that person must remain a private speculation – and it is only speculation. I wish wholeheartedly that this particular hunch proves correct, however, and that some day that person will step forward to finally reveal the truth about the disappearance of Ciara Breen.

There was a case in 2006 that was like a mirror image of the Breen case, in that we had the evidence, but we didn't have the supporting information needed to interpret it. This was the case of 'the Lambay man', which was followed with great interest by the media and the general public at the time.

It was nearing finishing-up time on a chilly and dull February evening, and I was looking forward to clocking off and heading home. But, as happened so often, a phone call put paid to that idea. The superintendent rang and instructed me to meet a fishing trawler at Skerries pier, because it was carrying some human body parts that had snagged in the nets while out trawling. I was the only detective on duty, so there was little choice as to who to send. I fired off the all-too-familiar 'late for dinner' message home, then took myself off on the short drive to Skerries.

As I stood on the pier, pulling my jacket tighter against the cold, the *Our Tracey* trawler bobbed into mooring. The nets were bulging, and there it was: a skull sitting on top of the final catch of the day. I gave my best unfazed expression to the fishermen, but really I was thinking to myself: *What in God's name am I going to do with Yorick?* I arranged for a local undertaker to retrieve the skull, which was done with the utmost respect, as if it were a full human body. Then I decided to hit the desk and do some research, because somehow – without a crime scene, a location, a body or a single clue – I was going to have to establish the identity of this person and how he or she had met their demise.

My research set me on the path of some experts who might be able to help with identification. I contacted Dr David Sweet at the University of British Columbia in Vancouver, Canada, who was a highly respected forensic scientist. He had worked with governments in various countries to identify remains found in mass graves, using the bones or teeth as a source of DNA. I sent him a sample of the teeth for testing.

In Ireland, I contacted the state anthropologist, Dr Laureen Buckley, and the state pathologist, Dr Marie Cassidy, who both examined the find. Dr Cassidy couldn't derive much information from the remains, but Dr Buckley was able to furnish me with some details. She concluded that the skull was that of a male Caucasian, between twenty-five and forty-five years old, and it had been in the water for around six to twelve months. I also contacted the state forensic dentist, Dr Paul Keogh, to ask him to conduct an examination in tandem with the work going on over in Canada. Dr Keogh told me that the skull had no fillings and that the teeth were healthy but slightly ground down, which suggested a foreign person, such as a North African, who was possibly partial to chewing nuts. From Dr Sweet we eventually received a full DNA profile from the teeth supplied to him. This was something our forensics lab wasn't equipped to do, but Dr Sweet was a world leader in his field and I was grateful for his input.

The breakthrough came when I discovered the work of forensic anthropologist Dr Caroline Wilkinson, who was then based at the University of Dundee in Scotland. Her work comprised full facial reconstructions based on partial evidence, and it was fascinating. I contacted her and she agreed to work on helping to solve the mystery. After an examination of the skull, she confirmed that it was within a forensic timeframe and therefore a full reconstruction would be possible. This was fantastic news, and I asked her to proceed with a clay reconstruction.

One month later I travelled to Dundee to see the results of Dr Wilkinson's work. I walked into her lab and came face to face with the man I was looking for. It was incredible – from the data extracted from the skull, Dr Wilkinson had rebuilt the man's facial features and moulded an exact likeness in clay. He was suddenly a real person. I took the clay head back to Balbriggan with me, and I looked at it a thousand times in the weeks that followed as I tried to put a name to the face. But, try as I might, I couldn't progress the investigation any further. The experts had yielded all the information they could divine from the skull, and that was all I had to go on.

As often happens, it was an unexpected phone call that opened up a new path. There was a lot of media attention on the case at this time, and stemming from this I received a call from a woman in Wales who had heard the story. Winifred Price had received a newspaper article from a friend in Ireland, who felt the story of the skull might hold answers for Winifred's own personal tragedy. The journalist had dug into the story and checked out all the people who had gone missing or drowned in the previous six months on either side of the Irish Sea. They had found what they felt was a match: David Price, Winifred's only son. He had gone missing six months prior to the finding of the Lambay Island skull. His torso had been washed up near Swansea, but his head had never been found. Could the skull be that of David Price?

Within a week, Winifred was standing face to face with me at Balbriggan station as I cradled a large brown cardboard box stuffed with polystyrene and shredded paper to cushion the clay bust. I lifted it out with care and Winifred asked to hold it. I passed it over to her and she held it close, gazing intently at every centimetre of it. I could see she was very moved, that tears were welling in her eyes, but she remained composed. I could see, too, that she was lost in thoughts and memories. She spoke gently to the clay bust, telling David how much she missed him. 'He had ears like that,' she said softly. 'Yes, they are like his ears.' She gazed and studied, felt, caressed, held the figure close to her nose. She wanted to sense his smell; she closed her eyes. I felt awkward witnessing this tender scene. I gave a half-hearted cough and said, 'I need to take a blood sample from you, as was agreed.'

It was strange, because all I wanted to ask her was 'Well, is it your son or not?' – which was the obvious question – but I could not. I already knew that the resemblance was not close enough to the picture she had shown me of her son, David. She had travelled on this pilgrimage from Swansea to Dublin looking for something that would give her solace. In the time that she held the bust, I could not help thinking that the resemblance didn't really matter. In that room, cradling that clay bust like a long-lost child, she had found something that had brought her a sense of peace. I looked at this scene and realized that I'd probably never know who the man really was, but at the same time I knew that this path I'd taken hadn't been in vain, because a grieving mother had been granted a last few minutes with her son, which is the fervent wish of every person who has lost a loved one.

I walked Winifred down to the front door of the station, and before she departed she held my hand tightly, thanking me for my kindness and understanding. I told her I would post the DNA results to her. She held my hand even tighter and smiled. 'You are a good man. I am sure you will.' She turned, her head held high, and walked in the direction of the bus station. She didn't look back. Even when she had walked a distance, she didn't look back.

The DNA results were not a match with Winifred's son. I did send her the results, but I didn't receive word back. I like to think that those disappointing results didn't change those moments of quiet love she'd experienced at Balbriggan station.

It's one of my regrets that I couldn't identify this young man. To this day, the only name for this victim is 'the Lambay man'; his true identity has been washed away by the waves. As with my other unsolveds, I still hope that one day I'll get one of those unexpected phone calls and a path will open up once again, this time leading to the truth.

In the case of the Lambay man, the media were helpful in spreading awareness of the case, which is how Winifred Price came to hear of it. But at the same time, the media was unhelpful in that it was a journalist who did research on people lost and presumed drowned in the area and then printed a photo of David Price next to the photo of the clay bust. That overstepped the boundary between helpful and unhelpful.

This is a constant bone of contention in detective work – the role of the media and how they affect the cases under investigation. The reality is that what gets written and printed about an ongoing case can seriously affect the investigation, therefore it's necessary for journalists to be very aware of what they are reporting and what slant they are putting on it. Gardaí know that the media have to do their jobs and have to make a living, but their actions can have serious consequences.

There's a now-famous photograph of me arresting Joe O'Reilly at his house, for the murder of his wife, Rachel. I had parked my car nearest to the house on purpose, so I could rush Joe out and straight into the back of it. But that didn't deter the photographers hiding in the hedge, who jumped out and snapped a shot of him being led away in handcuffs, firmly in my grip. The photograph was printed in the newspapers, in spite of the fact that An Garda sought an injunction to prevent its publication on the basis that it could prejudice a jury. In the event, of course, the media angle wasn't used in the trial at all, so the photo never appeared in the courtroom. Nonetheless, it's still used in journalism courses to show how 'optics' can play a role in court proceedings. That photo was the first instance in Ireland where a person was shown in handcuffs prior to being convicted of a crime. This is something the police and courts are careful about – the jury on any case is confined to the jury room with the express intention that their only view of the defendant is sitting with the defence barrister, not cuffed or restrained in any way. The O'Reilly photo is now used to explain why this is the procedure, and the thinking behind it. I hope that, in this way, it can do some good.

Of course, it's up to those working within An Garda to keep information contained for the sake of the investigation. On a major case, there can be between twenty and twenty-five detectives around the table in the incident room, and there's no way of knowing who they're talking to and what they're saying. Loose talk can be picked up on very quickly, especially in a small country like Ireland, and then you have titbits pored over and inaccuracies published for public consumption. This can create a horrible sense of mistrust among the team, which is detrimental to the running of the investigation. It can pose a huge problem, and is very disheartening for those who don't engage in it.

There were steps taken to combat this problem through the introduction of a dedicated press officer for every major investigation. This is usually the superintendent of the district, who is tasked with speaking at press conferences and liaising with the media throughout the investigation. If anyone rings up looking for information, the only person they'll be put through to now is the press officer, which is an excellent protocol. This way, the gardaí and the media can work together to ensure that the crime and the investigation are reported responsibly and with due respect for the course of justice and the rights of those being investigated.

The unsolveds are one source of regret, but there are wider disappointments I harbour from my years with An Garda Síochána. I know the organization has come in for a lot of criticism over the past few years, and while there are many things to commend about An Garda, I have to agree that there is much to criticize as well. I'm not into Garda-bashing, but it is important that the organization and its operations are examined objectively; that they are laid bare when they present barriers to progress, and are subjected to changes that are badly needed. And the key problem I could see was the tendency to elevate the wrong people into positions of decision-making and responsibility.

First, it's important to say that the issue of the wrong people going into senior jobs is not across the board by any means. I worked with gifted superintendents who were absolutely the right man or woman for the job – people such as Chief Super-intendent Christopher Mangan, who is now the divisional officer in Louth Division. He is by far the most experienced, innovative and forward-thinking policeman the division has ever had, and is highly respected by all the staff there. Also Chief Superintendent Dominic Hayes, now working in Carlow-Kilkenny Division. We worked together on the Whelan and O'Reilly cases, and I found him to be a gentleman and a solid decision-maker. He was never afraid to make a decision and progress a case as needed. He commands huge respect from his workforce, and he has tackled crime in his division using the same system as that put in place by Operation Scale in Dundalk District (which is explained in detail below). He is a man who can very much think outside the box. He also has the good of the public at the forefront of his mind at all times. It was a pleasure to work with him.

However, An Garda Síochána is a very large organization, with over 16,000 employees, so it's difficult to ensure that competence and experience win out every time. For some members, policing is a vocation; for others it's a career, which means treating it like a game of chess and outflanking your opponents rather than working as a team. It's like the Health Service Executive, that other behemoth public service – filled with fantastic people who are willing to work hard and deliver, but pressing down on them is a thick layer of managers who aren't always the best people for the job.

I want to acknowledge all that is good about An Garda Síochána, which is first and foremost the men and women who make up the force. They are the core of what makes An Garda an exceptional police force that provides an important and extensive service to the Irish people. There are some very bright and talented individuals in the ranks, and tapping into their skills is a key solution for the many problems besetting the force. But at the same time, if I'm being honest, I regret that I walked into a dysfunctional organization at the age of twenty-four and walked out of a dysfunctional organization at the age of fifty-seven. That's more than three decades without the changes that were – and still are – so badly needed.

I appreciate that managing an organization of this size is a challenge, but there's no point pretending we haven't all witnessed the McCabe scandal, the breathalyser test scandal, the urgent questions hovering over the careers of former Garda commissioners. There are operational challenges – and then there are wilful acts of disregard for competence, experience and achievement. Instead, given the deeply polit-ical nature of the force, those who are savvy operators and are good at allying themselves with people even higher up the hierarchy are seen as unquestioningly loyal and so rise in the ranks. Of course, many large organizations – private and public – are prone to this kind of 'corporate jungle'-type carry-on. But it's a real problem when the stakes are as high as they are in a police force.

The career of a garda is shorter than that of the general population, in that we must retire at sixty. I don't think that's a bad thing, because it's a stressful and demanding job and you can burn out doing it, but what is a bad thing is that people are just let go without any effort made to mine their knowledge and experience and put it to the greater good. This is a huge lost opportunity, and represents a brain drain that deprives young gardaí of experienced mentoring. I hope that some day soon this issue will be addressed, and a system put in place whereby retired gardaí can be utilized effectively, prior to and after their departure. When you have someone with thirty or forty years' experience, they are a repository of so much useful information. It should be a priority to tap into and use that wealth of knowledge for the good of the force. Speaking for myself, I can't think of anything that would give me greater pleasure than to have the opportunity to be involved in working with young gardaí, and I know many retired colleagues who feel the same way.

This sort of sharing of knowledge and experience is crucial because good management is at the core of every successful case prosecuted. The cases described here show again and again that the decisions made in the early stages of any investigation can make or break that case. The key thing about detective work is that it isn't all about solving the crime; it's about putting together related pieces of evidence that corroborate the allegation – and that will, crucially, hold up in court. That's why every 'i' must be dotted and every 't' crossed.

This requires not just a dogged mind that will pursue the truth, but also a very methodical mind that can categorize and tick boxes and make the links very clearly – so clearly that a jury has no problem following them. That's why it's hard to be a good detective; it requires the right and left sides of the brain to be working in harmony. And if you have the wrong people occupying the chairs of decision-making, if they got their backside on that seat through being willing to play the game rather than being brilliant at their job, then there is an immediate impediment to the work of those who *do* know what they're doing. But that shouldn't be happening. Those with the right skill sets need to be promoted and supported, so that they can ensure the highest standard of service delivery and the highest standard of training for up-and-coming officers.

The other issue that my colleagues and I have been repeating for years is the unsustainable caseload. Before my retirement in 2018, I was involved in fifty different cases at any one time.

The level of detailed attention required by each case means that this is plainly ridiculous. One case I was involved in, for example, had 190 complainants – just think of the logistics of that from an investigator's point of view; and that was only one case. This isn't just a personal issue of being overworked; it's a wider issue of respecting the requirements of the work and ensuring the highest standard of service can be delivered. If you have one DI working fifty cases, you cannot claim to be delivering a gold-standard service. This was implicitly acknowledged when I left, because I was replaced by two DIs to take on my caseload. Even so, I'm sure they're still tearing their hair out and feeling massively overworked.

There have been changes and improvements, of course, but more are needed. It was rumoured that, with the proposed changes in policing structures, An Garda would establish murder investigation teams (MITs) like those in the PSNI. In this scenario, a detective inspector would have a team of two detective sergeants and up to twelve detectives they could call on to take up an investigation anywhere in the country. In the PSNI, teams take on only two investigations at a time, as there is a health and safety requirement to protect the lead DI from overwork and stress. Their teams consist of ten people, with each team having a dedicated exhibits officer, incident room coordinator, digital expert, etc. This would be an important and very welcome improvement if it is adopted by An Garda, and I really hope that it is taken on. To my mind, it would lead to a better service to the public, and the unacceptably common occurrence of investigations not being handled properly would be eradicated.

What really bothers me about the problems endemic in the organization is that we have conclusively proven that An Garda has the ability and the talent to tackle crime very successfully, once the right structures and leadership are in place and a priority is placed on supporting and assisting good police work. We proved this through something we did in Dundalk District in 2016 – Operation Scale – which was a resounding success and seemed to pave the way for the future of policing in Ireland. Operation Scale was set up in response to the fatal shooting of Garda Tony Golden in October 2015, during what should have been a routine domestic call-out. Members had been campaigning for over two years for manpower increases, all to no avail. So when a colleague was shot dead while on duty, there was a huge outcry. Gardaí in Dundalk felt very let down by the force, by the lack of resources and the refusal to deliver more officers to a very stretched district. If those changes had been made, Tony Golden might not have died.

There was good reason for Dundalk District to feel they warranted a lot more input. It's a very difficult area to police given that it covers about one hundred square miles, as well as the fact that Dundalk is the third-largest town in the country, with a population of almost 40,000. There's also the border to contend with – there are thirty-six crossings in the district alone and a resulting constant back and forth between North and South, a lot of it criminal in nature. And as with any border town, people can be wary of the police and reluctant to cooperate with them. This makes Dundalk District a challenging area for gardaí, so the demand for increased resources and manpower was valid and based on definite need. Nonetheless, that help wasn't forthcoming.

After the death of Tony Golden, that changed – for a time, at least. Suddenly, resources and gardaí were pumped into the district as the powers that be fell over themselves in the race to be seen to be doing something to combat the ever-rising crime levels. The detective unit was tasked with putting in place an operation to tackle serious, organized and subversive crime through an intelligence-led operation.

This was music to my ears. We were given the key to the coffers and told to get on with it. And we did. We established Operation Scale, designed with a specific focus on reducing the crime rate. The method for achieving this was twofold: 1. disrupt the criminal activities of nominated targets; 2. prevent and reduce further criminal activity by bringing nominated targets to justice. Alongside it, I also set up an undercover arm utilizing ten plain-clothes detectives sent to us from Harcourt Street in Dublin. They went out onto the streets of Dundalk, infiltrated the drug scene and bought drugs from local sellers. An in-house garda who was born-and-bred Dundalk oversaw their work, identifying the sellers. Everything was recorded and categorized and the drugs bought were analysed, so it was all evidential. After twelve months, we had identified and arrested twenty-five dealers, all of whom were handed down nine-month sentences. It cleaned up the streets of the town and put a serious dent in the local drug operations.

We all worked together, pooling resources and information, and planned out our actions meticulously. I was very aware of the need for every action to be well executed so that we could prosecute successfully in court. As a result of our collective planning and focus, Scale was tremendously well run and structured, and we were all rightly proud of it. It illustrated, beyond any doubt, that the talent and ability were there and that we could tackle crime head-on and make a real difference. It was all there in the statistics, in black and white.

Over the time that Scale was in operation, we recovered over €1 million in illegal assets, including cars, houses, jewellery, drugs and cash. One of the key targets was the burglary rate, which was running at about 600 cases per year in Dundalk. The operation reduced that to about 270. From my point of view, that meant 330 people who were spared the trauma of a house burglary, 330 insurance claims that didn't have to be paid out, and 330 perpetrators and crimes that didn't have to be processed, investigated and included in an already heavily clogged system. It was win–win–win, every way you looked at it.

We got so good at digging away quietly that the criminals often didn't see us coming. I remember one case where we recovered illegal assets – a house and cars – from a dealer, and the first he knew about it was when he was pulled over on the road in another county and the car was taken from him, leaving him standing on the hard shoulder. Another major dealer couldn't believe it when we hit his house because he'd felt invincible until then. We found a CCTV unit recording inside the house that had helpfully captured lots of footage of him in the act of dealing drugs. After that, he got wise and put the CCTV outside. We hit the place again, and this time we used the footage to identify all the dealers and buyers coming to his door. We also found stolen property, firearms, smoke grenades – his house was an Aladdin's cave of stolen and illegal items. But the icing on the cake was the kilo of cocaine found in a sock in his girlfriend's car. A kilo costs about €80,000 to buy, and you double its value when you bag it up and sell it on the streets. So this old sock was worth more than my pension. He denied all knowledge of it – until we found his DNA on the sock and the game was up.

Alongside these hits and asset recoveries, we worked hard to build a positive relationship with the people of Dundalk and the district. We did up a leaflet explaining that we wanted to help the whole community to live safely and peacefully, but that we needed their help to achieve that. We'd set up checkpoints to check cars for tax, and if we found someone in contravention, we'd take them aside and talk to them respectfully – tell them to update their papers quickly and we wouldn't take it further. Then, while they were feeling the warm glow of our nice gesture, we'd press a leaflet on them and ask them to be there for us too. These efforts were appreciated by the community and relations improved hugely, with far more information coming in through the confidential line. It was working.

Operation Scale was one of the biggest achievements of my career – that's truly how I feel about it – but after twelve months we were told the plug was being pulled. The show of strength and 'doing something' had been put on successfully, and now they were closing the curtains, locking the doors and mothballing all the props. I was absolutely sickened by this decision. We had done all that was asked of us, we had proven that we were more than up to the task of putting some manners on the district, and just when it was all humming along beautifully and delivering incredible returns, it was shut down.

This is a stark example of the problem at the heart of An Garda Síochána. There is a gulf between those on the ground and those in the ivory tower of management. The force has incredible talent and very hardworking, dedicated people at its disposal, but it routinely denigrates their ideas, their work and their contributions, and in doing so alienates them. This severely damages morale and creates a disempowered body of men and women who can easily burn out, become resigned to the stale old status quo, and even become cynical. There is a pressing need for strong, joined-up thinking that will prioritize intelligently and lead from the front. Without that, the force will just keep haemorrhaging people, talent and ideas. Operation Scale was an inspired and slick bit of policing, and if there was a Scale in every district, you'd clean up the whole country and save an awful lot of heartache. But the force needs the leadership to recognize what's working and to fight for it. I know the desire is there among the gardaí themselves, who want to be effective and to make a difference. I could see that very clearly during Scale, when everyone was energized by the work, focused and dedicated, motivated by the improvements we could see happening before our very eyes. That could be how An Garda Síochána works, if the will was there at every level of the hierarchy and everyone pulled together in the same direction.

We know that to find meaning and purpose in your life is crucial to health (mental and physical), and for many of us – rightly or wrongly – work is central to what gives our life meaning. It is certainly that way in a job like policing. Though there were aspects of Garda management that frustrated me, I tried to remain focused on working my own patch in the very best way I could, so that at least my personal contribution was solid, no matter what was going on around me. It is very hard to be a good detective, but the cardinal rules I devised for myself were my bible, and they ensured every investigation I conducted was transparent and effective – and, in a huge number of cases, successful. Those five rules of investigation were:

1. Be honest in all dealings.
2. Be accountable at all times.
3. Be respectful of every single person you encounter, regardless of what side of the law they are on.
4. Be professional at all times.
5. Keep it simple – gather the evidence, evaluate the evidence, follow the evidence.

These rules ensure that an investigation is conducted methodically, intelligently, logically and properly. I put together this list of rules myself, based on observation and common sense; I learned from the good detectives around me, and tried to be the best detective I could be. It proved a very effective method, and I think it could apply to the organization as a whole, to show a way forward into working practices that value people, match the right people to the right job, and ensure that An Garda upholds its motto to the highest standard. I regret that the organization is, to an extent, broken, and that it often breaks people who work within it, but I am also very hopeful for the future of the force and its detectives and I believe that there are better days ahead. The scandals might be divisive and difficult, but they shine a light into dark corners and allow people to see clearly.

That's why I'm hopeful. And more than that, I'm rooting for them.

Acknowledgements

When I joined An Garda Síochána in the 1980s, I didn't know what was in store for me. I can say now that it has been a marvellous career, though being part of an organization that provides a service becomes more than a career – it becomes a way of life.

Like in most careers, or indeed in the normal course of life, you encounter those who leave a mark on you for various reasons – because they teach you important lessons, because their sheer professionalism is inspiring or because you admire their dedication to maintaining high standards – and because of this you will never forget them. I have been fortunate to have worked with some of the finest people you could ever meet during my investigations.

When I joined the force on 14 August 1985, I did so with fifty-nine others, all male enrolments. This group was divided into three classes of twenty recruits. I must acknowledge those nineteen men who eventually passed out with me in January 1986. All were decent, caring people, and without their company and good humour Templemore would have been a dreary place. My PD sergeant during my training was Michael (Mick) Mulryan, who prepared us as best he could for our days on the beat. He was understanding, and an easy man to get on with. I am grateful for his good teaching and how well he prepared us for the tough transition into our working lives.

My first station was Donnybrook in south Dublin, where I was stationed from January 1986 to October 1987. This was a station that covered a number of embassy residencies, which required twenty-four-hour protection, and there were twenty-five men on my unit who paraded at 5.45 a.m. each day on the early-morning shift. As a junior garda you were given the unenviable posts – standing outside buildings at all times of the day and night, with nothing happening. I must acknowledge my unit sergeant there, Sergeant Pat Malone, who was very fair and managed all of us without favouritism. He understood the boredom of what we did, and did his best to rotate the detail so we got to experience more police-friendly jobs that provided interaction with the public (concerts at the RDS, horse shows and the like). I appreciated his even-handedness and his understanding.

My roommate and fellow member who passed out with me, and who was also stationed in Donnybrook, was Garda Peter O'Hare – now Sergeant O'Hare. As naive young men we enjoyed the premises of fun and dance that Dublin provided. We spent all of our wage packets from our first week at Donnybrook in Leeson Street. I have not since paid £25 for a cheap bottle of wine anywhere, I'm glad to say. Peter was a good friend and we ended up at Drogheda station together several years later, which was lucky for me. I have greatly enjoyed Peter's friendship through all the years.

I was transferred to Blanchardstown station in 1987, and it was there that my career really began with my appointment to plain-clothes duties. Before that, I had spent almost three years in the patrol car as observer, alongside driver and colleague Garda Michael Cusack. I always admired Michael's bravery, particularly as he saved my skin on several occasions when confronted with violent and difficult situations. My first detective sergeant was Derek Byrne (now DI Byrne and formerly assistant commissioner), and it was he who put me into the ranks of the plain-clothes members and gave me my break. I want to thank him for his faith in me and for giving me the opportunity to get involved in major investigations.

Superintendent Michael McGlynn was another man I held in high regard. He worked out of Cabra station, at the time when it was the divisional headquarters for K District. It was a busy division but Michael McGlynn always made time for the plain-clothes section. It was in Blanchardstown that I began to learn my trade as an investigator, and here I must acknowledge Detective Garda John Lyons, now retired, from whom I learned so much. He may not have known it then, but he was the man I listened to and observed more than any other. He greatly influenced how I conducted investigations later in my career.

There are several gardaí I'd like to mention who served with me in Blanchardstown, but I am afraid that if I do so, I'll leave someone out. So I will simply say thank you to all the members on Unit B between 1987 and 1997 – in particular Detective Garda Dean Kerins and Detective Garda Martin Flood, with whom I worked closely before my promotion to uniform sergeant in Clones, County Monaghan. I remained in Clones until 1999, and I have to say it was quite a culture shock. It was a brand-new locality for me, and it was challenging to be in charge of a large unit on the border at the time of the foot-and-mouth scare. I want to thank all those on my unit in Clones as they kept me straight, as I did them. In particular, I would like to thank Garda Willie Gillard for his local knowledge and his shrewdness in dealing with certain individuals we encountered.

In 1999 I was transferred to Balbriggan station, where I took up the position of detective sergeant in charge of the detectives and plain-clothes members. These were by far the most enjoyable years of my thirty-three-year career with An Garda. Balbriggan was district headquarters, covering the areas of Garristown, Lusk, Rush and Skerries. It was during my time there that I investigated the high-profile murders of Mary Gough and Rachel O'Reilly, and I encountered some excellent and bright gardaí who contributed to both investigations. Detective Inspector Dominic Hayes (now chief superintendent) was an inspiration to me, as his approach to problems was direct and well thought out. He is an exceptional policeman with a great vision for the policing service, and I learned a huge amount from him. Detective Garda John Geraghty and Detective Garda John Clancy were two members who taught me an immense amount on piecing together evidence and producing a file for the DPP. The assistant commissioner at the time, Tony Hickey, was always willing to give his opinion on crimes we were trying to solve. Not only was he a gentleman, but he had also the passion and ability to lead people and investigations in a professional manner. I observed his approach closely and I learned from him. He was a huge loss to the force when he retired.

Among my own team in Balbriggan I must thank Detective Gardaí Peter McCoy, Robert Keogh and Richard Culhane as well as Garda Aaron Gormley, now a sergeant. I also want to thank Garda Aidan Holland, a senior detective who guided me in my early days at Balbriggan. Our superintendent at the time – and a man who could not be replaced – was Thomas Gallagher, a Leitrim man who possessed honour, insight and great ability as a detective. A calm and focused individual, he was a true leader. Working under him at Balbriggan was a happy time, even though we had murders that were difficult to investigate. His departure on retirement opened up a period of uncertainty, so I was grateful when I got promoted in 2008 and was sent to Drogheda station as a uniform inspector. I spent two years in uniform before being appointed to Dundalk as detective inspector. While in uniform, part of my duty was to present cases twice a week in Drogheda District Court and in this I appreciated the guidance of Inspectors Brendan Cadden and Michael Crowley, both now retired.

As detective inspector I had dedicated teams in Drogheda, Ardee and Dundalk. I had approximately forty-four officers under my remit to manage on a daily basis. I have to give credit to the detectives I worked with in Louth Division over the last eight years of my career. They were an exceptional bunch of people, always willing and able to carry out the work asked of them, without any quibbling. There are many I wish to thank.

The Drogheda Detective and Crime Unit was always busy, and it was said that, in Drogheda, serious crimes happened in threes – so if we had a murder or a serious incident, we always braced ourselves for an onslaught of work. Like all members of my teams, those in the Dundalk Detective and Crime Unit were resilient people with good moral standing and were always willing to carry out their tasks with dedication and professionalism. Detective Sergeant Nicholas Kelly was a man of encyclopedic local knowledge and a bedrock of sense in any situation. I relied on him in many a murder and serious crime investigation. Nicholas was a strong character and a good man – a team player who was worth two detective sergeants. I remember tasking Nicholas with tracing down a foreign national for whom there was an extradition warrant and whose whereabouts was unknown. Nicholas paid a visit to this man's house, where his wife stated that she didn't know where he was, that he worked at sea on the trawlers and that she couldn't help any further. An eagled-eye Nicholas noticed a painting of a trawler, framed and hanging in the sitting room. He noted the name of the trawler. He established it was an operational trawler and was due to dock in Galway Bay the following day. Equipped with his warrant, he waited for it to dock and his hunch proved correct. The man was lifted as he stood ashore. Nicholas was astute and certainly no fool. He did more for the people of Drogheda than any superintendent or member of authority within An Garda Síochána. His record on drug busts is the stuff of legends. Thank you, Nicholas.

Detective Garda Kieran Rohan was my incident room coordinator and he was always at the ready to set up an incident room and get the ball rolling. He would take on big investigations – sometimes two or three or more at once – and no matter what time of the night you might ring him, he was always obliging. He was a man I would bounce ideas off and I would listen keenly to his replies. He is an honest, decent, hardworking garda with great ability.

Detective Garda Maureen McFadden was the go-to detective for disclosure files. Maureen was so meticulous, precise and comprehensive in compiling these files that I enlisted her help for my Dundalk investigations as well. Thank you, Maureen, for your dedication and work ethic.

Detective Gardaí Seamus 'Rossie' Nolan, Sean Fitzpatrick, Brian Kearns, Ronan McMorrow and Donnie Corbett were the other detectives on the team, and I have to thank them for their loyalty to me. The plain-clothes crime unit consisted of Detective Sergeant Fearghal O'Toole and Gardaí Evan Connolly, Alan Connell, Amy O'Sullivan, Andy Corbett and Karl Mannion, and without their help the investigations would not have been completed to the high standard I demanded.

Dundalk District – or Fort Apache, as it is known – is a unique posting, and policing is at a different level there. The border with Northern Ireland brings its own problems, and unfortunately the policing of it led to the deaths of two of my colleagues – Garda Tony Golden and Detective Garda Adrian Donohoe, who was one of my team. The seriousness of the incidents encountered by the detectives and crime unit in Dundalk was equal to or above any other experienced by gardaí anywhere in the country, including Dublin. I saw gardaí come to Dundalk on transfer, and within a month they had to transfer back out because they felt there was nowhere as tough to police as Dundalk. Detective work on the border is very challenging, and it takes a certain type of garda to cope with it. I was blessed in that all those under my direction possessed an inner strength and a steely resolve to deal with whatever the border brought. I must thank the following for their dedication and professionalism and initiative, because whenever something serious happened, these people sprang into action without having to be told what to do: Detective Sergeant Kieran Reidy, Detective Sergeant Darren Kirwan, Detective Gardaí Joseph Ryan, Karen Coughlan, Pauric O'Reilly, Andy Barron, Paul Gill, Noel Mohan, James Kilgannon, Dave Devaney and Stacey Linnane. The crime unit in Dundalk was exceptional in solving crime and digging in when we needed help on the bigger cases. I greatly appreciated the help of Sergeant Ger Collins and Sergeant John Moroney, as well as Gardaí Stephen Byrne, Sean O'Callaghan, Garry Harris, Conor Mulcahy, Lisa McCabe and Keith Ginnitty.

Detective James Doherty is an incident room coordinator I hold in the highest regard, and he is now in his sixth year as coordinator on the murder of Detective Garda Adrian Donohoe. James, words cannot describe your dedication, ability and pure detective work. I relied on you so much and I always appreciated your friendship, humour and support. I hope you gave them fags up, James.

I also wish to thank my team in Ardee. Detective Sergeant Jim McCumiskey (RIP), Sergeant Peter Cooley, Detective Gardaí Michael Scanlon and Dave Leyton and Garda Yvonne Snell all worked tirelessly on several cases I investigated.

I took help from wherever I could get it, and I was often grateful for the assistance of the national support services, which included the National Bureau of Criminal Investigations. The skilled detectives of the NBCI were allocated to Louth Division to assist in some murder investigations and also with complex operations like Operation Scale. Detective Garda Philip Ryan of the NBCI devised and structured the operational system on Pulse, and he was an excellent administrator. We would not have had the success we had without the smooth running of the system he put in place. Also, Sergeant Ciaran Clancy of the Dundalk incident room compiled the strategy document for Scale and his knowledge of Garda procedures and systems was instrumental in its success. I will be forever indebted to Sergeant Clancy for his pure work ethic and the trust he put in me as an investigator.

Detective Gardaí Lorraine Travers and Pat Flood, both of the NBCI, worked with me on a major investigation involving 190 injured parties – a mammoth task. Their attention to detail in the statements they took was crucial, and I want to thank them for the hours and hours of work they put in. Also, Detective Liz McGarraity of the NBCI worked very hard to complete all the jobs allocated to her during a double murder investigation, and I appreciated her professionalism. Two other members of the NBCI I will never forget – because I worked tirelessly with them on a number of murder cases – are Detective Sergeant Mark Phillips and Detective Garda Jim McGovern. I have watched these two men work to a level of success you don't see many achieving, and their perception and attention to detail are second to none. They are true investigators. Detective Garda John Kissane of the NBCI was one of those detectives of the old stock, as we would say, but extremely focused on doing a good job. I am indebted to John for his help and banter over the years. Indeed, his skill at putting investigation files together is legendary in Louth Division. He even ended up in Romania with one of his murder files, liaising with the local police and judiciary. His was an inspiring level of commitment.

The Special Detective Unit in Harcourt Square frequented the border area in pursuit of dissident activity, and although I didn't always know what they were up to, they are men and women of great courage and the Irish people are indebted to them for all the explosives and firearms they recover and the people they bring before the Special Criminal Court. It's a dangerous job they do, and we all owe them a huge amount for doing it. Detective Gardaí Paul Flynn and Sean Finnegan, thank you for your help over the years.

Expertise from inside and outside An Garda Síochána is vital in any investigation. I worked closely with Ed McGoey, a Garda analyst, and relied on his ability to analyse vast volumes of documentation and distil them into a concise report – with diagrams and charts – that presented evidential material in a simple and comprehensive manner. Ed, you were invaluable to me, and I enjoyed your company very much. You are an important asset in any major investigation, and I hope you are still being utilized.

Garda Gareth Kenna and Detective Garda Ronan Diffley were two experts in the field of CCTV, and there are many murder cases that would not have been solved without their expert input. Gareth worked with unfailing dedication on cases where there were hours upon hours of footage to be examined, and he never failed to extract the evidence if it was there. He is a true professional. And the best evidence I ever heard given in the Central Criminal Court was by Detective Garda Diffley. He had compiled a video and a montage of stills for a jury in a murder case. He first outlined his qualifications – having a master's degree in Computer Technical Science and another degree in Computer Analytics, if my memory serves. I remember the judge stretching his head over the bench to get a look at this garda with all these qualifications. Anyway, Garda Diffley gave evidence of real time as against the time shown on the footage and stills. The defence barrister then rose to his feet to cross-examine him. 'Well, Garda Diffley, you corrected the time and you gave evidence of this. Did you use the talking clock?' Ronan's reply was priceless: 'No , I checked against the satellite that orbits the Earth, and its accuracy is to a billionth of a second.' As the barrister stared, Ronan proceeded to give the name of the satellite, the year it was launched and the names of weather experts and mathematicians who relied on that particular satellite for time. The defence barrister said, 'No further questions.' I always get a kick out of that story. Ronan, you are also a true professional.

There are some people you click with professionally and personally, and for me Detective Bobby Ogle was one such man. I worked with him for two years on the Irene White murder case, and Bobby impressed me with his foresight and his ability to pick up a detail that might have seemed irrelevant but in fact made a difference. I can honestly say that the Irene White case would not have been solved without Bobby's keen eye. Thank you, Bobby, for your great ability as a detective, but above all for your friendship and understanding of the bigger picture.

Another relentless investigator and incident room coordinator is Sergeant Mick Sheridan, who worked hand in hand with Bobby Ogle. I always said that with these two on my team, there was no crime we could not solve. Mick is a very clinical, honest investigator, and I hope he becomes a detective inspector at some stage as he is a very capable individual.

I have investigated quite a few murders and submitted files to the DPP, and I am sure they heaved a sigh of relief when they heard I was retiring. But I must thank Barry Donohoe and John Dolan, whom I dealt with often, because they always showed great decision-making skills with regard to my cases. I didn't always get my way as to what charges were to be brought or who was to be charged, but I respected their decisions.

I suppose this brings me on to the judiciary I had the pleasure of working with over the years. It is often said that judges live in ivory towers and don't know what is going on in the real world, but I can say from my own experience that this was not the case. In my opinion, not only are judges very bright but they are also very clued-in and remarkably adept at reading the true nature of a situation. I always found them to be courteous and civil, and they put a lot of victims and witnesses at ease with their manner. I also have high regard for the barrister community, and not only because I married one. I find their mental dexterity when conducting a trial to be fascinating. The cat-and-mouse questioning of a witness and the building of a defence are difficult skills to master. I always found when dealing with barristers that they were easy to get on with and thoroughly professional, even when

I was on the receiving end of those skills. As we always said, there were never any hard feelings.

There were people I admired from afar, and I know they influenced my thinking on criminal investigations. One was ex-Chief Superintendent John Courtney, who was relentless in his pursuit of solving a crime. We often spent hours chatting about crimes and how they were solved. He was a very interesting man, but sadly has passed away. I remember him fondly.

At my level of dealing with crimes of a serious nature I was open to encouragement, and Sergeant Niall Gillooly was one person who always gave me a boost. We trained together for the Gaelforce adventure race and enjoyed many a tough cycle around Gormanston/Stamullen and Drogheda. Niall, I enjoyed your company and your goodwill gestures, and they certainly helped me on my way.

Every crime scene needs to be examined, and investigators must be meticulous and exacting in their search for evidence. You only get one chance to read the scene, and the findings shape the SIO's thinking and decision-making. In Louth Division I had the remit of managing the divisional Scenes of Crime Unit. On murder investigations it was my call as to whether the GTB would be called in from Garda headquarters or whether it would be the local divisional SCU. The local team was excellent and I relied on them often. Sergeant Mick Kelly was in charge of the Louth SCU, which comprised four of the best and most experienced scenes of crime examiners in the country. Sergeant Michael Kelly, Detective Eric McGovern, Detective Aidan O'Hanlon and Detective Tony Boyle were exceptional in their work at serious crime scenes. I have watched them give evidence in the highest courts in the land without faltering. I thank them for their professionalism and their patience in taking direction from me. They were and are a good team.

One of the stakeholders an investigator must liaise with is the assigned forensic scientist. I have dealt with most of the scientists in the Forensic Science Laboratory (now Forensic Science Ireland), and in later years it was Dr Emily Jordan who was assigned to my cases. I must thank her for her understanding regarding my approach to DNA evidence. She is a pure gem in crime solving, and very pleasant to deal with.

Finally, I was a member in Louth Division for ten years, and in that time I saw chief superintendents come and go. Beyond any doubt, Chief Superintendent Christopher Mangan was like a breath of fresh air. An extremely experienced policeman and investigator, he – unlike others – had an understanding of what the plain-clothes and uniform sections needed in order to be able to do their jobs effectively. He was the first chief superintendent to specify as a priority that his staff and members would be kept safe on the job. He did all he could to make policing effective and with positive results for the public. He put his trust in me, and I don't think I let him down. He understood my methodology and approach to solving serious crimes, and I thank him for his support.

Part of my job was to liaise with foreign police forces, and I must thank all the PSNI officers I worked with as I always found them to be very helpful and professional. There were two officers I encountered who were special agents with the US Department of Homeland Security, Mathew Katske and Scott Crabb, and without them I could not have solved certain murders. They are both incredibly professional policemen with hearts of gold and huge ability. Thank you, Mathew and Scott.

It is difficult to mention everyone and I hope I did not leave anyone out, but to all those members I worked with, your efforts made a difference to people's lives – and that's what matters.

When you are asked to write a book, it's something you churn around in your mind, constantly asking yourself: *Can I do this?* Well, like most avenues I've taken in life, I've been lucky to meet people who helped and encouraged me in this task. I want to thank Penguin Ireland for the trust and confidence they placed in me, in particular Michael McLoughlin and Patricia Deevy. Their encouragement and faith in my initial scribbling I will not forget. My ghostwriter Rachel Pierce is a beautiful and talented person, without whom I could not have completed the task. I will miss our rendezvous in the Black Bull Inn for breakfast, and the mulling over chapter after chapter. I enjoyed your company and direction.

Detective Sergeant Dermot Nolan and Garda Vanessa Stafford of *Crimecall* were a huge help in the writing of the book, as they helped jog my memory on dates and times I appeared on the programme. Thank you for your help. Sergeant Ciaran Clancy agreed to read the book in draft form and his comments were extremely helpful. Thank you for your usual attention to detail, Ciaran.

Journalist Barry Cummins always told me there was a book in me and to go and write it, and I'm grateful for his encouragement.

Thanks to everyone who provided images for the picture inset. Copyright as follows: 3, 16, 18 and 19 – Ciara Wilkinson; 6, 15 and 20 – Tom Conachy; 4, 7, 10, 12 and 21 – INM; 5, 8, 9, 11, 13, 17 and 22 – Collins Photo Agency; and 14 – Niall Dorr's parents. All other pictures supplied by the author.

ACKNOWLEDGEMENTS

My family has always been a source of support, and I have to thank my brother David and my sisters Brenda and Elma for their words of encouragement about the task in hand.

I make no bones about it – I am married to a wonderful woman, Niamh, with whom I discussed my writing on a daily basis. Thank you, Niamh, for your patience and your encouraging words, and your faith in me to complete this book. Thanks also to my daughters, Cheryl and Jade, and my beautiful new addition, Doireann, whom I bored with extracts of the book on several occasions.

He just wanted a decent book to read ...

Not too much to ask, is it? It was in 1935 when Allen Lane, Managing Director of Bodley Head Publishers, stood on a platform at Exeter railway station looking for something good to read on his journey back to London. His choice was limited to popular magazines and poor-quality paperbacks – the same choice faced every day by the vast majority of readers, few of whom could afford hardbacks. Lane's disappointment and subsequent anger at the range of books generally available led him to found a company – and change the world.

'We believed in the existence in this country of a vast reading public for intelligent books at a low price, and staked everything on it'
Sir Allen Lane, 1902–1970, founder of Penguin Books

The quality paperback had arrived – and not just in bookshops. Lane was adamant that his Penguins should appear in chain stores and tobacconists, and should cost no more than a packet of cigarettes.

Reading habits (and cigarette prices) have changed since 1935, but Penguin still believes in publishing the best books for everybody to enjoy. We still believe that good design costs no more than bad design, and we still believe that quality books published passionately and responsibly make the world a better place.

So wherever you see the little bird – whether it's on a piece of prize-winning literary fiction or a celebrity autobiography, political tour de force or historical masterpiece, a serial-killer thriller, reference book, world classic or a piece of pure escapism – you can bet that it represents the very best that the genre has to offer.

Whatever you like to read – trust Penguin.